INDIGENOUS AUSTRALIAN YOUTH FUTURES

LIVING THE SOCIAL DETERMINANTS OF HEALTH

INDIGENOUS AUSTRALIAN YOUTH FUTURES

LIVING THE SOCIAL DETERMINANTS OF HEALTH

EDITED BY KATE SENIOR, RICHARD CHENHALL AND VICTORIA BURBANK

PRESS

Dedicated to the memory of Pippa Rudd
and David Daniels

Published by ANU Press
The Australian National University
Acton ACT 2601, Australia
Email: anupress@anu.edu.au

Available to download for free at press.anu.edu.au

ISBN (print): 9781760464448
ISBN (online): 9781760464455

WorldCat (print): 1257503258
WorldCat (online): 1256985969

DOI: 10.22459/IAYF.2021

Cover design and layout by ANU Press. Cover photograph by Julie Hall.

Contents

List of Figures

List of Tables

Contributors

Danielle Aquino is a public health nutritionist and dietitian with extensive experience in nutrition, child and maternal health, community development and program evaluation in northern Australia and Vanuatu. She has been involved in research investigating strategies to prevent anaemia amongst young children in northern Australian remote Aboriginal communities, and ethnographic research exploring Aboriginal parents' perspectives about children's food and eating practices.

Victoria Burbank PhD, FASSA, was a professor of anthropology at the University of Western Australia between 1994 and 2014. Drawing upon her experiences in the south-eastern Arnhem Land community of Numbulwar, she has published three books: *Aboriginal Adolescence*, *Fighting Women* and *An Ethnography of Stress*, along with a number of papers and book chapters. Now 'retired' she continues to draw on her expertise in psychological anthropology via public presentations, postgraduate supervision, reviewing and editing. She is currently working on her fourth book set in Numbulwar.

Richard Chenhall is Professor of Medical Anthropology in the Melbourne School of Population and Global Health at the University of Melbourne, Australia. Richard has conducted research with Indigenous communities and organisations for over 20 years in the area of the social determinants of health, alcohol and other drugs, sexual health and youth wellbeing. He is the author of *Benelong's Haven* and co-editor of the *Social Determinants of Indigenous Health*.

Daphne Daniels is the Deputy Chair of the board of directors for the Yugul Mangi Development Aboriginal Corporation. She is also the editor of the *Ngukurr News*, a role she has held for 20 years. Daphne has been engaged in research in her community since 1998, when she was a researcher on the South East Arnhem Land Collaborative Research Project.

Greg Dickson manages Kriol education programs in Ngukurr, NT, for Meigim Kriol Strongbala (a program of Yugul Mangi Development Aboriginal Corporation) and is an honorary lecturer at The Australian National University.

Mascha Friderichs works as lecturer in Public Health at Menzies School of Health Research, Darwin. Her PhD in Anthropology, awarded in 2019, focuses on Indigenous young women's beliefs about health and their interaction with the health system, considering specifically the interrelationships between health, culture and identity.

Trudy Hall lives in the Ngukurr community. She worked as a research assistant for the youth futures project, helping to facilitate body mapping activities with young women. She has also worked as a reporter on the *Ngukurr News*.

Angelina Joshua lives in the Ngukurr community. After completing her education in Darwin, Angelina worked as a community-based researcher supporting an infant nutrition project. She subsequently worked with the Ngukurr Language Centre, where she developed resources in her grandmother's language of Mara.

Kishan Kariippanon is a medical doctor and researcher in the healthy ageing field using a decolonisation framework, combining public health, design and innovation. He is a co-author in the *Oxford Research Encyclopedia for Global Public Health* for chapters on 'Traditional Medicine and Indigenous Health in Indigenous Hands' and 'Well-Being and Mental Wellness'.

Susan McMullen, worked for over 30 years as a nurse in remote settings including Timor and Numbulwar in the Northern Territory. She completed her PhD, 'Growing up fast: The social and reproductive health of young women in a remote Indigenous community', in 2014.

Pippa Rudd was a PhD student with the Menzies School of Health Research, conducting research into young Indigenous people's contact with the legal system. She was formerly a director in the NT Department of Justice.

Kate Senior is an Associate Professor of Anthropology in the School of Humanities and Social Science at the University of Newcastle. She has worked in collaboration with Daphne Daniels and the Ngukurr community for the last 20 years, with a particular emphasis on the lives and wellbeing of young people in the community. Research conducted for her Australian Research Council Future Fellowship provided the impetus for this publication.

Jared Sharp's background is as a criminal lawyer specialising in youth justice for Aboriginal legal services, principally the North Australian Aboriginal Justice Agency (NAAJA). Jared has been a long-standing advocate to address the human rights failings of the Northern Territory youth justice system. He was featured in ABC TV's *Four Corners* investigation into Darwin's Don Dale Youth Detention Centre, and was involved in the resulting Royal Commission into NT Youth Detention and Child Protection.

Bronwyn Turner lives in the Ngukurr community. She worked as a research assistant for the youth futures project, helping to facilitate body mapping activities with young women. She has also worked as a reporter on the *Ngukurr News*.

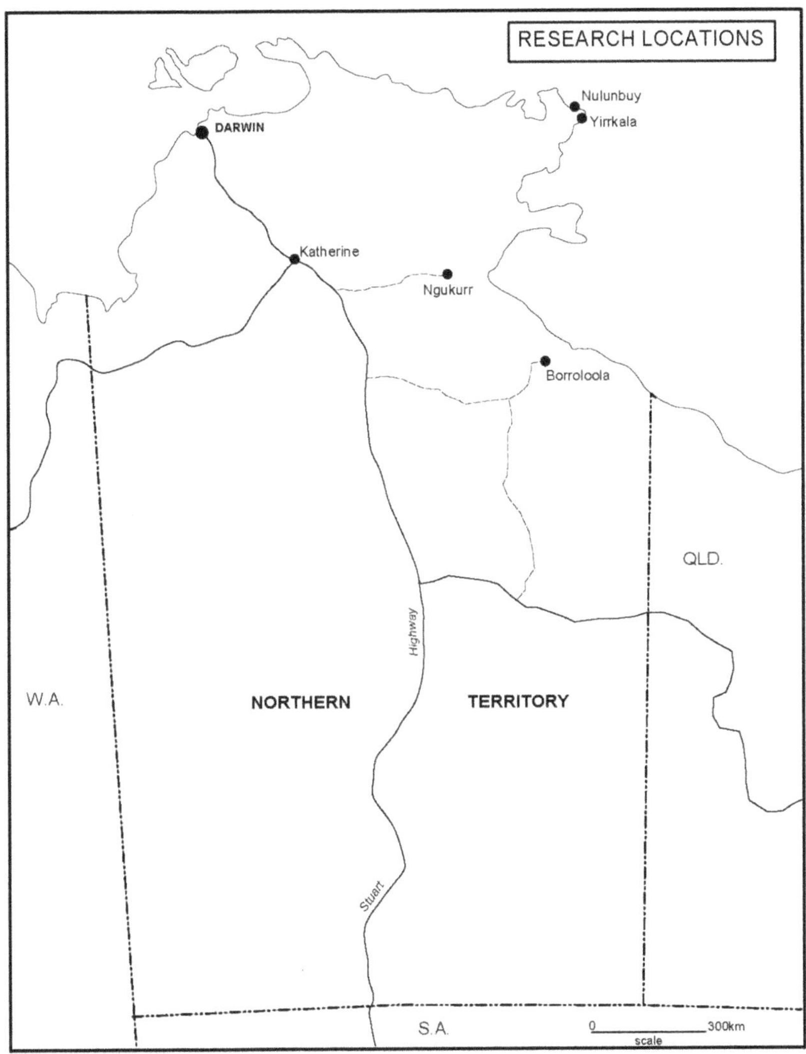

Figure 0.1: Map of research locations.

Source: Daniele Senior.

Introduction: Aboriginal Youth in the Northern Territory: Disadvantage, Control and Hope

Kate Senior, Richard Chenhall
and Victoria Burbank

> Perhaps the most important contribution of anthropology to the study of adolescence is the emphasis it puts on understanding the cultures within which adolescents operate. (Schlegel and Hewlett 2011, 287)

Young people are poised on the brink of maturity, of arriving at a life stage in which they are best able to contribute to the wellbeing of humankind or to do it great harm. Thus, it is vital that the challenges and possibilities of adolescence be well understood and addressed. In Australia, such understanding is most urgently needed with respect to Aboriginal youths. Not only must they adjust to their changing bodies and minds (e.g. Tanner 1990; Casey 2015), but, as Ute Eickelkamp (2011, 9) has observed, 'they need to cope with racism, discrimination, cultural insecurities, intergenerational trauma and the socioeconomic marginal status of their families'. They are also required to do all this in the complexity of intercultural environments that we argue must be included in our ethnography if we are to understand the challenges and achievements of these young people.[1]

1 Though defined variably, 'adolescence' is a term anthropologists have long used to refer to the transition between childhood and adulthood. Schlegel and Barry (1991, 10) use the term 'youth' to label a stage between adolescence and adulthood when 'a full social adulthood is delayed many years beyond puberty'; however, we find 'youth' and 'adolescent' sometimes used interchangeably and do so ourselves. Both of these terms may be contrasted with the word 'puberty', which refers to the physiological changes that take place around this time, most notably the onset of fertility (Tanner 1990). In contrast, labels like 'youth', 'adolescent' and 'teenager' are socially constructed life periods and are, therefore, variable across societies. For different usages of words for adolescence see: John and Beatrice Whiting's Foreword in Burbank (1988, xii), Tanner (1990, 58) and Schlegel and Barry (1991, 1–4).

Thanks to scholars like Merlan (1998, 2005) and Hinkson and Smith (2005), the recently rediscovered concept 'intercultural' (Vogt and Albert 1966) has provided a useful assist for portraying the circumstances in which Australian Aboriginal people live. We see an 'intercultural' space as a social environment constructed largely by the sustained interaction of at least two distinct populations, each of which brings to the interaction an ethos and associated identity derived from 'different forms of experience, knowing and practice' (Merlan 2005, 174). Due to their different histories and the consequent inequalities of knowledge, wealth and status, the respective bearers of these different traditions, may, as is clearly the case between Aboriginal and non-Aboriginal Australians, have more or less power over others, and themselves, in this space. The difficulties of Aboriginal youth, we cannot help but assume, arise, in large part, from their often disadvantaged positions in these intercultural interactions. However, it is not cultures that meet, but individuals (Vogt and Albert 1966, 61), and individuals invariably have varied experiences, however much shared their histories may be. Thus, it is these individual experiences that are created by, and brought to, intercultural encounters. We also recognise that each of the communities represented in this collection has arisen from a distinct series of intercultural encounters and events, and each occupies a different physical and social environment. Many of these responses, as demonstrated in the following chapters, are grounded in resilience and adaptability, and are ones in which young people uniquely draw upon their skills in both the traditional and globalised world (see also Allen et al. 2014). This collection presents accounts of youths as individuals, or as part of groups, coming of age, and engaged in and accompanied by positive and negative experience in various intercultural spaces.

The Vicious Cycle of Social Disadvantage

Anthropology can be seen as the study of human behaviour and experience in a larger context, whether that context is delineated as a particular set of sociocultural circumstances and/or as the evolutionary history of humankind. We would like our readers to understand that most of the young people and adults of whom we speak in these pages are living in intercultural circumstances that can fairly be described as risky, uncertain and stressful. These are circumstances that clearly arise from inequality, subordination and control, and have long been associated with an array of problems, some of which are discussed in these papers: inadequate education, precocious pregnancy, delinquency, violence, high rates of incarceration, poor health and associated high mortality rates (e.g. Wilkinson and Pickett 2010; Burbank, Senior and McMullen 2015).

Diane Austin-Broos (2011, 11) has said: 'To grasp the circumstance of remote Aboriginal people requires an understanding of both cultural difference and inequality'. In the last few decades, academics have paid considerable attention to the latter condition. In so doing, some have identified social arrangements and processes they have labelled as 'the social determinants of health' (Brunner and Marmot 1999; Marmot and Wilkinson 1999) and as 'structural violence' (Farmer 2004). These conceptualisations enable us to better identify at least some of the reasons why the fortunes of particular human lives are far better or worse than others. In this effort, we recognise the importance not only of cross-cultural but also intersubjective translation. Because the factors we identify are external to the person, notice of them alone can only presume specific effects (see Burbank 2011, 12–20, 80). Therefore, we attempt to understand youths' experiences of the complex sociocultural environments that affect their current and future lives though firsthand engagement with them.

The social determinants of health are generally understood as any set of circumstances or events that cause unhealthy stress—that is, an unhealthy activation of the human stress response.[2] This causes a 'fight or flight' response that has served humanity well, but, in our current environments, its prolonged activation, in circumstances that we can rarely fight against or flee from, leads to ill health, self and socially destructive behaviour and, possibly, early death (Marmot and Wilkinson 1999; Sapolsky 2004; Wilkinson and Pickett 2010). Typical examples of these circumstances include protracted experiences of discrimination, subordination and control (e.g. Kawachi and Kennedy 2002; Wilkinson and Pickett 2010). Institutions and social arrangements that create these inequitable and unhealthy experiences have been described as forms of 'structural violence' (Farmer 2004). These may be specific institutions, such as prisons, and

2 We are not saying that all ethnography should include relevant discussion of biological factors. Anthropology is, after all, enriched by its notoriously interdisciplinary practice; anthropologists routinely find illuminating material for their ethnography in areas as diverse as the health and biological sciences, economics, education, various philosophical arguments and myriad other domains.

practices, such as prison regimes of security, punishment and rehabilitation. They may be forms of social inequality, such as rigid class or caste systems. Racism is an apposite example of this latter form of structural violence: here a political entity, such as a nation-state, subjugates a segment of its population on the basis of perceived difference, whether physical, cultural or both (Gravlee 2009; Paradies 2016).

Unhealthy stress is generated by the relative powerlessness these arrangements entail (see Sapolsky 2004). Humans may be especially stressed by negative judgements made by others when they have little control over an outcome (Dickerson and Kemeny quoted in Wilkinson and Pickett 2010, 38). These arrangements and the stresses they generate are often, if not always, accompanied by relative poverty. Hence poverty's manifestations, in such things as poor housing and nutritionally inadequate diets, may be understood as outcomes of structural violence, as may the premature morbidity and mortality in populations that systems of inequality disadvantage (Carson et al. 2007; Marmot 2011). Powerlessness and poverty also lead, sometimes directly, sometimes indirectly, to behaviours that further disadvantage already disadvantaged populations. Such behaviours and their consequences found in Aboriginal Australia include truancy, premature child-bearing, vandalism, substance abuse, suicide[3] and forms of violence and delinquency that lead to incarceration (Burbank, Senior and McMullen 2015; Senior and Chenhall, 2006; Senior and Chenhall 2008a; Senior, Chenhall and Daniels 2006). The contributors to this volume identify and discuss the impact of intercultural arrangements characterised by prolonged histories of discrimination, subordination and control by outsiders that are found in these communities and that either contribute to or hinder the emergence of disadvantage, affecting the lives of the youths who inhabit the pages of this book.

3 In their global survey of inequality and its correlates, Wilkinson and Pickett (2010, 175) have noted that the relationship between suicide and social inequality is an unexpected one. More suicide is to be found in relatively egalitarian societies. We suggest that although Aboriginal Australians usually occupy a subordinate status in Australia, the communities in which they often reside, especially, perhaps, in remote and rural Australia, are characterised by an ethos of egalitarianism (e.g. see Burbank 2014).

Aboriginal Young People in the Northern Territory

Recent research has demonstrated that, throughout Australia, all-cause mortality for Aboriginal young people is double that of non-Aboriginal youth, with approximately 60 per cent of all deaths related to intentional self-harm and road traffic injury (Azzopardi et al. 2018). The Northern Territory has the lowest overall median age of all states and territories at 32.4 years (Australian Bureau of Statistics [ABS] 2016). It also has the highest rates of youth suicide, teenage pregnancy, substance misuse and imprisonment (Australian Institute of Health and Welfare [AIHW] 2015).

Aboriginal youth in the Northern Territory are often defined by the deficits in their health and wellbeing as measured by routinely collected data (e.g. AIHW 2015). For example, notification data in the Northern Territory in 2016 shows that young people aged 15–24 have the highest burden of sexually transmitted infections (Kirby Institute 2018, 93; NT Government 2016). Their rates of teenage pregnancy are seven times higher than the national rate for all teenage women (Li et al. 2006). The high rates of substance abuse (Clough et al. 2004; Senior and Chenhall 2008a; Senior, Chenhall and Daniels 2006) and suicide (ABS 2010) among Aboriginal youth are also recorded. Many Aboriginal youths are described as experiencing poverty, including unhealthy and inadequate diets and substandard and overcrowded housing (Seemann et al. 2008; Brimblecombe et al. 2013). These experiences are described as influencing school attendance, educational outcomes, unemployment and incarceration (Government of Australia 2010). These measures of health and wellbeing are centred on the values of the dominant non-Aboriginal population and rarely include values that Aboriginal people regard as essential for wellbeing (Senior 2003). Values related to family, connection to country and engagement with traditional practices are absent from these indicators (Chenhall and Senior 2018).

Guidance and Control of Youth, Past and Present

As the statistics presented in the last section indicate, the life circumstances for young people in the Northern Territory can be challenging and responses to these may cause consequences that reverberate throughout an individual's life. It may be a time when young people have more freedom to act and, at the same time, are more vulnerable to harmful influences. The developing youth brain, which enables acquisition of greater social-cognitive and social-affective intelligence, may render young people more vulnerable to such influences and encourage risk-taking behaviours, especially when peers are present (Blakemore and Mills 2014, 197–98; Chein et al. 2011; Crone and Dahl 2012, 646; Worthman and Trang 2018, 452). And, as Schlegel and Hewlett (2011, 286) suggest from their exhaustive review of the literature, 'adolescents whose lives are lived at the intersection of two cultures' may have even greater difficulties. This is clearly a time when adult guidance and control are more important than ever, yet may be tested by the adverse effects of intercultural settings.

The forms of government characteristic of pre-colonial Australia have long been a topic of debate,[4] for, as John Bern (1979, 127) has observed, no anthropologist has encountered an Aboriginal society untouched by colonial intrusion. These debates have been further complicated by the considerable social and environmental variability in which the myriad Indigenous language groups are located. Clearly, however, Aboriginal peoples have employed, and continue to employ, forms of social control apart from those imposed from outside. Much like Mervin Meggitt (1962, 247) and Robert Tonkinson (1974, 63), we think it safe to say that, currently, 'Aboriginal' social control is exerted largely through the 'family',[5] on the one hand, and religious practice, on the other, although the legitimacy and effectiveness of both have been severely undermined by the progressive encroachment of Western laws, social arrangements and material goods into these communities.

In past times, guidance and control of youth appears to have been effected largely thorough 'puberty rites' or 'initiation'. The following is an account of the kind of ritual that once took place on Melville Island, off the northern shores of the Northern Territory, when a girl reached menarche:

> I first married to Black Joe when I small girl. He grew me up [introduced to sexual activity]. He made me woman with his finger. One day I think I'm woman [the first menstrual flow]. I little bit shamed. I go bush all alone. I sit down. Nanny Goat Jenny follow

4 For overviews of these debates see Bern (1979) and Hiatt (1996).

5 'Family' is the Kriol/Aboriginal English word used in south-east Arnhem Land to distinguish a set of 'close' kin from all other kin. In anthropological terms, 'family' is known as a 'kindred' (see Shapiro 1979, 57).

> me up. Look about. Find me. She say, 'You muringaleta?' I say no. Five times she say it. By and by I say 'Yes'. She cry cry. Make me cry. She get pandanus and kill [strike] me on arms and back. She make tight rings on my arms, ala same pukamani (mourning). Can't touch food or drink. Might be by and by swell up. One week stay in bush. Someone tell Black Joe, 'Rosie muringaleta!' Everyone happy. Paint up. Get girl-spear and hold it in front. Can't look at husband. He come up behind and kill me with tokwiinga (feather ball). Then I run. Kneel by tree. Husband grab me on shoulder. Tree marked overhead. Ambrinua (son-in-law) get spear. Can't talk husband rest of day. (Goodale 1971, 47)

As Jane Goodale (1971, 47), who heard this story in 1954, tells us, via this ritual activity Rosie not only became a Tiwi 'woman', she became a mother-in-law. Mother-in-law bestowal,[6] practised at one time in a number of Aboriginal societies, illustrates a form of control over young people no longer available to Aboriginal adults. This form of bestowal meant that, from birth, girls were, in effect, married, and might join their husband at a pre-pubertal age (Shapiro 1979, 111–14). It ensured that girls, like Rosie, had a husband long before they might be interested in finding their own sexual and marital partners. Even when mother-in-law bestowal was not employed, Aboriginal people recognised that early marriage for girls was a means of preventing incorrect unions, an important concern in societies organised around designated kin statuses (e.g. Burbank 1987, 1988; Warner 1937, 65). These are derived from the principles of patrifiliation and matrifiliation—that is, on the recognised connections between a man and his child, and a woman and her child (Scheffler 1978, 13–38). Kin identity is also ideally derived from a legitimate conjunction of paternal and maternal statuses expressed in a 'straight' marriage. If a girl becomes pregnant by a partner regarded as 'wrong', people might ask: 'How are you gonna call the child? What's the child gonna be?' (Burbank 1987, 232). Mother-in-law bestowal, or the early bestowal of young children, apparently did much to circumvent the possibility of unrestrained sexual behaviour that might not only restrict youths' futures but also disrupt the social order.

6 In times past, a widespread Aboriginal practice was to bestow a young female upon a man as his mother-in-law. This meant that when this young girl married and if she had at least one girl, her daughter would be given to her son-in-law in marriage. There appears to have been variations in this practice, for example, at Numbulwar a man might be given all the daughters his mother-in-law bore, whereas the Arunta son-in-law would only receive a woman's first daughter (Spencer and Gillen 1899, 559 in Shapiro 1979, 104).

Mother-in-law bestowal was once practised by the Aboriginal groups who today live at Numbulwar, initially established as the Rose River Mission. This practice appears to have been abandoned by the time that the Nunggubuyu/Numburindi settled there in 1952. In its place, women, along with their mothers and mothers' brothers, were said to have betrothed their daughters when they were infants or small children, then eased them into marriage with their promised husband sometime before menarche. Such arrangements, however, were not in accord with the Australian Commonwealth's 'standards of life', and their practise was discouraged (Burbank 1987, 227–28; 1988, 52). By 1981, although at least 18 adolescent girls were known to have been betrothed, only one had married her 'promise' (Burbank 1987, 229). Not only were Aboriginal marriage practices largely dismantled, but also the settlement provided an environment that supported youth strategies, as opposed to those of their elders. For example, the co-educational school, which all youths were expected to attend, provided a venue apart from most Aboriginal adults where adolescent boys and girls might meet. The settlement also enabled the formation of youth peer groups, an unlikely demographic possibility in pre-settlement times given the size of local groups throughout most of the year (Biernoff 1974, 274–76). Peers assisted girls in liaisons regarded as illicit by adults, acting as 'mailman', delivering messages to desired partners (Burbank 1987, 230–31; 1988, 104–05; cf. Senior and Chenhall 2008b).

Not many years after a Methodist mission was established at Millingimbi in 1923, the anthropologist William Lloyd Warner lived for several years among a group of Yolngu people he called the Murngin. His detailed ethnography includes an extensive discussion of the rites of passage through which male Murngins had to pass in order to reach adulthood and ritual seniority. This process began with circumcision. Between the ages of six and eight, boys might be taken from their mothers and other female relatives in a mock battle between men and women. This performance began the Djungguan ceremony's version of circumcision. Including the time the initiates spent travelling to invite other relatives and clans to their initiation, this ceremony might last for a period of up to three months. The mock battle marked a boy's separation from his family; until his marriage he could not live with them, although some contact was allowed. Instead, he resided in the men's camp along with a population of teenagers and older men, all of them unmarried. Male visitors travelling without their wives also stayed in the men's camp. Segregated from women, the camp was a place of education where senior men instructed their juniors. The newly circumcised were introduced to the etiquette of gender relations and reprimanded when they were not conducting themselves as they should. They were taught about 'totemic emblems', 'mythology', and 'group mores and traditions'. Warner (1937, 117) says of these teachers: 'Such authority is more explicit here than one finds it in almost any other part of the Murngin behaviour, with the possible exception of the ceremonial ritual'.

Initiation did not end with the circumcision ceremony. There was at least one other ceremony necessary for adulthood[7] and several others required to achieve a senior ritual status. Instruction did not cease either. In the circumcision ceremony the initiates were told:

> You must not use obscene language. You must never tell a lie. You must not commit adultery, nor go after women who do not belong to you. You must always obey your father and respect your elders. You must never betray the secrets that you have learned from us to the women or the boys who have not been circumcised. (Warner 1937, 278)

And messages of this kind continued to be delivered as young and older men progressed through the series of initiation ceremonies. During these years, young males were subjected not only to painful physical operations, but also to threats, food and speech taboos, periods of fasting and exclusion from their seniors' 'men's business'. But, as just mentioned, they were also instructed and they were nurtured. For example, in the circumcision ceremony, boys were carried just as infants were and adult males lay beneath them and held them in their arms while the operation was performed. Both during the ceremony and afterward they were 'watched over most carefully' by older men:

> This attention is given both to keep them away from the women and because it is felt that during a circumcision initiation, a boy should have every luxury given him and the best of everything that the group has to offer. (Warner 1937, 279)

In his resuscitation of Roheim's ideas about psychosexual development and initiation in Central Australia, Morton (2011, 40) has reacquainted us with the concept of 'mitigated' aggression—'aggression tempered by

7 A young man might marry when he grew a moustache and beard, that is, before he completed the range of initiation.

fellow feeling and sympathy' (Roheim quoted in Morton 2011, 40)—an attitude that Myers has described as 'a specific conflation of "authority and "nurturance"' (Myers quoted in Morton 2011, 40). These Murngin ritual practices and the segregation of unmarried males, both of which might also be described as the practise of 'tough love', were clearly an attempt to guide and control young men, although they were undoubtedly motivated by other intentions as well. As a number of anthropologists have suggested, initiation into religious life—a process that could take years—was a bulwark for a gerontocratic form of sociality (Bern 1979, 125; Hiatt 1985; Keen 1982, 621; Rose 1968, 207). Initiation, however, does not seem to have been entirely effective in this respect and young males have been thought of as sexual miscreants in the past (e.g. Meggitt 1962, 234; Hiatt 1965, 107). Perhaps they are thought to be even more so in recent times (e.g. Sackett 1978).

Beyond this control, ceremonies have other value and continue to be routine in the three remote communities represented in this collection. The question, however, is can they, in intercultural circumstances such as those of Borroloola, Ngukurr and Numbulwar, not to mention the town of Katherine, still hold the same meaning for performers and audiences, and how compatible are they with many of the sociocultural innovations introduced by the encompassing polity? Myrna Tonkinson (2011, 223) has said of Western Desert, Mardu adolescents:

> Sex, marriage, parenthood and family formation are aspects of life characterised by conflicting ideas and practices. Young people's practices do not fit neatly within either traditional Mardu or contemporary Australian norms.

For decades, anthropologists have been observing youths who are disinterested in the ritual life of their communities, at best. For example, discussing the challenges of staging a Jabaduruwa at Ngukurr in the early 1970s, Bern (1970, 17) observed:

> A more general factor was the increasing European influence, particularly on the younger men … [T]he men were doubting the efficacy of totemic myths and questioning the relevance of ceremonial performance.

Among other things, the authority that ceremonial practice previously bestowed on senior men may have been undermined by the changing settlement economy. No longer did sustenance come largely from the land, control of which was exercised in these rituals, but instead from wages and welfare (see Bern 1979, 127). This kind of youthful disaffection is not restricted to Ngukurr. From his work at Wiluna in the Western Desert, Sackett (1978, 116) provides another example of the effect of outside influence on the perspectives of young men with an account of one youth facing circumcision:

> The boy having grown up in the new environment of mission school versus camp, saw [circumcision] in a different light, however. Those positive elements both mystical and pragmatic, which had prepared his father and father's father are no longer present. The supporting myths were largely unknown and those known were sceptically received. Unlike in the past when there would have been no alternative to his following the law.

This process of disaffection is clearly not confined to Aboriginal youth in the Northern Territory.

Aboriginal Australians have long understood the importance of guiding and controlling their youth, no doubt seeing that what transpires during this life stage can have major effects on adult health and wellbeing as well as on the health and wellbeing of the social body (Sawyer et al. 2012, 1631, 1637). Today, however, many Aboriginal youths live in circumstances in which adult guidance, if not control, of adolescent minds and behaviour is either absent or without efficacy. Aside from the radical disruption of their communities and past forms of control, we argue that today this is due, in large part, to the conflicts inherent in intercultural settings, especially ones characterised by such extreme power inequalities as those found between Aboriginal and non-Aboriginal Australians. Thus, within the period of adolescence, which may, in Aboriginal communities, extend into what Westerners consider childhood and adulthood,[8] youths are necessarily making choices that have the potential for harmful long-term consequences with little adult guidance or supervision.

Adults in the communities we include in this volume attempt to regulate youths' unlawful sexual behaviour and pre-empt other forms of delinquency; they are clearly searching for effective forms of social control. As the examples above indicate, in previous times social arrangements largely ensured that young people were placed in situations where

8 At Numbulwar, for example, at least in the recent past, girls were regarded as 'young girls', that is, as adolescents, as soon as their breasts began to develop, regardless of chronological age. Neither adolescent boys nor girls were regarded as adults until they were married and had children (Burbank 1988, 4).

adults were their constant companions and guides, whether this was a young woman being supervised by her husband and senior co-wives, or an adolescent boy in the men's camp in the company of senior men. Papers in this volume illustrate the challenges accompanying these intercultural settings that have created the circumstances in which youths are engaging in behaviours that undermine their communities and their futures. They also illustrate efforts on the part of both young people and adults, the latter both Aboriginal and non-Aboriginal, that may move these communities towards useful solutions or exacerbate the problems of youth.

The Importance of Ethnography

There has necessarily arisen a substantial literature on harmful youth behaviour in Aboriginal Australia that includes attention to their early sexual initiation, substance abuse and other adverse behaviours (e.g. Azzopardi et al. 2018; Blair, Zubrick and Cox 2005; Clough et al. 2004; Chenhall and Senior 2009; Thompson, Zhang and Dempsey 2012). Such efforts provide vital information, much of which has inspired this volume. In contrast, and not surprisingly, there is a relatively small contemporary ethnographic literature that focuses on Aboriginal young people: the seemingly universal reserve of youth in adult company does not usually meld with the method of participant observation. Still, some have managed to engage youth in the field. Besides our own previous work (e.g. Burbank 1987; 1988; Senior and Chenhall 2008a; 2008b), we note Maggie Brady's (1992, 95) ethnographic treatment of youth petrol sniffers in the Northern Territory, Central Australia and Western Australia, which she sees as a means of addressing a 'major crisis of self-image and identity'. Gary Robinson's (1997) examination of the dynamics of separation and individuation in the context of changed marriage arrangements in Tiwi families inevitably led to his engagement with Tiwi youth. Three papers on youth found in Ute Eickelkamp's (2011) collection on childhood and adolescence also illustrate the complications of the latter life stage, created, at least in part, by rapid social change. David Brooks (2011) casts the most positive light on the situation of Aboriginal youth, seeing Ngaanyatjarra social arrangements and 'tjukurrpa-thinking' as ameliorative factors for life trajectories in less than ideal circumstances. In her thoughtful discussion of Mardu youth, Myrna Tonkinson (2011) suggests that premarital pregnancy may not necessarily shunt a teenage girl off into a life of dysfunction, though it is not ideal in terms of health and education. Such a pregnancy may instead create or revive the kinds of ties that ground the social cohesion and resilience upon which so many observers of Aboriginal Australia have remarked. Marika Moisseef (2011) theorises racism's effects on the person, based on her experiences in South Australia, ethnographic literature on Central Australia and her experience as a clinical psychiatrist. Her efforts remind us of what can be a significant characteristic of the intercultural settings in which Aboriginal youth attempt their transitions to adulthood. A collection on *People and Change in Aboriginal Australia* (Austin-Broos and Merlan 2018) provides us with two more studies of youth. In his richly detailed ethnographic account, John Mansfield (2018) suggests that, lacking social legitimacy and desiring personal autonomy, male youths at Wadeye reimagine themselves as non-persons, at least in the local scheme of things, modelling themselves on figures from the outside world's heavy metal scene. In her study of the effects of removing youth from Mornington Island in order that they might study on the mainland, Cameo Dalley (2018) circumvents the difficulties of relying exclusively on conversations with young people. She speaks not only with youth but also with adults who not long before had themselves studied outside the community. Among other things, she found that the youth who benefited the most from this arrangement, according to Western standards, were the children of mixed unions, that is, one of their parents was a non-Mornington Islander. It is predominantly these students who, as adults, now live in nuclear families and are employed in Western occupations. Each of these papers reminds us that youth is a complicated life stage, further complicated for Aboriginal youth by the intercultural spaces in which they are coming of age. The papers also highlight the need for complex representations of these young peoples' lives and environments. It is just such representation that we hope this volume presents. We also hope that it will add to the small but growing understanding of Aboriginal adolescence and inform both Aboriginal and non-Aboriginal people concerned about the futures of Aboriginal youth.

Fieldwork is the sine qua non of ethnographic research. Its principle technique, participant observation, requires living in the community of study and participating in community life. It also requires paying close attention to what is being done and said, what activities are taking place and the characteristics of the setting—in a word, the world as it is at the moment of observation.[9] Participant observation is usually accompanied by the use of other techniques such as self-reflection, autoethnography, linguistic analyses, interviews, questionnaires and other eliciting devices (the reader will find examples of these in the chapters that follow). Of course, extensive and detailed notes are kept of as much of what transpires as possible.

When working in urban settings, as several of the contributors to this volume have done, the community of study may not be as circumscribed or assessable as is the case when research is set in a remote community. Over the last few decades, in particular, anthropologists have become quite adept at doing 'fieldwork' in unconventional locations including health services, courtrooms and prisons, as the reader will soon discover. Even work in remote communities, however, may sometimes take the anthropologist beyond the boundaries of a local setting. For many of us, our work today may be extended during shared expeditions to locations outside the study community, via telephone conversations and social media contact.

The Chapters

The editors of this book have had a long engagement with exploring the lived experience of the social determinants of health with a particular focus on young people. This scope was extended by including insights from PhD students and community researchers, which were discussed at an Australian anthropology conference in 2016. The majority of chapters in this book focus on remote communities in the Northern Territory, including Ngukurr, Yirkala and Numbulwar. Authors discuss the conditions in these communities in which the youth population live, and the changes and controls to which they are subjected. Authors also illustrate the potential for local conditions and large structural and political changes to influence Indigenous lives and life chances. These effects, however, are not limited to remote community contexts. Indigenous youth experience similar conditions in more urban settings. This collection includes studies of young people living at Borroloola, Katherine and incarcerated in the Don Dale Youth Detention Centre at

9 This can be done, of course, only to the extent that it is possible without distressing or disturbing people.

Darwin. It thus enables us to present a panoramic view of Aboriginal youth in the Northern Territory, and the disadvantage, conflict, health statuses and hope that characterise many of their lives.

Most of the contributions to this volume attempt to reflect the firsthand experiences of Aboriginal youth. Ethnographic research has enabled us to focus on individual lives and reveal something of youth perspectives. We have sometimes been able to provide accounts of their actions, decisions and motivations and thus present material with the potential to help the non-Aboriginal segment of Australia understand the reasons behind actions considered to be problems. We have also been able to provide at least the beginnings of an 'experience near' grounding for appropriate and effective policy and programs of support. The editors of this volume have long-standing collaborations with several remote Aboriginal communities and engaged people from these communities as co-researchers to provide direction to the research process and to collaborate in the production of these chapters.

This collection begins with a short autobiographical piece by Angelina Joshua, a young woman from Ngukurr, that frames the first five chapters, all of which are located in this community. Joshua tells us how she negotiates the kinds of social factors that often characterise remote Aboriginal communities: seemingly irrelevant schooling, overcrowded housing and substance abuse. Most painfully, she describes losing her mother at age seven and her father and grandmother as a young adult, losses of a kind that are widespread in Aboriginal families and communities. In this life story, we see how people who might have the greatest interest in, and ability to guide and control, specific youths are lost before their time. A shortage of not only willing but also able adults appears to be one of the factors behind the problems youth both create and face today. Angelina is a long-term research associate of Senior and Chenhall and has been involved in various projects since her youth. She attended the conference in Melbourne and gave a version of her chapter to frame the other papers.

In Chapter 2, Chenhall, Senior and Aboriginal colleagues from Ngukurr, Trudy Hall, Bronwyn Turner and Daphne Daniels, explore the hopes, dreams and plans of a group of young women in Ngukurr. Young women in Ngukurr worked with the authors on a body mapping activity that encouraged them to empathise with a hypothetical character and think deeply about that person's choices and future. This revealed important information relating to their hopes and dreams with respect to their future aspirations for work and relationships. Although young women's narratives of their futures and the choices available to them remained very limited, the visual method provided an important insight into the way that young women were engaging in a radical re-imagination of self. This chapter also serves as an introduction to the Ngukurr community and its circumstances to frame the chapters that follow.

Placing their discussion of youth leadership at Ngukurr in the context of three generations of leaders, Senior and Chenhall's conversations with young men help them identify young peoples' understanding of leadership, the ways they enact it and the disjunction between their own, the Ngukurr community's and the larger society's ideas of who Aboriginal leaders should be and what they should do. Here we find a portrayal of the difficulties that Aboriginal adults may face in the governance of their community. We also find a unique, though imperfect, solution: self-governance by the young themselves.

The next two chapters, by Danielle Aquino and Greg Dickson, present happier, though not uncomplicated, pictures of young peoples' lives. Aquino's work, focusing on youth food choice in Ngukurr, demonstrates the difficulties of food importation and how this challenges health promotion statements around healthy diets. This chapter portrays the kind of environmental complexity in which outsider information and entrenched local practice may collide, the kind of encounter often noted in accounts of intercultural settings characterised by inequality and rapid change. Nevertheless, a growing appreciation of 'traditional' foods may be countering what appears to be a universal human appreciation of fat and sugar (Breslin 2013) and local norms regarding the proper response to children's demands, including demands for unhealthy kinds of food. Dickson, a linguist, examines young people's knowledge and use of bush medicines in the community of Ngukurr, including their knowledge of traditional language terms for various plants and their associated uses in healing. He challenges views that such knowledge is deteriorating and portrays the considerable extent to which young Aboriginal people know about, and use, bush medicines. His research indicates the persistence of at least some forms of Aboriginal knowledge, a notable example as Western medicine has been practised at Ngukurr for over 100 years. He may be providing us with an example of a youth-generated maintenance of cultural tradition that may sometimes be found in intercultural settings.

Moving the focus away from Ngukurr to the nearest regional centre, Friderichs's paper describes young peoples' knowledge about, and use of, both Western and Aboriginal forms of health care. Her ethnographic study is located in Katherine, another town populated by both Aboriginal and non-Aboriginal people, but one that is somewhat larger than Ngukurr and closer to Darwin, the Northern Territory's largest urban centre. Its intercultural nature is of particular interest with regard to the diversity of its Aboriginal population and the various identities held by the youths with whom Friderichs worked. Not surprisingly, she found an array of diverging and overlapping ideas about health and healing available to Aboriginal young people. The variety of this information undoubtedly affects what they know about health and the choices they make with regard to it. Like Dickson and Aquino, Friderichs presents the complex and contradictory information that Aboriginal youth receive in the intercultural settings they inhabit and the difficulties these present to those desiring to create appropriate forms of guidance.

Sue McMullen and Kishan Kariippanon continue to paint vivid pictures of the life circumstances of Aboriginal youth. McMullen's paper compares sexual activity and pregnancy in two other towns in south-east Arnhem Land, further east towards the Gulf of Carpentaria. The furthest, some 437 km south-east of Ngukurr, is home to both Aboriginal and non-Aboriginal people, and, with a range of liquor outlets, is known for both violence and alcohol abuse. This is a significant part of the context in which youth pregnancy and child-bearing occur and the life prospects of 'young girls', that is, young females, may be established. In Kariippanon's study, which is set in the remote Yolngu community of Yirrkala and an associated outstation, we see an example of intercultural sociality that surrounds both the anthropologist and the youth he is there to understand. We are able to see the circumstances that lead to his conclusion that social media, rather than enhancing the youth experience, may be exacerbating some of the long-existing problems they face. His study also illustrates some of the ways in which new technology can undermine adult control of youth misbehaviour, though such technology may also promise new ways of exerting it.

In 2016, Darwin's Don Dale Youth Detention Centre, largely populated by young Aboriginal offenders, became the focus of national attention with the Australian Broadcasting Corporation's *Four Corners* program's public exposure of young inmates' mistreatment. This was followed by the Royal Commission into the Detention and Protection of Children in the Northern Territory in 2016–17. Just years before this inquiry, Pippa Rudd had been engaged in an ethnographic study of the juvenile justice system in Darwin when she lost her battle with cancer. The chapter on juvenile (in)justice was completed by Kate Senior and Jared Sharp. Drawing on Rudd's field notes and interviews with three 18-year-old Aboriginal inmates of the Don Dale correctional facility, the authors trace the pathways in and out of the correctional system as they are perceived by its youth prisoners. Although it is not unusual for young Aboriginal people to spend some time in jail, and these youthful inmates sometimes compare it favourably with life 'outside', incarceration is far from an ideal condition for a developing young human. While this chapter is based in Darwin, these experience of youth incarceration would be well known to youth in remote communities. It presents an intercultural space that has not often been examined, particularly from the perspective of young people themselves.

The final chapter in this book, by Burbank, draws on autobiographical material that covers a 30-year period from a senior Numburindi man. Sawyer's story allows Burbank to address the question of guidance and the benign control of adolescent behaviour in another intercultural space. This paper suggests the importance of individual motivation in the domain of self-control, a factor that needs to be considered in the construction of programs and policies, but one that is highly individualised.

We anticipate that readers will find in this book a greater understanding of the day-to-day lives of at least some Aboriginal young people, and some of the adults who care for or neglect them. We also anticipate that readers will finish the collection with a better understanding of the circumstances, processes and factors that affect youth health, wellbeing and future prospects in their intercultural environments. We hope that readers will, at least, glimpse the multiplicity of these circumstances, processes and factors, and the complexity of their interaction. We also hope that readers will consider whether or not future policies and programs of intervention or assistance advantage these youth and their seniors in their already beset circumstances:

> [Most] important is the creation of conditions where Aboriginal people have enough incentive and motivation, and enough capacity to change, to make improvement in their own lives. Large numbers have done so. (Sutton 2009, 12)

References

Allen, J., K. Hopper, L. Wexler, M. Kral, S. Rasmus and K. Nystad. 2014. 'Mapping Resilience Pathways of Indigenous Youth in Five Circumpolar Communities'. *Transcultural Psychiatry* 51 (5): 601–31. doi.org/10.1177/1363461513497232.

Austin-Broos, D. 2011. *A Different Inequality: The Politics of Debate about Remote Aboriginal Australia.* Crows Nest, NSW: Allen & Unwin.

Austin-Broos, D. and F. Merlan, eds. 2018. *People and Change in Aboriginal Australia.* Honolulu: University of Hawai'i Press. doi.org/10.21313/hawaii/9780824867966.003.0001.

Australian Bureau of Statistics. 2010. 'Causes of Death Australia, 3303.0'. Canberra: ABS.

Australian Bureau of Statistics. 2016. 'Australian Demographic statistics, 3101.0'. Canberra: ABS.

Australian Institute of Health and Welfare (AIHW). 2015. *The Health and Welfare of Australia's Aboriginal and Torres Strait Islander Peoples 2015.* Cat. no. IHW 147. Canberra: AIHW.

Azzopardi, P., S. Sawyer, J. Carline, L. Degenhardt, N. Brown and G. Patton. 2018. 'Health and Wellbeing of Aboriginal Adolescents in Australia: A Systematic Synthesis of Population Data'. *The Lancet* 24 (391): 766–82. doi.org/10.1016/S0140-6736(17)32141-4.

Bern, J. 1970. *Field Report on Social Anthropological Research At Ngukurr, Northern Territory, December 1979 to June 1970.* Canberra: Australian Institute of Aboriginal Studies.

Bern, J. 1979. 'Ideology and Domination: Toward a Reconstruction of Australian Aboriginal Social Formation'. *Oceania* 2: 118–31. doi.org/10.1002/j.1834-4461.1979.tb01948.x.

Biernoff, D. 1974. 'Pre and Post-European Designs of Aboriginal Settlements: The Case of the Nunggubuyu of Eastern Arnhem Land'. *Man-Environment Systems* 4 (5): 273–82.

Blair, E. M., S. R. Zubrick and A. H. Cox. 2005. 'The Western Australian Aboriginal Child Health Survey: Findings to Date on Adolescents'. *Medical Journal of Australia* 183: 433–35. doi.org/10.5694/j.1326-5377.2005.tb07112.x.

Blakemore, S-J. and K. Mills. 2014. 'Is Adolescence a Sensitive Period for Sociocultural Processing'. *Annual Review of Psychology* 65: 187–207. doi.org/10.1146/annurev-psych-010213-115202.

Brady, M. 1992. *Heavy Metal: The Social Meaning of Petrol Sniffing in Australia.* Canberra: Aboriginal Studies Press.

Breslin, P. A. S. 2013. 'An Evolutionary Perspective on Food and Human Taste'. *Current Biology* 23 (9): R409–R418. doi.org/10.1016/j.cub.2013.04.010.

Brimblecombe, J., M. Ferguson, S. O'Dea and K. O'Dea. 2013. 'Characteristics of the Community-Level Diet of Aboriginal People in Remote Northern Australia'. *Medical Journal of Australia* 198 (7): 380–84. doi.org/10.5694/mja12.11407.

Brooks, D. 2011. 'Organization within Disorder: The Present and Future of Young People in the Ngaanyatjarra Lands'. In *Growing Up in Central Australia: New Anthropological Studies of Aboriginal Childhood and Adolescence*, edited by U. Eickelkamp, 183–213. Oxford: Berghahn Books.

Brunner E. and D. Marmot. 1999. 'Social Organization, Stress and Health'. In *Social Determinants of Health*, edited by E. Brunner and D. Marmot, 17–23. Oxford: Oxford University Press.

Burbank, V. 1987. 'Premarital Sex Norms: Cultural Interpretation in an Australian Aboriginal Community'. *Ethos* 15: 226–34. doi.org/10.1525/eth.1987.15.2.02a00040.

Burbank, V. 1988. *Aboriginal Adolescence: Maidenhood in an Australian Community.* New Brunswick, NJ: Rutgers University Press.

Burbank, V. 2011. *An Ethnography of Stress: The Social Determinants of Health in Aboriginal Australia.* New York: Palgrave Macmillan. doi.org/10.1057/9780230117228.

Burbank, V. 2014. 'Envy and Egalitarianism in Aboriginal Australia: An Integrative Approach'. *The Australian Journal of Anthropology* 25: 1–25. doi.org/10.1111/taja.12068.

Burbank, V., K. Senior and S. McMullen. 2015. 'Precocious Pregnancy, Sexual Conflict and Early Childbearing in Remote Aboriginal Australia'. *Anthropological Forum* 25 (3): 243–61. doi.org/10.1080/00664677.2015.1027657.

Carson, B., T. Dunbar, R. Chenhall and R. Bailie, eds. 2007. *Social Determinants of Aboriginal Health.* Crows Nest, NSW: Allen & Unwin.

Casey, B. 2015. 'Beyond Simple Models of Self-Control to Circuit-Based Accounts of Adolescent Behaviour'. *Annual Review of Psychology* 66: 295–319. doi.org/10.1146/annurev-psych-010814-015156.

Chein, J., A. Duston, L. O'Brien, K. Uckert and L. Steinberg. 2011. 'Peers Increase Adolescent Risk Taking by Enhancing Activity in the Brain's Reward Circuity'. *Developmental Science* 14 (2): F1–F10. doi.org/10.1111/j.1467-7687.2010.01035.x.

Chenhall, R. and K. Senior. 2009. 'Those Young People All Crankybella: Indigenous Youth Mental Health and Globalization'. *International Journal of Mental Health* 38 (3): 28–43. doi.org/10.2753/IMH0020-7411380302.

Chenhall R. D. and K. Senior. 2018. 'Living the Social Determinants of Health: Assemblages in a Remote Aboriginal Community'. *Medical Anthropology Quarterly* 32 (2): 177–95. doi.org/10.1111/maq.12418.

Clough, A. R., P. D'Abbs, S. Cairney, D. Gray, P. Maruff, R. Parker and B. O'Reilly. 2004. 'Emerging Patterns of Cannabis and Other Substance Use in Aboriginal Communities in Arnhem Land, Northern Territory: A Study of Two Communities'. *Drug and Alcohol Review* 23 (4): 381–90. doi.org/10.1080/09595230412331324509.

Crone, E. and R. Dahl. 2012. 'Understanding Adolescence as a Period of Social-Affective Engagement and Goal Flexibility'. *Nature Reviews Neuroscience* 13: 636–50. doi.org/10.1038/nrn3313.

Dalley, C. 2018. 'Mobility and the Education of Aboriginal Youth Away from Remote Home Communities'. In *People and Change in Aboriginal Australia*, edited by D. Austin-Broos and F. Merlan, 130–45. Honolulu: University of Hawai'i Press. doi.org/10.1515/9780824873332-008.

Eickelkamp, U. 2011. *Growing Up in Central Australia: New Anthropological Studies of Aboriginal Childhood and Adolescence.* New York: Berghahn Books.

Farmer, P. 2004. 'An Anthropology of Structural Violence'. *Current Anthropology* 45: 305–25. doi.org/10.1086/382250.

Goodale, J. 1971. *Tiwi Wives: A Study of the Women of Melville Island, North Australia.* Seattle: University of Washington Press.

Government of Australia. 2010. *Closing the Gap: Prime Minister's Report.* Canberra: Commonwealth of Australia.

Gravlee, C. 2009. 'How Race Becomes Biology: Embodiment of Social Inequality'. *American Journal of Physical Anthropology* 139: 47–57. doi.org/10.1002/ajpa.20983.

Hiatt, L. 1965. *Kinship and Conflict: A Study of an Aboriginal Community in Northern Arnhem Land.* Canberra: Australian National University Press.

Hiatt, L. 1985. 'Maidens, Males and Marx: Some Contrasts in the Work of Frederick Rose and Claude Meillassoux'. *Oceania* 56: 34–46. doi.org/10.1002/j.1834-4461.1985.tb02106.x.

Hiatt, L. 1996. *Arguments about Aborigines: Australia and the Evolution of Social Anthropology*. Cambridge: Cambridge University Press.

Hinkson, M. and B. Smith. 2005. 'Introduction: Conceptual Moves towards an Intercultural Analysis'. *Oceania* 75 (3): 157–66. doi.org/10.1002/j.1834-4461.2005.tb02877.x.

Kawachi, I. and B. Kennedy. 2002. *The Health of Nations: Why Inequality Is Harmful for Your Health.* New York: The New Press.

Keen, I. 1982. 'How Some Murngin Men Marry Ten Wives: The Marital Implication of Matrilateral Cross-Cousin Structures'. *Man* 17: 620–42. doi.org/10.2307/2802037.

Kirby Institute. 2018. *Bloodborne Viral and Sexually Transmissible Infections in Aboriginal and Torres Strait Islander People: Annual Surveillance Report 2018.* Sydney: Kirby Institute, UNSW.

Li, S. Q., S. Guthridge, E. Tursan d'Espaignet and B. Paterson. 2006. *From Infancy to Young Adulthood: Health Status in the Northern Territory 2006.* Darwin: Department of Health and Community Services. Accessed 8 June 2021, digitallibrary.health.nt.gov.au/dspace/bitstream/10137/84/1/infancy_to_young_adulthood_2006.pdf.

Mansfield, J. 2018. 'Murrinhpatha Personhood, Other Humans and Contemporary Youth'. In *People and Change in Aboriginal Australia*, edited by D. Austin-Broos and F. Merlan, 117–29. Honolulu: University of Hawai'i Press. doi.org/10.1515/9780824873332-007.

Marmot, M. 2011. 'Social Determinants and the Health of Aboriginal Australians'. *Medical Journal of Australia* 194 (10): 512–13. doi.org/10.5694/j.1326-5377.2011.tb03086.x.

Marmot, M. and R. Wilkinson, eds. 1999. *Social Determinants of Health.* Oxford: Oxford University Press.

Meggitt, M. 1962. *Desert People: A Study of the Walbiri Aborigines of Central Australia.* Sydney: Angus and Robertson.

Merlan, F. 1998. *Caging the Rainbow: Places, Politics and Aborigines in a North Australian Town*. Honolulu: University of Hawai'i Press. doi.org/10.1515/9780824861742.

Merlan, F. 2005. 'Explorations towards Intercultural Accounts of Socio-cultural Reproduction and Change'. *Oceania* 75 (3): 167–82. doi.org/10.1002/j.1834-4461.2005.tb02878.x.

Moisseef, M. 2011. 'Invisible and Visible Loyalties in Racialized Contexts: A Systemic Perspective on Aboriginal Youth'. In *Growing Up in Central Australia: New Anthropological Studies of Aboriginal Childhood and Adolescence*, edited by U. Eickelkamp, 213–38. Oxford: Berghahn Books.

Morton, J. 2011. '"Less Was Hidden among These Children": Geza Roheim, Anthropology and the Politics of Aboriginal Childhood'. In *Growing Up in Central Australia: New Anthropological Studies of Aboriginal Childhood and Adolescence*, edited by U. Eickelkamp, 15–48. New York: Berghahn Books.

Northern Territory Government. 2016. *NT Guidelines for the Management of Sexually Transmitted Infections in the Primary Health Care Setting*. Darwin: Sexual Health and Blood Borne Virus Unit, Centre for Disease Control. Northern Territory Government.

Paradies, Y. 2016. 'Colonisation, Racism and Aboriginal Health'. *Journal of Populations Research* 33 (1): 83–96. doi.org/10.1007/s12546-016-9159-y.

Robinson, G. 1997. 'Families, Generation and Self: Conflict, Loyalty, and Recognition in an Australian Aboriginal Society'. *Ethos* 25 (3): 303–32. doi.org/10.1525/eth.1997.25.3.303.

Rose, F. 1968. 'Australian Marriage, Land-Owning Groups, and Initiations'. In *Man the Hunter*, edited by R. Lee and I. DeVore, 200–09. Chicago: Aldine. doi.org/10.4324/9780203786567-25.

Sackett, L. 1978. 'Punishment in Ritual: "Man Making" among Western Desert Aborigines'. *Oceania* XLIV (2): 110–27. doi.org/10.1002/j.1834-4461.1978.tb01382.x.

Sapolsky, R. 2004. 'Social Status and Health in Humans and Other Animals'. *Annual Review of Anthropology* 33: 393–418. doi.org/10.1146/annurev.anthro.33.070203.144000.

Sawyer, S., A. Rima, L. Bearinger, S.-J. Blakemore, B. Dick, A. Ezeh and G. Patton. 2012. 'Adolescence: A Foundation for Future Health'. *Lancet* 379: 1630–40. doi.org/10.1016/S0140-6736(12)60072-5.

Scheffler, H. 1978. *Australian Kin Classification*. Cambridge: Cambridge University Press. doi.org/10.1017/CBO9780511557590.

Schelgel, A. and H. Barry. 1991. *Adolescence, An Anthropological Inquiry*. New York: The Free Press.

Schlegel, A. and B. Hewlett. 2011. 'Contributions of Anthropology to the Study of Adolescence'. *Journal of Research on Adolescence* 21 (1): 281–89. doi.org/10.1111/j.1532-7795.2010.00729.x.

Seemann, K., M. Parnell, S. McFallan and S. Tucker. 2008. *Housing for Livelihoods: The Lifecycle of Housing and Infrastruture through a Whole-of-System Approach in Remote Aboriginal Settlements*. Alice Springs: Desert Knowledge Cooperative Research Centre.

Senior, K. 2003. 'A Gudbala Laif? Health and Wellbeing in a Remote Aboriginal Community—What Are the Problems and Where Lies The Responsibility?' PhD thesis, The Australian National University, Canberra.

Senior, K. and R. Chenhall. 2008a. 'Lukumbat Marawana: A Changing Pattern of Drug Use by Youth in a Remote Aboriginal Community'. *Australian Journal of Rural Health*, 16: 75–79. doi.org/10.1111/j.1440-1584.2008.00956.x.

Senior, K. and R. Chenhall. 2008b. '"Walkin' about at Night": The Background to Teenage Pregnancy in a Remote Aboriginal Community'. *Journal of Youth Studies* 11 (3): 269–81. doi.org/10.1080/13676260801946449.

Senior, K., R. Chenhall and D. Daniels. 2006. '"Stuck Nose", Reasons to Sniff in a Remote Aboriginal Community'. *Contemporary Drug Problems* 33: 451–72. doi.org/10.1177/009145090603300306.

Shapiro, W. 1979. *Social Organization in Aboriginal Australia*. New York: St Martin's Press.

Spencer, B. and F. J. Gillen. 1899. *The Native Tribes of Central Australia*. London: Macmillan.

Sutton, P. 2009. *The Politics of Suffering: Aboriginal Australia and the End of the Liberal Consensus*. Melbourne: Melbourne University Press.

Tanner, J. 1990. *Fetus into Man: Physical Growth from Conception to Maturity*. Cambridge, MA: Harvard University Press.

Thompson F., X. Zhang and K. Dempsey. 2012. *Northern Territory Midwives' Collection. Mothers and Babies 2007*. Darwin: Department of Health.

Tonkinson, M. 2011. 'Being Mardu: Change and Challenge for Some Western Desert Young People Today'. In *Growing Up in Central Australia: New Anthropological Studies of Aboriginal Childhood and Adolescence*, edited by U. Eickelkam, 213–38. Oxford: Berghahn Books.

Tonkinson, R. 1974. *The Jigalong Mob: Aboriginal Victors of the Desert Crusade.* Menlo Park, CA: Cummings Publishing Company.

Vogt, E. and E. Albert, eds. 1966. *People of Rimrock: A Study of Values in Five Cultures.* Cambridge, MA: Harvard University Press.

Vogt, E. with the assistance of M. J. Arth. 1967. 'Intercultural Relations'. In *People of Rimrock: A Study of Values in Five Cultures*, edited by E. Vogt and E. Albert, 46–82. Cambridge, MA: Harvard University Press. doi.org/10.4159/harvard.9780674865082.c5.

Warner, W. L. 1937. *A Black Civilization.* New York: Harper. doi.org/10.2307/2262587.

Wilkinson, R. and K. Pickett. 2010. *The Spirit Level: Why Greater Equality Makes Societies Stronger.* London: Bloomsbury Press.

Worthman, C. and K. Trang. 2018. 'Dynamics of Body Time, Social Time and Life History at Adolescence'. *Nature* 554: 451–57. doi.org/10.1038/nature25750.

1

Living the Social Determinants of Health: My Story

Angelina Joshua

My name is Angelina Joshua and I was born in 1987 in Ngukurr. Ngukurr is a small community in south-east Arnhem Land. It takes about eight hours to drive from Ngukurr to Darwin and our nearest large town is Katherine, or K-Town to the locals. I'm the youngest child in our family. There are seven of us: two older brothers and four older sisters. My mum was from Oenpelli, an Aboriginal community near Kakadu, and my dad was from Ngukurr.

When I was little, I remember always being with my brothers and sisters; they were always home and looking after me. They gave my dad time to do his job and to put food on the table. Growing up, my life was the best. I wouldn't ask for anything else, because I have an amazing family. I also remember going to school; I went nearly every day because my dad said it was important. Sometimes I didn't want to go, but I didn't have any choice; I had to go.

My mum passed away when I was about seven. I don't remember her at all, but sometimes I think about going to visit her country around Oenpelli. Dad had to look after us, but he had my older brothers and sisters and my three grandparents to help. They had to help because he often had to leave Ngukurr for meetings. Dad was the housing officer and before that he was the town clerk.

I was going to school every day, but I didn't ever learn to read and write as a child. It wasn't until I was in high school that I finally learnt to read: I was 13 or 14. A new teacher came in and brought literacy and numeracy into the school. We did writing on the board and we read the book *Lockie Leonard* (Winton 1990). We did that book in school and it was really amazing when I actually learnt to read—this was when I was 14. It was really hard at first. I was always saying 'I don't know this word, I don't even know what it means'. It was really hard man. I look back at it now and it's hard to imagine not being able to read. I love reading.

My dad was the boss in our family. He was strict in a good way. I'd say to him, 'I want to go to the disco', and he would stop and have a think and then say, 'No you are staying at home'. He wouldn't give me the opportunity to go out prowling at night. I didn't have a boyfriend; I wasn't allowed to have a boyfriend. No boyfriends and no prowling. I didn't like it much then, watching all my friends walk about at night. Now I think it was good to be different. Now when I'm at Ngukurr, I look at all the girls and boys, all my old friends, and they all married up now with kids. I don't know how they feel; they are always caught up with their kids who are crying all the time. But I'm free. I see boys telling their wives what to do and if they don't do it, they get beaten. I am lucky because of my dad. I thank my dad for raising me up to be a talented woman. There is one thing I worry about; I didn't learn much about culture.[1] My dad was more interested in me learning at school than teaching me things about culture.

When I was 13, my dad got married again. I didn't feel comfortable calling someone new 'mum'. Actually I didn't feel comfortable at all, because I had grown up without a mother. We lived with her and her three kids; sometimes there were 10 children in the house. I was lucky that I had other family to stay with in Ngukurr and I could get away sometimes when it felt really overcrowded and noisy. Now the kids are part of the family; we have all grown up and we understand.

When I was 16, I went to boarding school in Darwin. I wouldn't say it was difficult. It was alright, even normal. There were lots of kids from different communities there. Sometimes we would fight, but not as much as the fighting that goes on now. But maybe I had too much fun at boarding school. I got expelled for being a bad girl and going out and looking

1 By culture, Angelina means traditional Aboriginal culture, including knowledge of her country and dreamings, knowledge of her obligations through kinship as well as the appropriate songs and dances.

for alcohol. I was always looking for alcohol. I would meet my friends and it was amazing; we would do this and that and I was the leader. My friends would all follow me and that's why I got caught all the time. I didn't really learn much. I had a bad attitude and I gave the house parents and teachers a bad time. They would say 'you are a talented young lady, I know you can learn and listen more, you've just got that attitude woman!'

It was a lot of fun, but I got expelled and got sent back home. Dad was really cross with me. He went to his office without talking to me and when he came home he said: 'Tomorrow you have got to look for a job, you are not going to eat and sleep under my roof and not work for a living'. I was just about to turn 18.

So, I went and got a job as an assistant teacher at the school. I loved the kids and they loved me, but I didn't really know what I wanted to do. I was always thinking about other jobs. I worked at the council for a bit and then I ended up with lots of jobs around the community; I just kept moving from one to another. I left work for a while and I couldn't find another job, so I was at home doing nothing. Then a position came along with Sunrise Health Service. They were running a nutrition program in the community, where they gave iron supplements to children. They had a vacancy for a community-based worker. I took that job in 2005 and I have been eight years on and off with that mob.

Then, one day, something really big and bad happened to me. I had been in Darwin and Katherine for training for the nutrition project. It was the last day and we were at the resort in Katherine and we were drinking. I had a couple and I fell and I started having a seizure. It was lucky I was with my friends; they rang my supervisor and she came running. The ambulance came and took me straight to Darwin and straight into the operating theatre. They cut my head open and I had an operation to drain out all the blood. I was in a coma. Then they flew me to Adelaide while I was still in a coma. When I woke up, I couldn't remember anything, not anything, not even my name or what had happened to me or my age. My brother came down to Adelaide to look after me.

The accident affected my memory and my right leg. I remember being in hospital fighting for my memory and trying to walk again. It was the scariest thing for my brother. I don't know if it was scary for me because I felt so supported; my brother was there and my teacher, Jacinta, drove all the way from Melbourne to be with me. They were supporting me and my family all the way until I got strong again. I don't know what I would do without Jacinta. The best day of my life was when I was able to take steps again. That's when my physio organised another doctor to work with me and throw my walking frame away. We went to the gym to do some work and they said 'time to get rid of the frame'. I started to get really scared. I thought I might fall and bump my head again. But they did a good job; it was amazing. They said: 'I'm going to do this and you copy me'. They were hopping and running and I thought 'Oh my gosh, I can't do this', but they said, 'Yes you can, just take it slowly'. I thought he was crazy, but I took my first two steps and it made me feel really good inside. I just went for it. I was proud of myself; it was the best thing that ever happened in my life to walk again. I still remember it and think about it. I walked back to my room and I didn't use the frame. My brother saw me sitting there with a big smile saying, 'We are going back home'.

The accident changed my life. Before the accident, I was a really heavy smoker and I drank a lot of alcohol. It was heavy drinking. I drank all the hot stuff: rum, Jim Beam, vodka. I was drinking so much, but I was just being me. It was nothing to do with being worried; I just liked drinking and being drunk. But maybe if I didn't have such a good family, I would be drinking because of stress—lots of people do. Now I'm a new person. I get up early in the morning and I go to work.

When I came home to Ngukurr, my memory wasn't that strong, but gradually it all came back; being home really helped. I started work again and I had lots of opportunities including the opportunity to go and live and work in Darwin. In 2013, I lost the most important people in my life. I lost my dad, he was 58, and my grandma. It was so much pain. I couldn't think or work; I was really, really down. Then another girl died and it was all too much. She was so young and the loss of her really hurt. I couldn't keep going. I kept getting these voices in my head. Dad's voice kept me from breaking loose. I was going backwards. Losing my dad was really painful. I was living in Darwin and I wanted to experience new things, but my family were calling me, calling me back home. They were saying 'It's not the same without you'. It made me really sad. I missed my best friends, hanging out with them and laughing, and I missed my brothers and sisters. I didn't have anyone to talk to. It was a really hard time. I was experiencing city life, but I didn't really like it. At least I gave it a go.

It's good to be back home in Ngukurr; being home is just great. I didn't work for a month and then I said to myself 'I need to be thinking and working for my brain to work again'. A linguist came to my place and said that they were looking for a part-time language worker. I said that I'd love to do that because I didn't have any job. Now I have a part-time job at the Language Centre. The hours suit my life. I don't want to work full time and get stressed and hurt my brain again. It's fascinating because we are learning my grandma's language.

I am living with my sister, but I would love a place of my own. My sister has three kids and they all bring their friends around and make a lot of noise, which drives me crazy. I wish that the house wasn't so crowded; it gets so hard, especially when you want to use the stove and the shower. It's a good life now, though. I'm feeling calm after lots of ups and downs. It's so much better than when I was drinking and smoking and had all that attitude.

References

Winton, T. 1990. *Lockie Leonard Human Torpedo*. UK: Bodley Head Children's Books.

2

Defiance in the Detail: Young Women's Embodied Future Selves

Richard Chenhall, Kate Senior, Trudy Hall,
Bronwyn Turner and Daphne Daniels

Introduction

> All of us are doomed to the life of choices, but not all of us have the means to be the chooser. (Bauman 1998, 86)

Future thinking, which may encompass ideas of hopes, aspirations, concerns and fears, has become an important focus of anthropological interest, with authors suggesting that such a focus stems from global feelings of crisis and uncertainty (Kleist and Jansen 2016). Within this larger global perspective, people also develop their own personal sets of hopes and aspirations. The ambitions of these are largely constrained by the opportunity and experience that individuals and groups have to imagine potential life paths (Appadurai 2013). People living in impoverished environments are expected to have a limited set of choices regarding their lives, because their experiences and their opportunities to enact change are constrained. But, as Hoffman (2017) argues in her study of youth in Haiti, limited options may reduce outcomes, but not necessarily the desire to make change. Disadvantaged people do not necessarily suffer from a 'poverty of aspiration' (Hoffman 2017, 18).

Young people are often the focus of studies about futures, hopes and aspirations, as they are in the process of actively constructing their own futures; indeed, the words 'youth' and 'aspiration' are often combined to inform a discourse of future planning that revolves around education, tertiary opportunities and a successful career. Implied is a step wise plan, in which each action leads to the next desirable outcome. Young women in Australia expect to have lives that are different from those of their mothers and grandmothers—they expect to be involved in the labour force and to delay marriage and motherhood until their late 20s (Wyn and Woodman 2006)—which implies a step-by-step rendering of their futures. As Kenway and Hickey-Moody (2011, 152) point out, this consideration of aspirations, which appears deeply embedded in educational policy, fails to recognise 'how complex and diverse aspiration is and how it is rooted in social, cultural and spatial inequalities'. Harwood et al. (2017) have recently described research in which they engaged disadvantaged young people in discussions about their educational futures, including how they imagined their post-school educational options. Importantly, these young people conceptualised the future as being 'both distant and fragile' and only to 'be dealt with seriously *after* the pains of the present, inflicted by schooling have been managed' (Harwood et al. 2017, 132, original emphasis). Implicit in this is the suggestion that disadvantaged young people, whose present lives are problematical and unpredictable, are too busy responding and reacting to the present to make concrete plans for the future. For Indigenous youth living in Australia's remotest regions, a range of structural inequalities resulting from colonisation, poverty and a history of exclusion from participation in economic, education and governance processes has resulted in the poverty of available choices (Senior and Chenhall 2008, 2012) or, in Appadurai's terms, a reduced 'capacity to aspire':

> If the map of aspirations (continuing the navigational metaphor) is seen to consist of a dense combination of nodes and pathways, relative poverty means a smaller number of aspirational nodes and a thinner, weaker sense of the pathways from concrete wants to general norms and back again. (Appadurai 2013, 189)

In 2008 and 2012, two of us published some of the results of our study of young women's present lives and future aspirations in the remote Aboriginal community of Ngukurr in the Northern Territory (Senior and Chenhall 2008, 2012). We drew on material that we had collected through our extended periods of ethnographic engagement in the community from 1999 to 2008. In our earlier papers, we discussed the limited range of options available to young women, their limited conceptions of future selves, and their limited agency to either make or imagine a different type of future. We concluded that:

> Young women's agency examined within the context of a culture which is bound in age and gender hierarchies would appear very limited … community living requires a series of compromises from the young women. (Senior and Chenhall 2012, 384)

The young women in our study described feeling trapped by what they considered to be traditional gender roles; they also considered escaping from these roles to be impossible. For example, one young woman commented that the only way she saw to avoid this was to 'go to Melbourne and get a sex change operation' (Senior and Chenhall 2012, 383). This possibility aside, it was clear from what the young women had to say that they thought that leaving the community would not enable them to take up opportunities unavailable to them in their own communities. Young people talked about the strong pull that the community and their families had on them, and made it clear that they could never consider living anywhere else (Senior 2003; Senior and Chenhall 2008). The limited range of choices available to young women in remote communities is also a strong theme of McMullen's research, described in Chapter 7 of this volume. This chapter presents findings from further work conducted with a group of young women in a remote Aboriginal community for whom the opportunities to engage, or even imagine engaging, in the sorts of trajectories set out in educational policies are very limited.

Working with Young People in Ngukurr

Between 2014 and 2016, we revisited Ngukurr to work with young people around their aspirations for the future. We combined participant observation with a series of workshops that included a body mapping workshop and a photovoice project, in which young people were asked to take pictures of the 'most important things in their lives and what they wanted their future lives to look like'. Twelve young women participated in the project and eight young men. The young men were enthusiastic about the photovoice project and embarked on producing photographs for a book to describe their lives, values and aspirations (Senior and Chenhall 2017; see also Chapter 3 of this volume). Although few of the young men had completed schooling, they had a clearly thought-out process whereby they would be recognised as the future leaders of their community (Senior and Chenhall 2017). As with Kenway and Hickey-Moody's (2011, 153) 'Boys with Aerial Vision', they had viewed the community strategically, located an opening in the political structure and determined a step-by-step approach to achieve their plans, which included a series of meetings to consider their approach—which was to burst into the community's imagination and ensure their efforts were continually noticed and reaffirmed.

Although the young women also participated in the photovoice project, the method that caught their attention and enthusiasm was the body mapping workshop. They enjoyed the combination of storytelling and creativity. In this exercise, a series of hypothetical scenarios were developed and these were used to guide discussions and the decoration of life-sized body maps (for more details, see Senior and Chenhall, 2017) with groups of up to five young women at a time. The stories framing the discussion linked to their work on the body map and were designed to elicit information about how the girls imagined their character's (the body map's) hopes, dreams and plans for the future. Following Nilsen (1999), we decided to distinguish between hopes, dreams and plans, assuming that hopes are more tangible than dreams and that plans are more concrete paths to action.

We worked with three groups of young women and each group was composed of three to five participants. The ages of the young women were between 15 and 18. One young woman had a one-year-old baby and the remainder said that they were in a relationship. One of the workshops was conducted at an outstation 17 km outside the community, where several families had gathered for the holidays. The remaining two were conducted in the main community of Ngukurr. The young women were presented with a series of scenarios developed from our previous ethnographic work (Senior and Chenhall 2008, 2012) and in consultation with young women who had previously been involved in the research. These included the story of Lucy who returned to Ngukurr after being away at high school for two years, Cathie who lives in Ngukurr with her mum and dad, Sarah who thinks she may be pregnant and Julie who is a single mother with a one-year-old baby. Of these, the stories of Cathie and Sarah were chosen by the groups as characters to work on. The story of Lucy was dismissed as being 'a bit boring' and the story of Julie (although suggested by our participants) was thought to be unrealistic. They said that a 16-year-old with a baby would be married. In local understandings, a young woman is married or 'all married up' when she moves in with her partner (see also McMullen, Chapter 7). As discussed later in the paper, a single state was something that young women aspired to, but they did not think it was possible at such a young age.

The young women were encouraged to spend time developing their characters and to think deeply about what sort of person their character was as they decorated her body. We wanted them to develop a rapport with their character and immerse themselves in the unfolding narrative. Our previous research alerted us to the importance of involvement as a means of developing an empathetic response (Senior and Chenhall 2017; see also Johnson 2012). As the young women drew their person's feelings and thoughts on their body map, they also engaged in discussion about the issues that their character was feeling. For example, in each of the stories, the words 'dumps her partner' are written. This statement, however, was framed by extensive discussions about how partners could be abusive and how a young woman might work up the courage to leave their partner. It was vital to capture these discussions among the young women as well as their visual depictions of their character. We worked as a team (Senior, Daniels, Hall and Turner) to determine the key themes arising from these sets of data, and then crosschecked our interpretations with the young women from the community who were participants.[1]

Contemporary Life for Young Women Living in the Ngukurr Community

The community of Ngukurr is home to 1,000 Indigenous people and a small population of non-Indigenous people who work in institutions such as the school and the health clinic. Ngukurr is extremely remote: it is 750 km from the capital city of Darwin and 300 km from the nearest town of Mataranka. The town of Ngukurr was established by the Christian

1 Ethics approval for this project (which includes the work with the young men discussed in Chapter 3) was granted by the University of Wollongong Ethics Committee (UOW 2015/197) following extensive community consultation about the project. The lives of young women in the community were a cause for concern in the community and had been the catalyst for the earlier research (2008 and 2012) into young women's lives and aspirations. In this case, community elders noted that there were very few opportunities for young women to talk about their lives and that they often felt lonely and isolated.

Missionary Society in 1908 in response to what they saw as the 'desperate plight' of Aboriginal people in the region who had suffered at the hands of encroaching pastoralists (Chenhall and Senior 2018). The mission bought together people from seven different language groups who now speak the common language of Ngukurr Kriol. Although Christian conversion was considered by the missionaries to have been largely unsuccessful, many of the values they instilled continue to influence Ngukurr life, such as modesty or emphasising a modest form of dress. For older women, this is usually an A-line dress (a zippy or pocket dress) and for younger women a long skirt or baggy shorts and t-shirt (Senior and Chenhall 2008, 274). Older women continue to enforce these standards among the younger women in the community.

The dirt road into the community and the two river crossings were often flooded during the wet season (November–March) making access impossible. By 2018, however, bridges had been built over the two most flood-prone river crossings, making year-round access by car possible for the first time. This has meant that travelling out of the community, even just to the closest town of Katherine, has become increasingly possible for young people. Ngukurr now also has a bus service linking it with the coastal community of Numbulwar as well as Katherine and Darwin.

Ngukurr's conditions are similar to those of other remote communities, with high levels of premature mortality and preventable disease (Senior and Chenhall 2013). People live in circumstances of deep poverty and, although there have been recent attempts to improve local housing conditions, houses are often extremely overcrowded. Educational outcomes, although improving, remain considerably lower than those of non-Indigenous Australia, with very few young people receiving a Year 12 secondary education. Some young people undertake training in certificate-level courses after their school education.

Changes in local government have had an important impact on people's lives. In 2008, the Ngukurr community, previously administered by a local government council, became part of a super-shire. The community was then administered from Katherine, 350 km away. This change eroded local decision-making and meant that initiatives, such as organising a sporting event, were the responsibility of workers from the shire, rather than the community (Sanders 2013).

In 2009, we described the frustrations expressed by youth in the community who were only able to obtain brief glimpses of a globalised youth culture and lacked the technology to engage more fully with it (Chenhall and Senior 2009). Although access to mainstream media, especially print media, was still extremely limited, Facebook and other social media were pervasive and accessed through people's mobile phones. Access to social media had considerably extended people's social networks and provided a means of exposure to life beyond Ngukurr (see also Kariippanon, Chapter 8, this volume).

Relationships were a source of tension for the young women (Senior and Chenhall 2012) and they continued to have babies and get married very young. Although babies are highly valued, they are accompanied by a loss of freedom for the young women as well as incorporation into the family of their partner. Despite this, negotiating and planning relationships—a domain in which they are able to make choices and have some sense of control—remains a high point in young women's lives (Senior and Chenhall 2008). Those in relationships talked about young men as being controlling and violent. There was some acceptance of violence in relationships as seen in the words of a 14-year-old girl:

> Sometimes their wives are lazy and don't know how to cook or clean around the house. And they answer back their husbands when their husband is saying the right thing. When they answer back their husband gets cross and starts hitting them. I think it's their own fault because they should listen to their husband and what they say to them. (Senior and Chenhall 2012, 380)

On a return visit to Ngukurr in 2016, it appeared that relationships continued to be associated with the hopes and dreams of young women. The preadolescent girls played endless clapping games to what, at first, seemed like a familiar chant. On closer inspection, the words had been changed to reflect local interpretations of marriage:

> Sittin' in the Apple tree
> My boyfriend said to me:
> Kiss me
> Hug me
> Tell me that you love me
> Marry me
> Choke me
> Boom! (Senior field notes 2016)

When asked why a marriage ends in choking, the young girls commented, 'that's what boys are like, always jealous and bossy of their partner' (Senior field notes 2016). We were interested to explore further young women's perceptions of young people's relationships in the community, but also to explore their hopes, dreams and aspirations for their lives in the future.

Exploring the Body Maps

The character depicted in Figure 2.1, Cathie, is in a relationship with a young boy in Ngukurr. She is dressed in a tank top, which is decorated with a large heart that exposes her bellybutton and a matching long flowery skirt. She wears earrings, eye make-up and nail polish. Another heart near her shoulder has the words 'feels good inside' written over it.

Cathie's key hope is that she doesn't get pregnant, as 'getting pregnant will spoil her plans'. She also hopes that she does well at school. Her plans are to 'go to school and learn how to be a nurse'. This was considered by the girls to be a desirable career because of the benefits that it would bring to her family: 'When you are a nurse, you know what to eat and she can live for a long time'. The group of young women constructing Cathie added the category of 'worries' to their list, arguing that young girls worry about the things that might spoil their plans for the future. Cathie worries that her boyfriend will tell her what to do and that he will force her to leave school and that he may want her to have a baby.

We believe that these young women were speaking of their dreams when they were imagining Cathie in five years time. They said that 'she won't have a baby', and that she will, by this time, have 'dumped her boyfriend' and found a 'good man in Darwin'. The young women said that to accomplish her dreams Cathie would have to leave the community: 'she will go away for a long time, and don't come back, maybe to Darwin'.

The scenario chosen by the group who created the young woman shown in Figure 2.2 was that of Sarah, which was a vignette of a girl in a relationship who was worried that she might be pregnant.

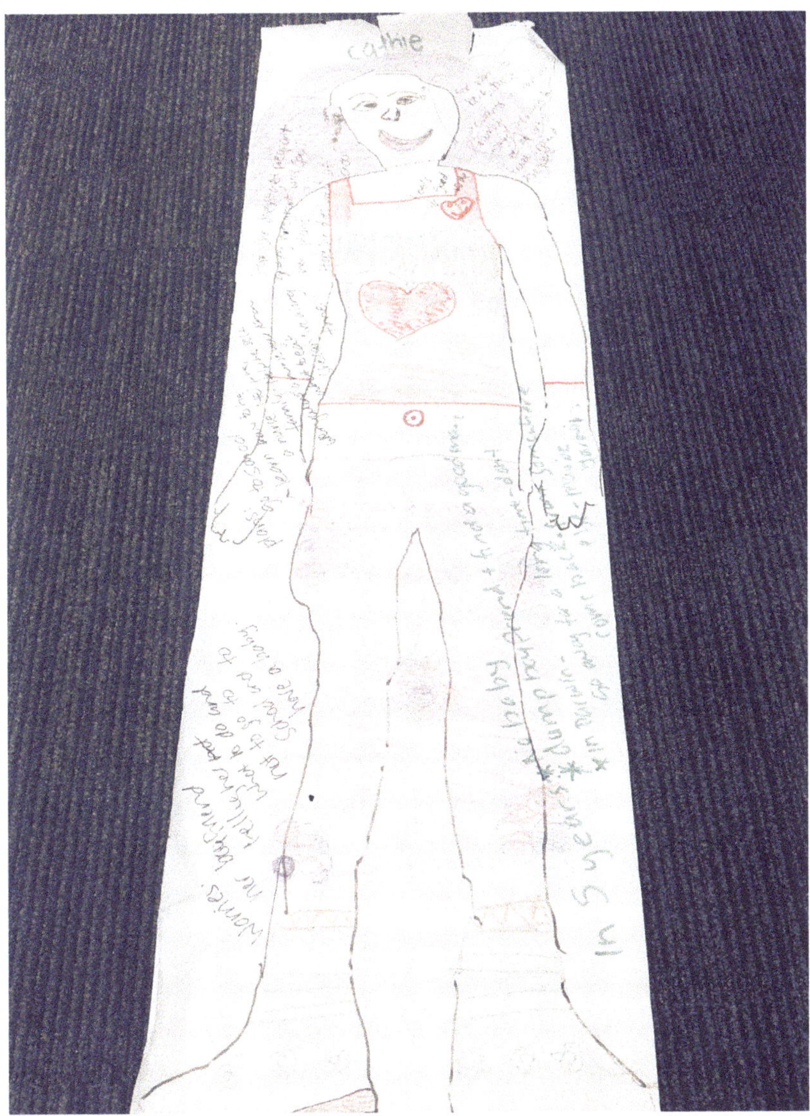

Figure 2.1: Body map Cathie.

Source: Photograph by Kate Senior.

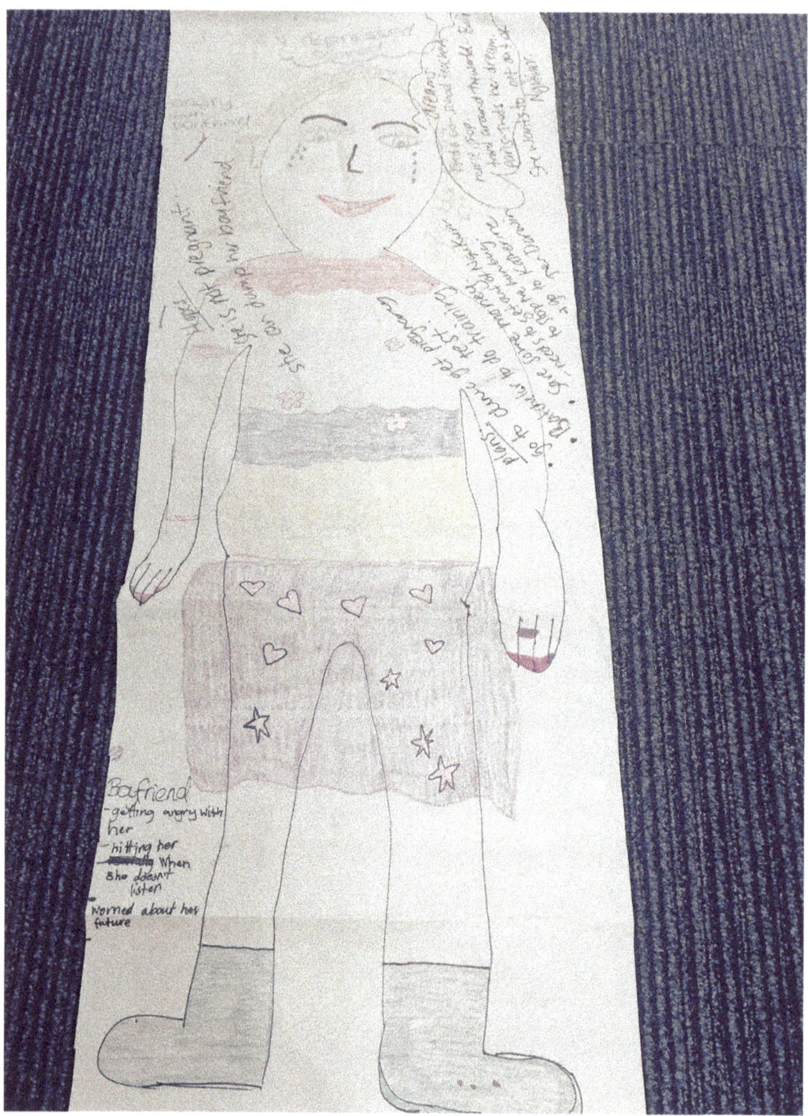

Figure 2.2: Body map Sarah.

Source: Photograph by Kate Senior.

As with the previous body map, considerable attention was paid to her clothes. She is dressed in a flowery tee-shirt and a short skirt covered in hearts and flowers. She has make-up on as well as jewellery (a ring and a bracelet), her fingernails are painted and her hair is dyed blonde. Unlike the character in the previous body map, she is obviously unhappy, with tears pouring from her eyes and the words 'depressed' and 'scared' written about her head. Her key hopes are that she is not pregnant and that she can 'dump her boyfriend'. Her angry, jealous boyfriend is drawn beneath her left foot. He is saying 'stop going to school, stop dreaming about what you gonna be. I want you to have a baby; I want you to stay at home with me'. The young women summed up this behaviour with the statement: 'Boys are bossy'. Her plans are to go to the clinic and get a pregnancy test and then (if the test is negative) to go to the Batchelor Institute of Indigenous Tertiary Education[2] to do some training. She will need to plan to save money: 'She needs to get out of Ngukurr to stop the Humbug'. The participants explain that she will not be able to save money unless she moves away from what anthropologists call a 'demand sharing environment', in which 'everyone' has the right to ask her to share her resources. She plans to go to Katherine first and then to Darwin.

Her dreams are 'to find a job, maybe a school teacher, a nurse or work at the shop'. She wants to travel 'around the world, Bali first and then Paris, Paris that's her dream'. She wants to get out of Ngukurr. In the future, she'll be living in town, she'll have her own house and she'll be earning her own money. She will be single, or she'll have a relationship with someone from outside the community. The young women in the group say 'you gotta get out of here to find a good man'. They say Sarah 'worries about her future'. She worries that her boyfriend will get angry with her and hit her 'when she doesn't listen'.

The third group also chose the scenario of Sarah who has just found out that she is pregnant. As with the other body maps, Sarah is depicted in pretty, feminine clothes, with make-up and nail polish. She was initially depicted wearing a very short skirt, but the girls decided to make it a knee length skirt 'because she is pregnant'. The foetus is shown in Sarah's uterus.

2 The Batchelor Institute of Indigenous Tertiary Education provides both vocational and higher education. It is based in the town of Batchelor near Darwin, but has annexes across the region, as well as providing training in communities.

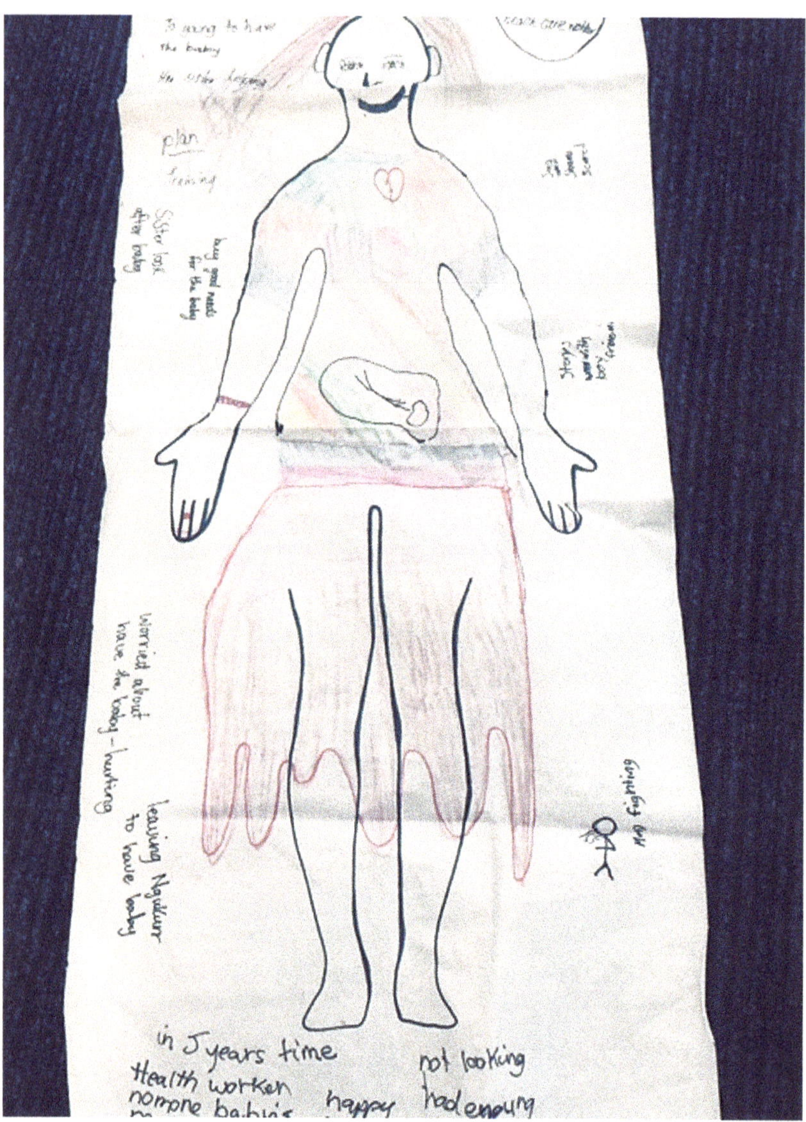

Figure 2.3: Body map Sarah.

Source: Photograph by Kate Senior.

Sarah is worried and frightened. She is crying because she is scared of being pregnant at age 16 and of the potential pain of having a baby, as well as having to leave the community for the birth (see McMullen, Chapter 7, this volume). She thinks she is too young to have the baby and she is upset because her parents are fighting about it. Her sister is prepared to help her.

Sarah's hope is centred on the behaviour of her current boyfriend. She hopes that her boyfriend 'changes' and that he 'stops smoking drugs'. She plans to do some training and thinks that her sister may be able to look after the baby. She plans to save some money to buy 'good things for the baby'. She also plans to stay with her current boyfriend while she has the baby. She dreams of being a 'good mum' and maybe 'a health care worker'. In the future she dreams that she will have no more babies and no husband. 'She's not looking, she's had enough. She's happy being single'.

Discussion

As Beck (1992) famously commented, the contemporary, globalised life is a project that must be planned. But what chance do these young women have to plan their lives? Despite their engagement in schooling, which highlighted future educational and career possibilities, their embodied futures remain constrained by what other people—notably their partners—expect them to be. The young women's short-term hopes centre around events, which they consider largely unpredictable, but which they hope *will not* happen, such as pregnancy and beatings from their boyfriends. In these young women's environments, the meaning of hope seems very different from the ability to perceive positive futures (Bishop and Willis 2014). Such responses, however, echo Harwood et al.'s (2017, 132) discussion of tenuous futures when those anticipating them are negotiating difficult environments.

Becoming pregnant, the young women say, would spoil their dreams for the future. But what are these young women's dreams? Each of the three groups of women that participated in the body mapping exercise talked about future careers as being an important dream. Among the limited range of suggested careers was becoming a health worker or a nurse. These suggestions were very similar to those suggested by young women in 2000–04 (Senior and Chenhall 2012). In both studies, the participants lacked clear articulations of what such jobs might entail and the steps required to obtain them. Acknowledgement of the steps that the young women would have to take to achieve these goals was missing in their accounts. They did not appear have what Kenway and Hickey-Moody (2011, 154) describe as 'aerial vision':

> They have foresight. Their life-lines are connected to future opportunities through the logic of 'if'—'if I do this now, then' … they understand cause and effect and operate in terms of actions and consequences.

Nor did the young women display the confidence demonstrated by the young men (see Chapter 3, this volume) to carve out a different kind of future.

In the young women's stories, careers would somehow happen if they went away 'for training', which was not well understood or articulated. The young women provide much clearer descriptions of the things that are holding them back—the things that prevent them from achieving their personal dreams. They describe being constantly 'humbugged' for money and the impossibility of saving. They said that their boyfriends put pressure on them to stay home and have babies. In their stories, the only way to address this problem is to leave and head for the big city of Darwin. This is in marked contrast to the young women in the previous study who wanted to 'live in Ngukurr until I die' (Senior and Chenhall 2008). Ten years later, young women talk about the potential freedom of leaving the community, which includes the freedom to work and to save money, to choose a boyfriend who respects them or to choose to be single.

This freedom, they argue, is both well-deserved and hard-won. As one group stated of their character (who was by then 19 years old) 'she is going to be single, because she has had enough'. Leaving the community, however, is a very difficult choice. Underpinning these young women's life stories are deep commitments to their families. One group talked about the young woman's sister who would help her look after the baby. Another group talked about their character wanting to be a nurse, because the knowledge that this person acquired through their training would be good for the family—'when you are a nurse you know what to eat and you can live a long time'. A concrete example of the importance of family is provided by Angelina Joshua (see Chapter 1, this volume), a young woman who has experienced leaving the community. Her story is one of isolation and the pain of being continually called back by her relatives:

> I was living in Darwin and I wanted to experience new things, but my family were calling me, calling me back home. They were saying 'It's not the same without you'. It made me really sad. I missed my best friends, hanging out with them and laughing, and I missed my brothers and sisters. I didn't have anyone to talk to. It was a really hard time. I was experiencing city life, but I didn't really like it. At least I gave it a go.

The young women's ideas about leaving the community and living in Darwin or Katherine are like their ideas about having a career, in that they are conspicuously lacking in detail. In one of the stories, living in Darwin (which is a reality for some Ngukurr residents) is described in the same sentence as travelling the world and going to Paris. For these young women, moving away is conceived as a necessary act required for creating a different kind of life—one that remains in the realm of dreams. Despite their limited articulation, these plans are significant for our understanding of these young people, as they represent a clear departure from earlier views from this age set. With regard to the ethnographic literature, such plans address the emerging theme of mobility as a key to changes in young people's lives (Hoffman 2017, 23).

Talking about leaving the community is a radical idea and one that may be difficult to achieve. There are, however, more immediate indicators of young women's propensity to imagine their lives in ways that are not controlled by authority—for example, the radical imagination described by Kenway and Fahey (2009, 114). Evidence for this is not in the words or thoughts that are ascribed to the characters, but in the way the images themselves are depicted by the young women.

At a superficial level, the young women depicted in these body maps may be assumed to be seeking relationships. They pay conspicuous attention to their appearance, including wearing make-up and jewellery, and are dressed (at least by the standards of the community) in provocative ways. Young women in Ngukurr have access to globalised images of youth culture through social media and are increasingly aware of the clothing choices of young people outside the community. Importantly, the images they create are dressed in an entirely different way to the young women who created them, who all wore baggy shorts and loose fitting tee-shirts in sombre colours, were unadorned by either make-up or jewellery, and seemed to be trying to look as inconspicuous as possible. The bodies that they created, when understood in the language of relationships in the community, take on a completely different meaning:

> Young married women are expected to stay at home and do housework. When they are married they are expected to wear dresses past their knees. Married women are not allowed to shave their legs, pluck their eyebrows or wear earrings. (Senior and Chenhall 2012)

Paradoxically, the dreamed feminine figure, in a floaty dresses or midriff-exposing top, is a figure of emancipation and globalisation. She is a young woman who is not wearing the 'ugly clothes' expected by her partner and is, instead, expressing her personality and her sexuality through her clothes. Such provocative depictions of young women can be considered as acts of defiance when young women are expected to present themselves in the most inconspicuous way possible, so as not to provoke the jealousy of their partner. When considered in light of the constant reinforcement of the need for modest dress instilled by older women in the community, these images are also defiant.

In many ways, the young women's depictions embody Zournazi's (2002) ideas about hope being a useful concept to think about in the present, rather than encompassing a set of utopian ideas about the future. Hope is not the same as optimism, as hope resides in the sphere of uncertainty. Indeed, Zournazi argues that it is the uncertain nature of hope that provides its most important characteristic—the opportunity to experiment:

> To speak of hope is therefore to speak of the not yet become 'seeds of change', connections in the making that might not be activated or obvious at the moment. (Zournazi 2002, 221, quoted in Anderson 2006, 745)

In their detailed depictions of what they could look like, and the detailed attention they gave to the pattern and colour of clothes, the shoes embellished with flowers and stars, and the styling of hair and make-up, the young women are experimenting with something that they have 'not yet become' (Anderson 2006, 741). During the process of experimenting, they begin to imagine a range of other freedoms, such as having a career or moving away from the community.

Conclusion

In this chapter, young women's relationships emerge as a limiting factor in their lives. One young woman articulated this in her comment that '[boys say] stop dreaming what you gonna be'. Yet, it is in the area of relationships that the young women describe a step-by-step approach to life planning that involves a current boyfriend, possibly a baby, and then a move away from the community to be either single or to find a 'good man'. It is the final stage of this imagining—in thoughts about moving away from the community—that represents a new departure for these young women. Leaving the community was considered to be one of the worst possible outcomes in a person's life in the 2008 and 2012 studies, due to people's deep feelings of connection and support from family. However, moving away is largely uncharted territory for them, as few of them have experienced any lengthy residence outside of the community. Ideas about living without a partner are also tentative, as very few single women exist as potential role models in the community (with the exception of older widows).

The possibilities of a radical re-imagining of self, however, occur not in the young women's stories, but in the visual depictions of their characters. A preoccupation with pretty clothes, hair, jewellery and make-up may be assumed to be unsurprising for teenage girls, but in this setting, they are an act of defiance. No young woman in a relationship would be allowed by her partner to present herself in such a way. Therefore, the depictions of the young women's characters reinforce their partly formulated dreams of leaving the community to live a life in which such choices are possible. The body maps and the stories associated with the depicted characters alert us to the complexity and subtlety of aspiration for these young women, which would be easy to overlook from a conventional aspirations perspective.

References

Anderson, B. 2006. 'Becoming and Being Hopeful: Towards a Theory of Affect'. *Environment and Planning D, Society and Space* 24 (5): 733–52. doi.org/10.1068/d393t.

Appadurai, A. 2013. 'The Capacity to Aspire: Culture and Terms of Recognition'. In *Culture and Public Action,* edited by R. Vijayendra and M. Walton, 59–84. Stanford: Stanford University Press.

Bauman, Z. 1998. *Globaliszation: The Human Consequences.* London: Polity Press.

Beck, U. 1992. *Risk Society: Towards a New Modernity.* London: SAGE Publishing.

Bishop, E. C. and K. Willis. 2014. '"Without Hope Everything Would be Doom and Gloom": Young People Talk about the Importance of Hope in their Lives'. *Journal of Youth Studies* 17 (6): 778–93. doi.org/10.1080/13676261.2013.878788.

Chenhall, R. and K. Senior. 2009. '"Those Young People All Crankybella": Indigenous Youth, Mental Health and Globalisation'. *International Journal of Mental Health* 38 (3): 28–43. doi.org/10.2753/IMH0020-7411380302.

Chenhall, R. and K. Senior. 2018. 'Living the Social Determinants of Health: Health Equality and Life Style Choices in a Remote Aboriginal Community'. *Medical Anthropology Quarterly* 32 (2): 177–95. doi.org/10.1111/maq.12418.

Harwood, V., A. Hickey-Moody, S. McMahon and S. O'Shea. 2017. *The Politics of Widening Participation and University Access for Young People: Making Educational Futures.* United States: Routledge. doi.org/10.4324/9781315736921.

Hoffman, D. M. 2017. 'Against All Odds: The Ethnography of Hope among Haitian Youth in Difficult Circumstances'. *New Directions in Educational Ethnography* 13: 15–33. doi.org/10.1108/S1529-210X20150000013001.

Johnson, D. R. 2012. 'Transportation into a Story Increases Empathy, Prosocial Behaviour and Perceptual Bias towards Fearful Expressions'. *Personality and Individual Differences* 52: 150–55. doi.org/10.1016/j.paid.2011.10.005.

Kenway, J. and J. Fahey. 2009. 'A Transgressive Global Research Imagination'. *Thesis Eleven* 96 (1): 109–27. doi.org/10.1177/0725513608099122.

Kenway, J. and A. Hickey-Moody. 2011. 'Life Chances, Lifestyle and Everyday Aspirational Strategies and Tactics'. *Critical Studies in Education* 52 (2): 151–63. doi.org/10.1080/17508487.2011.572828.

Kleist, N. and S. Jansen. 2016. 'Introduction: Hope over Time—Crisis, Immobility and Future Making'. *History and Anthropology* 27 (4): 373–92. doi.org/10.1080/02757206.2016.1207636.

Nilsen, A. 1999. 'Where is the Future? Time and Space as Categories in Analyses of Young People's Images of the Future'. *Innovation: The European Journal of Social Science Research* 12 (2): 175–94. doi.org/10.1080/13511610.1999.9968596.

Sanders, W. 2013. 'Losing Localism, Constraining Councillors: Why the Northern Territory Supershires Are Struggling'. *Policy Studies* 34 (4): 473–90. doi.org/10.1080/01442872.2013.822704.

Senior, K. 2003. 'A Gudbala Laif? Health and Wellbeing in a Remote Aboriginal Community—What Are the Problems and Where Lies The Responsibility?' PhD thesis, The Australian National University, Canberra.

Senior, K. and R. Chenhall. 2008. '"Walkin' about at Night": The Background to Teenage Pregnancy in a Remote Aboriginal Community'. *Journal of Youth Studies* 11 (3): 269–81. doi.org/10.1080/13676260801946449.

Senior, K. and R. Chenhall. 2012. 'Boyfriends, Babies and Basketball: Present Lives and Future Aspirations of Young Women in a Remote Australian Aboriginal Community'. *Journal of Youth Studies* 15 (3): 369–88. doi.org/10.1080/13676261.2012.663890.

Senior, K. and R. Chenhall, R. 2013. 'Health Beliefs and Behaviour, the Practicalities of "Looking After Yourself" in an Australian Aboriginal Community'. *Medical Anthropology Quarterly* 27 (2): 155–74. doi.org/10.1111/maq.12021.

Senior, K. and R. Chenhall. 2017. '"More than Just Learning about the Organs": Ethnographic and Participatory Approaches as a Basis for Understanding, Communicating and Learning about Sex and Relationships'. In *The Palgrave Handbook of Sexuality Education*, edited by L. Allen and M. L. Rasmussen, 95–144. London: Palgrave.

Wyn, J. and D. Woodman. 2006. 'Generation, Youth and Social Change in Australia'. *Journal of Youth Studies* 9 (95): 495–514. doi.org/10.1080/13676260600805713.

Zournazi, M. 2002. *Hope: New Philosophies for Change*. NSW: Pluto Press Australia.

3

'They Don't Dance Corroboree Any More': Youth Relations to Authority, Leadership and Civic Responsibility in a Remote Aboriginal Community

Kate Senior, Richard Chenhall and Daphne Daniels

> What do you see as the future for young people in Ngukurr?
>
> No future, they are all *munanga* [non-Indigenous people] types, growing in a house, with a fence and electricity. I didn't grow up like that, I had a tyre and a tree for a hospital. They don't learn Aboriginal way, it's too hard for them. Everything you learn is hard, I see no future, they don't dance corroboree, they don't sleep around the fire. I want to see Aboriginal people be Aboriginal people. This is my purpose in life. (Edward, senior male, July 2015)

Introduction

This study of young people's leadership aspirations begins with a corroboree, which was part of the initiation ceremony for three young boys. This was the final corroboree before the boys were to be circumcised the following day. Circumcision marks the end of a period of exclusion from the mainstream world, after which the boy is reintegrated into society as a man. During his period of removal, he has been taught traditional law, and sacred objects and knowledge are revealed to him. Ivory (2009, 128), in his study of Indigenous leadership, explains that this rite of passage is 'vital to being considered an adult male and progression towards becoming a leader'.

At dusk, the boys and their families gathered at the small settlement of Urapunga, about 20 km from Ngukurr, and waited for the dancers from Numbulwar to arrive. This period was marked by uncertainty; the women said they were unsure about where to sit or what their role would be (and were in fact moved several times until everyone was satisfied). There appeared to be considerable unease about the timing of the ceremony's start; the men had said it would begin in the late afternoon, but nothing had been heard about the whereabouts of the dancers from Numbulwar by nightfall. Ceremonies such as this were infrequent in Ngukurr and this may have heightened people's anxieties about their ability to ensure that it was conducted properly. Such anxieties are not a new feature of Ngukurr society. In 1970, Bern described the hesitance of the Djungaii (managers) in the conduct of the Jabadurwa ceremony because they were 'unsure of their ability' (Bern 1970, 18).

As it got darker and darker, people became more and more anxious, and periodically the men would call out. Finally, their calls were answered with short bursts of digeridoo and song and a large, old, flatbed truck pulled up disgorging a surprising number of people, the men carrying spears and digeridoos. The little boys, who were about eight years old, sat at the front of a bower shade. The Red Flag Dancers from Numbulwar led the dancing, the men acting as though they were pushing the boys forward, the women as though they were trying to bring them back to their world with the actions of hauling in a net. These dances were followed by short explosive ones by small groups of men, appropriate to their own skin and clan. There was considerable reluctance from the local residents to take part in the dancing, some of the women said that they did not feel confident dancing in public, others practised tentative steps at the side of the gathering. Only a few older people attempted any public display, which was met by nervous laughter from the spectators. By 11 pm, there was no sign that the ceremony would end soon, and it was explained that the boys would be cut (circumcised) tomorrow after being kept awake all night by the singing and dancing. This ceremony was an important and highly anticipated community event, but, as the opening quote indicates, there was a feeling among older men that such ceremonies were no longer respected by many people in the community, particularly younger people.

Figure 3.1: Corroboree at Urapunga, July 2015.
Source: Photograph by Kate Senior.

For Bern (1979b, 120), the organisation and performance of such rituals 'dramatizes structural differences both among initiated men and between them and the uninitiated'. Rituals affirm older male authority over young men and celebrate their political power. Bern (1979b, 126) argues that, unlike women, who must be placated to assist the men in rituals, youth acquiesce because one day they will also rise to this position of power. However, his description of the organisation of a ceremony in Ngukurr points to a degree of ambivalence among the young men:

> A more general factor was the increasing European influence, particularly on the younger men. This had a contradictory effect. On the one hand, the men were doubting the efficacy of totemic myths and questioning the relevance of ceremonial performance, while on the other hand, they were becoming increasingly aware of its being a unique Aboriginal possession. (Bern 1970, 18)

As mentioned above, the initiates at this particular corroboree were young, only about eight years old; their powers to resist the authority of the older men were, therefore, extremely limited. Older men, women and little children were present, but there was a conspicuous absence of youth, particularly young males. Edward's lament that young people don't dance corroborees anymore can be understood in a political context: the young men are not respecting the authority of their elders. Is this to be understood as a lack of respect for all authority or are young people specifically questioning the ritual authority of the mature men of the community?

This chapter explores power, authority and responsibility in the secular realm at Ngukurr, paying particular attention to the experiences and aspirations of a group of emerging young male leaders. Youth and leadership are not considered to be mutually compatible categories in Aboriginal communities, in which political power is often considered to be the domain of mature men (Bern 1979a, 1979b). The mainstream literature demonstrates an increasing apathy towards civic and political involvement among young people generally (Youniss et al. 2002), caused in part by a range of structural barriers, such as access to employment, that prevent effective involvement (Bessant 2004). What, then, are the political motivations of the young men who do not attend ritual events such as that described above?

To address this question, we contrast the leadership efforts of older community members with those of one group of young men, under the age of 25, and ask how each cohort defines and enacts their political presence. The contrast we employ is provided by individuals from three generations of one family. The first is from an elderly male, Edward, who described himself as having been a leader for much of his life; the second is from his daughter, Edna (in her 40s), who tried but failed to become a leader; and the third is from their grandson and son, Edwin (in his early 20s), who is the focal member of a group of young men describing themselves as a gang. This chapter describes how these individuals rose to positions of leadership and the actions and values underlying their decisions.

In each generation, leadership was enacted in different ways in response to broader sociopolitical contexts. Edward was put forward by the older generation in the community (who gained their respect and authority from the religious sphere) to interact and engage in the developing bureaucracy of the self-determination era. He was placed in the intercultural spaces of community councils and government meetings that involved 'politicking' between the Aboriginal community and governmental and other outside processes. His daughter, Edna, played a similar role but in an environment that saw the devaluation of Indigenous self-management with leadership roles that had very little power. Edna's son, Edwin, has pushed away from leadership in the intercultural space of community management, instead embracing a new style of leadership—one that takes in Indigenous culture and connection to land and community, but aspires to increasing mobility and globalised forms of expression.

Leadership and Authority

Studies of political organisation in Aboriginal societies have always been fraught, with debate ranging from the assertion that Aboriginal tribes had no formal apparatus of government (e.g. Meggitt 1962) to claims that political leadership was restricted to the religious sphere (e.g. Berndt and Berndt 1969; Elkin 1938; Strehlow 1947) In *Kinship and Conflict*, Hiatt (1965) summarised the different conceptualisations of Aboriginal leadership in the literature and argued that men's leadership has often been related to their courage, strength and force of character, but that their authority resides in the domain of ritual. The path to becoming a leader begins early in a young boy's life, with older men identifying particular characteristics and nurturing those who possess them. The process in Port Keats is described by Ivory (2009, 131–32):

> From an early age a child's development is overseen firstly by their parents and then increasingly by their uncles and aunts. Others observe a boy's behaviour, demeanour, and decisions are made as to when they will commence the formalised rites of passage.

A process such as this is described by Myers (1976, 556) as 'looking after'. Initiation is the rite of passage that transforms the young boy into a man and a future leader (Ivory 2009). Post initiation, an individual's rise in status is largely determined by ceremonial attainment and a capacity for taking responsibility for others (Ivory 2009, 129).

Bern (1979a, 1979b) wrote extensively on the leadership and politics of the Ngukurr community. He describes the mature men's control of religion and ritual and, through it, control of 'the relations of production': 'Within the Aboriginal social formation religion is the determinate structure. The social formation has a developed political structure in which the mature men occupy the dominant position' (Bern 1979a, 131). During the end of the mission era and into the period of self-determination, leadership at Ngukurr required people to be active in the secular world. Bern, in 1970, described five councils or committees that required Aboriginal involvement. These included the station council, which administered the general running of the community; the citizens club, which ran the shop; the entertainment committee; the school council; and the church council (Bern 1970, 11). Each of these provided opportunities for individuals to demonstrate leadership and develop individual standing, but they also required a range of different skills focused on mainstream education and cross-cultural communication. In Port Keats, Ivory (2009) showed how authority was deferred in some areas from older men to middle-aged men who had the necessary educational skills to perform the new roles. In the committees described by Bern (1970), membership was dominated by males over 40. Women were minimally represented in all committees (with the exception of the church committee). The only committee in which women achieved equity of membership with men was the school committee. Later, both the church and the school became important avenues for women to demonstrate leadership (O'Donnell 2007).[1]

In his analysis, Bern sees secular power as something derived from religious authority and, because acquisition of religious knowledge is a gradual process (controlled by older men through initiation), only mature men can assume this power. There were situations, however, in which younger men were able to exert their influence on the older men. A key example is the Ngukurr strike (9 March – 6 April 1970), which saw Ngukurr workers leave their positions and take their children out of school until their demands for fair wages and control of their land were met. It is clear that, although older men were designated as the frontmen of the strike, it was the younger men who were most insistent on change. Bern (1976, 220) talks, for example, of the 'caucus decision by the young men to go on strike' and says that: 'The young men had taken the decision to strike based in their assessment of gains to be made, their world view, and their own propensity to oppose authority.' Although older men controlled the religious domain, the young men, on this occasion, exerted considerable political power, which the older men, at least initially, accepted.

1 Issues of women's leadership were largely ignored until Bell (1983) challenged the notion of women as second-class citizens and described their maintenance of a rich ritual life on which the sustenance of the group depended. Bell points out, however, that the change from nomadic existence to living in settlements disrupted women's power base due to men's classification as breadwinners and the head of households by outside observers.

A Changing Context for Leadership in Ngukurr

The period covering the lives of the three generations of leaders in this chapter encompasses a range of different contexts and opportunities. Edward's story begins when missionaries withdrew from the community and handed control back to the Northern Territory Government. His story coincides with increasing levels of Aboriginal activism and a commitment to self-determination. At a very young age, he was chosen by the elders to become a leader in secular affairs and the world of non-Aboriginal politics. This leadership was outside of the religious sphere and was dependent on Edward's skills in straddling Aboriginal and non-Aboriginal domains. The community was administered through a local community government council with representation from each of the seven clan groups, yet the community remained restricted in its capacity to make decisions. Outsiders, mainly non-Aboriginal people, occupied management, governance and skilled positions within the community and the council itself was administered by a non-Aboriginal town clerk. Notwithstanding Aboriginal leaders' expectations that they could make decisions about their community, their ability to do so was often undermined. For example, in 2001, the leaders initiated a carefully planned intervention to combat petrol sniffing in the town (Senior and Chenhall 2007). Through a series of public meetings, the leaders were able to mobilise the interest of the community and work collectively with it to develop a program that was acceptable. They were adamant that their decisions would be supported by the council:

> Decision must come from the community, and then Council can act of it. River Town is number one sniffing community, what are people doing about it? The decision has to come through the community and then we will push it through Council. If the Council make the decision on their own, then the community may not like it. (Senior and Chenhall 2007, 320)

Regrettably, the efforts of the community leaders were not recognised by the largely non-Aboriginal staff representing the key agencies in the community, and the intervention failed to be supported.

Edna witnessed many of these events in her early adult years; however, by the time she was in a position to become a leader, the context had changed dramatically. The structures of the community government council and the town clerk had been disbanded and the community had been amalgamated with others to became part of a 'super-shire', administered from Katherine, 300 km away. Shire representatives took over the running of various institutions and programs in the community. The health clinic, formerly run by the Northern Territory Government, became part of a regional health board, also administered from Katherine. These structures gave opportunities for Ngukurr residents to be involved in regional boards, but effectively removed decision-making from the local community (Sanders 2013). Superimposed over all these changes was the Northern Territory Emergency Intervention in 2008, which brought a range of new institutions, particularly those focused on infant and child care, and regimes, including income management and alcohol prohibitions, to Ngukurr (see Hinkson 2017). Out of this regime of control and regulation, a new form of leadership has been articulated by young people in the community—a style that distances itself from both religious and political authority and connects to a civic sense of duty and globalised forms of identification.

The View of the Older Generation

Edward is now confined to a wheelchair—we manoeuvred him with difficulty to the front step of his house to talk. Inside the house, the room was bare apart from a partially dismembered bullock that attracted a swarm of flies. His lifetime of prominence in the community had clearly not resulted in any obvious material gains. In 1999, when Senior (author one) first met him, Edward was a man to be feared; he was notorious for sacking town clerks and removing people's permits to enter the community. Even the sight of his Land Cruiser could strike fear into the hearts of meddling *munanga*. An encounter with Edward usually included a monologue on community issues and Northern Territory politics, but, on this particular day, he didn't recognise Senior: 'Ah my girl, that dress, I thought you were lady from the mission'. With the help of his daughter, he remembered and they fell into their usual conversation about political issues in the community.

Senior asked Edward to tell the story about how he came to be a leader. Edward said he was chosen by the men in the community. This was something about which he felt deep ambivalence. He was clear that this was the decision of elders in the community and not one he made himself. Somehow, they were able to divine the intrinsic qualities of a future leader in him when he was still an infant:

> When I was only six years old they pointed at us and made us a leader—'you are going to be a leader of this place'. I didn't feel good, was just a young fella, then in 1959, I was voted a leader, I was only 13 years old, it was very hard for me, I used to call meetings every month, not a *munanga* thing, an Aboriginal thing. When I became 15, I became a strong leader, in 1961 they built a big office; the Council Office and they put me in there.

Edward's story resonates with Myers' (1976) concept of 'looking after', in which young males are nurtured by older men and, through this, are made into leaders (see also Ivory 2009, 127). It is clear that the authority of the elders remained, while the 'young fella' was sent in to deal with secular affairs and non-Aboriginal politics. Edward's achievements in this world are significant: for example, he was a driving force in the Aboriginalisation of the school in 1978, when all the non-Aboriginal teachers were removed and trained local teachers took over responsibility (Senior 2003):

> I said to teachers, this is no good, go to Sydney to Melbourne, get out! But they disobeyed my orders. Then I took their permits away from the teachers. I told them again, 'get out!' Then they galloped!

He was also a driving force behind the community strike in 1970 (Bern 1976), which was an effort to achieve fair wages and recognition of Aboriginal ownership of the land:

> I said to them, 'we'll go on strike, take all the children out from schools'. They thought I was joking. 'You've got to pay us and then we will work for you'.

A commitment to self-determination is clear throughout his narrative:

> I wanted to see Aboriginal people in charge of everything. Aboriginal people should be the people you consult, Aboriginal people should run the meeting.
>
> Did you achieve this?
>
> I achieved it, I reckon, people would say 'He's right that old fellow'.

Edward's narrative is punctuated by conflict; he characterised his life as being one in which he constantly had to fight to get things done. These fights were both internal (with other senior men in the community) and with outside authorities. He also admitted that there were times when it all became too much and he would leave the community and live in the nearby outstation of Urapunga. By the time of our conversation in July 2015, he considered that there was very little left of his legacy. His daughter had tried to become a leader, but became exhausted by 'being bullied by the men'. In Edward's view, no one else was motivated enough to fight for changes in the community:

> Do you think there is much of what you achieved left?
>
> Nothing, it's falling apart, council doesn't work, we don't have elections, I feel down hearted and I feel no good inside because I feel like people will fall down. Now no one knows where they are going, while I'm still alive people have to change, they have to own this place, make sure they get the jobs—they can do it, but they are too lazy.

Edward's leadership was clearly very different to the ritual authority discussed by Hiatt (1965), as his efforts were largely directed to governing the non-religious sphere of the community and included managing both Indigenous and non-Indigenous residents. However, his selection as a future leader at an early age by the older men resonates with the traditional practices of 'looking after' described by Myers (1976), Keen (1994) and Ivory (2009). His influence was wide and the extent of his influence outside the Ngukurr community was made very clear at his funeral in 2015, which was attended by the Northern Territory chief minister as well as the police commissioner.

The Middle-Aged Leader

Edna, Edward's daughter, has also been active in community leadership. She was an elected member of the community government council, which was the key decision-making body for the community until 2007, and is a member of a range of community advisory boards. She is respected by her family and thought to be an important role model in the community. When Edna's daughter spoke about her, she said: 'This is my mum … she is a strong woman. I would like to be like her and go to school and study.'

When she was in her mid-20s, Edna was pushed forward by her father to take part in a community research project. During that time (1999–2004), she became the editor of the local community newspaper and was increasingly involved in local politics. She was also the deputy leader for her tribal group on the council and a member of the local school board. In 2005, she became a member of the local community-controlled health board and, in 2007, became the deputy council leader. This central role of a woman in the intercultural affairs of the council and community business, traditionally the realm of men, was a significant shift. In 2008, the Northern Territory Government decided to create 'super-shires' and Ngukurr became administered from Katherine. Positions with real authority within the local government organisation were no longer available; however, Edna remained a representative on the Roper Gulf Shire and the Stronger Futures Committee. She felt uncertain about her roles within these organisations; she was unclear about what they were and how much authority they afforded her. Ultimately, and despite numerous opportunities to be involved in structures of governance within the community and, later, the shire, sometimes in roles that offered significant opportunities for leadership, her participation did not result in meaningful involvement and, in most cases, decision-making remained controlled by a non-Indigenous person.

Edna continues to be sought out by outsiders as an important person to talk to about community issues. She acknowledges that, although women often have such status, they are rarely considered to be leaders in the same way as men. Similar to descriptions of female leadership in other remote communities, Edna was chosen by her father to become a leader for the community on the basis of her having completed high school. However, she found that while she was often consulted, she had little authority to make decisions. She explained: 'They see me as a leader, but leadership is still a men thing.'

Edna talks about leadership as a struggle. This struggle became particularly acute when the administration of the community shifted from the local government council to the Roper Gulf Shire. Sanders (2013, 48) describes the difficulties that community representatives face within such structures, especially the requirement to consider policy and structural issues rather than advocating for change in their communities. Edna saw her role as a councillor in terms of having to learn to do things 'the non-Aboriginal way': 'Me, I've been struggling, learning both ways. In the other way you have to work with white people, understand how they work.'

Ultimately, Edna was exhausted by her efforts and her perception that she was being constantly undermined by older Aboriginal men and non-Aboriginal people in the community. Her source of leadership was connected to her father's generation. She was selected by her father to take on a leadership position and the role of mediator between the community and outside agencies. However, her being a woman was problematic, not only because of the very dominant place men hold over public forms of leadership, but also because of the increasing governmental regulation and lack of power installed in various official roles.

Edna considered that young people in the community were apathetic about taking on leadership roles, despite the fact that they were a well-educated generation: 'There is nothing for young ones. They are just bored, rely on drinking and smoking as their hobbies and then when opportunities do come up they are not interested.' She constantly remarked on the need for what she described as 'governance training' for people in the community, and particularly young people, so that they could be better equipped to take responsibility for decision-making within the community.

Youth Leadership and Civil Participation

Ivory (2009), in his research on Aboriginal governance at Port Keats, says that a study of how power is acquired, distributed, wielded and sustained is fundamental to a study of leadership. We argue that it is also necessary to consider how power is recognised and acknowledged. Young people's efforts to exert power in Aboriginal worlds are largely invisible to the outsider and often to older people in their own community, unless such efforts are characterised by violent and destructive acts. At Wadeye, for example, youth power was exerted though gang behaviour (Ivory 2009). In their study of youth leadership, Youniss et al. (2002, 124) pose the question:

> Are young people being well prepared to take on civic responsibly in this new, changing global reality? Ultimately, we will be placing the world into young people's hands. Will they be prepared and what can be done to facilitate their preparation?

Despite the importance of young people being prepared to take on such roles, they are often characterised as having limited commitment to citizenship (France 1998, 97). However, this may not be due to disinterest. The interest and willingness of young people to be involved in civic responsibilities in their own communities is hampered by their lack of rights and by the structural barriers they encounter when they try to attain positions that may afford them some decision-making capacity. As France (1998, 108) explained: 'Young people's willingness to undertake certain forms of responsibilities both within the local community and in the labour market has been undermined by experiences of exclusion and exploitation.'

According to Bessant (2004), considerable governmental efforts have been made to encourage the leadership of young people and to ensure they are exposed to participatory and democratic processes via the development of forums such as youth round tables and youth advisory groups. However, Bessant observes that forums such as regional youth committees and round tables that aim to inform policymaking in Australia face important limitations that may result in young people's continued cynicism about their roles. Youth are aware of the tokenistic aspect to their participation, in which participation and opinions are heard but not treated as serious contributions:

> Unless young people are confident that their opinions will be treated with respect and seriousness, they will quickly become discouraged and dismiss the participation process as ineffective with all the implications this has for the confidence in the democratic processes as they grow into adulthood. (Bessant 2004, 400)

Bessant also points out that youth forums are rarely initiated by young people themselves and that young people are not elected representatives, but are appointed to their positions. Further, even once involved, young people have 'minimal opportunities for agenda setting' (Bessant 2004, 400). There are also equity issues to be considered, such as which young people are selected and whether they are equipped to influence policy (Bessant 2004, 401; see also Augsberger et al. 2017). Young people from remote Aboriginal communities may occasionally have roles as youth representatives on local health boards, but they are very unlikely to be selected as members of youth round tables at regional or even national levels. They may have developed strong leadership skills and be respected by their peers for taking on leadership roles but remain unnoticed outside of the Indigenous domain.

The View of the Younger Generation

Edward's grandson and Edna's son, Ethan, has been constantly exposed to community politics from his childhood, watching both his grandfather's and mother's leadership efforts. His memories of his mother's experiences of being bullied and marginalised are particularly acute. Educated to Year 11 at boarding school in Darwin, Ethan is now in his early 20s and has a wife and a baby daughter. He has made a conscious decision to move away from what he described as 'the cultural side' of life in Ngukurr, which means that he avoids participation in ceremony.

For Ethan, and many other people in Ngukurr, ceremony is linked with sorcery. Reprisals using sorcery were of particular concern after the death of a relative:

> We all got sick from thinking about sorcery after our father died. They blame everyone and families tell us more. It makes us more crazy, making us feel sad all the time and it makes us sick.

This move away from the 'cultural side' is effectively a move from the only recognised structure within the Aboriginal domain that provides opportunities for the demonstration of leadership.

Edward's perception of Ethan's apathy and laziness, and Edna's lack of opportunity, stand in marked contrast to Ethan's own account of his civic activities with a group of friends—a group they call a gang or 'crew': the 'Bad T Boys' or 'Bad Ts'. Youth gangs are common in remote Aboriginal communities and have been described as a form of emergent leadership by Ivory (2009, 295), who explains the rationale for gang formation in Port Keats in the following way:

> By rebelling, creating sub structures and causing mayhem they were not only forcing their own community to take notice of them, but they were also creating a form of resistance against the dominant society represented to a large degree by the church, something which they believe their fathers in embracing the church had not done.

The gangs described by Ivory are characterised by their belief in violence and destruction, but also by their respect for tradition, particularly in the areas of kin and kinship obligations and affiliation to country (Ivory 2009, 302). Edwin's account of his gang articulates a very different underlying philosophy, one directed towards non-violence. The commitment to some forms of traditional knowledge are similar between both groups. Numbering between six and 13 at various times, the Bad Ts are all in their early 20s. All were schooled in Darwin, although none completed their education. At the time of this study, all were unemployed, although some had had short-term, part-time jobs. Most were married with young families. One member had spent a considerable period of time in jail. All were members of prominent Ngukurr families whose fathers and grandfathers were known leaders in both the secular and religious spheres.

The Bad T Boys expressed doubts about adult leadership in the community; in their opinion, the older men spent too much time deferring to a range of non-Aboriginal people, such as shire representatives. Here again there are resonances with the situation described by Bern in 1970 and with the rationale provided for the development of gangs in Port Keats (Ivory 2009):

> The few leaders left are weak, only do things that are good for their families. One of the things about jealousy is that there is jealousy of people who have the ear of the whitefellas. Then the other leaders get jealous.

We were able to observe elders' lack of authority in the non-Aboriginal sphere on several occasions, such as the failure of community leaders to implement a petrol-sniffing project due to a lack of support from the non-Aboriginal community described above (Senior and Chenhall 2007). More recently, an elder was engaged to meet with a group of youths to talk about issues affecting their lives, such as jealousy and domestic disputes. This meeting was considered to be of upmost importance by the young men involved. However, on the day of the meeting, a shire representative arrived unannounced and required the elder to meet with him. The young men commented that their needs were 'pushed aside' so that the 'whitefella' could be accommodated.

Issues of youth leadership were a particular focus of our research at Ngukurr in 2014–15 and we conducted a series of in-depth interviews with adult leaders and young people. During this time, we also asked young people to participate in a photovoice project. Photovoice, developed by Wang and Burris (1997) and Wang et al. (1998), is a participatory qualitative methodology that aims to support grassroots action. For our project, participants were asked to take pictures of 'things that were important for young people in the community'. The photos were then collaboratively interpreted, and narratives developed to explain the relationship of the photos to the research theme. The young men who participated in the photovoice story ultimately produced their own book, which described the history and aspirations of the gang, or 'crew', and its members. Some of their photos were simply of each other, assuming gangster-like poses, but many expressed the values that underpinned their activities, such as helping old people and providing food for them. Such values also include participation in Aboriginal culture, with an emphasis on going to the bush and hunting and fishing for bush tucker. They talked about the importance of children learning about such things, as well as values such as sharing. For example, a picture of three children with bottles of soft drink and packets of salty plums was not a statement about nutrition, but one about the importance of children learning to share highly valued goods (see Figure 3.4).

Figure 3.2: The Bad Ts. 'This is my gang, my crew. We look after each other. We are a famous crew in Ngukurr.'

Source: Photovoice project, Ngukurr, 2015.

The young men took this photograph (Figure 3.2) to illustrate the leaders of their gang and show their mastery of gang-like poses and attitudes. They talked about the formation of the gang while they were still at school and the strategies they developed to be recognised in the community:

> There were a lot of 12–13 year olds back in those days, but the gangs were 16–17 year olds. We were the first ones to make a kid's gang. We said, 'We are a pack, call us the Woody T Boys'. We thought let's go to the Disco, we can go and get dressed and walk in as a gang. We had no tattoos or nothing, so we made a dance instead. We practised all day. We all dressed like gangstas and went down to the rec hall. It was packed with people. Not so much anymore. We went home, relaxed a bit and then went to get dressed. Went to disco and made a dance group. It went well and all the crowds said: 'We didn't know you boys could dance. Have you ever heard of krump?'
>
> Yes, I have.
>
> We first invented it. Nobody dance krump here before. We put it to the new generation in Ngukurr. No one danced like that. I seed it on video. We invented it in Ngukurr. Famous, went all the way out to Numbulwar. Famous, we famous crew in Ngukurr.

Without access to the visible trappings of gang identity (e.g. tattoos or distinctive clothes), the group decided to differentiate themselves through their knowledge of youth culture, which had been made possible for them by spending time away from Ngukurr at school in Darwin. Other elements of consumerism and youth culture were also important for their identity; for example, one member's gang name was 'Rusty T' because of his Rusty-branded cap (again purchased in Darwin), which was obviously a treasured possession. Once they had achieved recognition in the community, they met to decide how to make the most of their fame:

> So, what happed then?
>
> We were all about love, respect and families, being a good person, talking to old people. We had a talk at the hill over near the school and we made a pact. We said, 'We are famous now, everyone know us.'

Figure 3.3: 'This place is important, because this is where we go to talk and make decisions.'

Source: Photovoice project, Ngukurr, 2015.

Figure 3.3 is taken from the small hill on the edge of the community. The young men described this as 'their place', saying that it was the place that they went to go to talk and make decisions. This photograph symbolises the processes that the young men associate with leadership, including attempts to represent the ideas of the group and voting on appropriate courses of action and the leadership structure of the group.

The gang has had three different leaders since its inception in 2004. The current gang leader, Ethan's cousin and close friend, talked about the responsibility he felt when taking on the leadership and the values that he brought to the position:

> It was me then after the second boss got married. Respect was from when W was the boss, I continued the same rules when it came to me. No fighting. He [W] questioned us: 'Are you going to be like other gangs with fighting?' We taking care of community. It's a pretty big community, but we are strong. It was in my head, not to fight, to go fishing for the old people, talk to old people, learn culture. We do respect white man law and black man law and mix it all together and make it strong. Everything comes easy to us. We give people a lot of things.

Figure 3.4: 'It's important to teach children to share, we teach them that.'
Source: Photovoice project, Ngukurr, 2015.

A driving factor in the formation of the Bad T gang's identity was a commitment to non-violence. They were also clear that they were not going to be involved in drug dealing, unlike many of the other gangs in the community. The actual activities of the collective were not as clearly defined, but involved an idea of doing things that were of benefit to the community, drawing on what they defined as key values, which included an ethos of sharing and looking after people, both of which may fairly be described as quintessentially Aboriginal values. Figure 3.4 was taken to illustrate the importance of 'children learning how to share'. Another key value is the maintenance of some (non-religious) cultural knowledge, such as hunting and gathering bush foods. The most important function, however, appears to be the mutual support that gang membership provides for its members.

The young men in the Bad Ts said that they wanted to avoid violence in the community. However, this was not always the case, as one young person spoke about being sent to jail in Darwin for domestic violence:

> I was in there (jail) for three months.
>
> Could you tell me what you did?
>
> Yes … I threw a bottle at my wife. It hit her on the head. It was a half-bottle of Coke. It was my last warning, I was on good behaviour. They put me in for three months. When I came out my son is gone and my wife is gone. Since I get out I got to be a man, strong.

The loss of his son is a particular source of grief for this young man. The rhetoric surrounding the values of the gang is all about 'doing good for families and our children', but this individual never sees his child. The fear that his gang members would think he had let them down added to his anxiety. Ethan said that he did let the gang down, and that they were 'sad and upset' because he was the 'boss' and was expected to set a good example:

> How did it feel for the gang?
>
> Ethan: Everyone was sad and upset, he was the boss.
>
> Gang Leader: When I came out of jail, I spent time with him … He said, 'If you have worriness, come down to me, I give you a feed.'

Gang members talked about the importance of closely monitoring an individual's behaviour before they allowed them to become a member of the gang. For example, in the following story, they mention such things as ensuring trust and exerting dominance by getting the younger person to buy things for them. At the same time, they also talk about checking up on the potential gang member's education, which echoes the 'looking after' ethos that is part of male nurturance of initiates:

> Then there's J, we call him Boney Man. He's a real skinny fella. He joined in 2006, we started the gang in 2004. He came up to us and we made a pact. We tested him to see if we could trust him. He's been good, buying things for us, we seen to his education as well. Checked that his education is alright.

Internal social capital is high within the group. Members talk about looking after each other and watching for symptoms of 'worriness' or depression:

> We call him the A-Train, because he smokes like a train. He's been through stuff. His wife left him. He's got mental health stuff, depression. We try to help him, we talk to him. He is back to where he was. We always talk, spent all day with 'im yesterday. That's how we took the darkness from him, talk to him, hang out with him, tell him who he was, that he belonged to family and to Woody T. Tell him: 'If you don't see love from your parents you see love from us'. He's 'bin thinking, thinking and then he said 'I know who my boys are'. A-Train has been alone for a long time, he's a good man, a good fella. He's back now.

The Bad Ts' form of leadership is different to that of preceding generations. This is partly the result of the lack of leadership opportunities in the community described earlier; however, these young men have also turned away from both the religious authority of their grandfathers and the form of leadership taken up by their parents in the intercultural domain of community governance. Instead, their leadership is relational, drawing on non-religious aspects of culture to engage civically within their community. Underlying this is a connection to globalised forms of culture centred around their gang, albeit in their own local form.

J, a gang member, painted an optimistic view of the future in which their kids would assume positions of leadership and continue to respect culture. Ethan had a more nuanced viewpoint. He considered a range of external influences that would impact upon his children's future (see Figure 3.5):

> What do you think the future will be like for them (the children) in Ngukurr?
>
> J: We'll be old! (Laughter). I think if we teach them, teach them cultural stuff, kids will be good leaders when they are our age. Ngukurr will be a great place, our kids will be leaders like us. Gonna be strong, gonna be there for his kids, I think our kids will be like us.
>
> Ethan: I see it different.
>
> How do you see it?
>
> Ethan: Things are making it hard, the Government, the Intervention, drugs …
>
> J: But it makes a big difference if you are strong like this.

Figure 3.5: 'Our children's futures: our kids will be strong like us.'
Source: Photovoice project, Ngukurr, 2015.

Discussion

Edward, the male elder, provided an extensive history of his role as a leader. He described acting alone and in opposition to community views. His story is one of constant conflict and struggle and periods of exhaustion and withdrawal from the community. His story is also one of recognition of his power and his capacity to enforce change in the community, albeit sometimes reluctantly, from non-Aboriginal people and government authorities. Edward was a leader during the era of self-determination after the missionaries left the community—a period of assertion of Aboriginal rights and an emerging knowledge that leaders would have to be active in both the Aboriginal and non-Aboriginal domains. In 1969–70, there were five councils or committees within Ngukurr, each composed of both Indigenous and non-Indigenous people (Bern 1970, 3). However, Aboriginal autonomy was restricted to the religious sphere and, even within this sphere, male participation was influenced by non-Indigenous values, particularly from the conflict some people felt between their adoption of Christianity and ritual participation (Bern 1970, 18).

By July 2015, Edward considered the community's future to be bleak. He saw no young people with the skills to take on future leadership positions. His daughter Edna was experienced in the processes of representation and decision-making and had received considerable encouragement to take on positions of leadership in the community; she held numerous positions on both community and shire-based structures of governance, but her level of authority was limited. Uncertain of the authority she had to make decisions, she usually found herself deferring to a non-Aboriginal person. As a woman, she felt that her various leadership roles were not respected by the men in the community. By 2020, however, significant changes were taking place. Edna had significantly more leadership opportunities, which she attributed to local government structures taking responsibility for activities, such as the Community Development and Education Program (CDEP), which were formerly administrated by the shire.

Both Edward and Edna tried to work within the system and to forge relationships with non-Aboriginal structures of authority. Despite some wins, which included the decision to make the community alcohol free in 1969 and the Aborginalisation of the school, they were repeatedly reminded of the difficulty of sustaining interventions, or, as in the situation exemplified by the community decision to address petrol sniffing (Senior and Chenhall 2007), to ensure that their interventions were recognised beyond the Indigenous domain.

Disillusioned with the leadership of adults in the community, Ethan's generation have adopted and Aboriginalised another Western form of leadership—the gang. Their leaders have arisen from the collective. The Bad Ts are motivated by the failure of adult leaders to adequately protect Aboriginal interests and what they see as the constant deferral to non-Aboriginal authority. Importantly, the Bad Ts stand in contrast to the gangs in Port Keats and other youth gangs in Ngukurr who fight, destroy property and take drugs. They say that they place a high value on the preservation of Aboriginal culture and traditional knowledge. Because the gang is not defined by violent or destructive acts, their existence and actions are not visible to authorities outside the community. The rhetoric of the gang leaders emphasises respect for other people and culture and places importance on democratic processes: the youths meet and vote on decisions. They say that they play a significant role in 'taking care of the community', but it is difficult to ascertain how influential they are in this space. Certainly, community members talk about them and describe them as 'good boys', but there are few examples of what they actually do. Mutual assistance appears to be a characteristic of the group. This was indicated in stories about helping others get through difficult times, such as going to jail, the break-up of relationships and mental health problems. Their values of 'looking after' each other extend to their care of their own wives and children and their relationships within the community.

This form of leadership aligns with descriptions of 'youth leadership' that emphasise the importance of group processes and collective action rather than models that highlight the personality and qualities of specific individuals (see Dempster and Lizzio 2007). Significantly, this relational leadership has been described as emerging in post-industrial globalised contexts (Houwer 2016). An adaptive form of leadership, it emphasises collaboration between group members who work together with strong moral and ethical grounding (see Haber 2011). It has been described by Clarsen (2019) as existing among the young men depicted in the film *Black As*—a self-made documentary about four young Yolngu men on a hunting trip. As the young men move through their country, they embrace certain elements of modernity, evidenced through their fixing and modifying of vehicles, and reject other elements of a post-industrial society, evidenced through their humorous recreations of commercials of 'Aboriginal' bush products. Citing Marcia Langton, Clarsen (2019, 161) describes these young men as embodying the 'new permissiveness atypical of the old tradition'.

This is true for the Bad T Boys presented in this chapter. The young men articulated their strategic approach to becoming recognised as a unified gang. They capitalised on their connections to a globalised youth culture, which were made possible by spending time away from the community in Darwin. Access to a branded cap or knowledge of a new dance style may seem trivial to outsiders, but such things have significant currency in a community where access to a globalised youth culture is minimal (Chenhall and Senior 2009). Although such strategies may have resonance with local youth, they are unlikely to affect strategic decisions in any wider context. Unlike Edward and Edna, the gang operates purely within the Aboriginal domain (see Trigger 1992). Their actions are not likely to be noticed by non-Aboriginal people. But their participation in the Aboriginal domain is limited by their avoidance of ceremony. Instead, they have constructed their identity by drawing upon some aspects of traditional culture including values of caring for each other and maintaining traditional skills such as hunting. These values have been combined with their knowledge of a globalised youth culture and access to highly valued material goods. They are less exposed to the conflict of non-Aboriginal and Aboriginal domains that affected both Edward and Edna, but their ability to enact any change is minimal. Beneath the bravado of their rhetoric—'Our kids will be strong leaders like us'—a more thoughtful commentary indicates that they feel powerless to address many of the major issues influencing the community, which they see as coming from outside: 'the intervention, drugs'. Despite developing some political and management skills, including knowledge of democratic processes and being motivated by a principal of community development, these young men are unlikely to be noticed as potential representatives for youth round tables or forums, or to be seen as the next generation of leaders in their community. Their actions are doubly invisible because they live in a remote community and because they are young within a system that recognises age as an important prerequisite for leadership. Their ethos of non-violence will not even provide them with the notoriety associated with the Port Keats gangs.

Conclusion

Contrary to the mainstream expectations of young people and the expectations of their own families, the group of young men presented in this chapter are not apathetic with regard to leadership and civic responsibility. Nor are they ignorant or dismissive of traditional culture, which appears in their values and decision-making, despite their avoidance of the performative aspects of culture, such as ceremony. Rather than submitting to a situation in which cultural knowledge is controlled by older men, they have decided what aspects of cultural knowledge are important to them, and what aspects they can avoid.

They have not been thrust into their roles by elders; rather, they have reimagined and enacted such roles for themselves. They have embraced a key set of values to underpin their activities and they emphasise the importance of democratic processes. They could be supported and nurtured to become influential voices in their communities. But they face an identity issue: from the perspective of outsiders, young men in remote Aboriginal communities, if they are not recognised for their sporting prowess, are often defined by their problems, their criminal activities, their violence, their use of drugs and alcohol. From the perspective of elders in their own communities, young people may be recognised as agitators, but older people are those who take responsibility and ownership of decisions. However, what is clear from this study of three generations of leadership is the continuity of structural determinants that place Aboriginal people in positions in which they have very limited authority and opportunity to make decisions about own their lives and communities. Since mission times, various structures have existed to encourage participation, but these were never entirely within the Aboriginal domain. The only sphere in which men have autonomy away from non-Aboriginal direction is the religious domain, and yet, even in this area, people's capacity has been greatly affected by non-Aboriginal beliefs, particularly those of Christianity.

References

Augsberger, A., M. E. Collins, W. Gecker and M. Dougher. 2017. 'Youth Civic Engagement: Do Youth Councils Reduce or Reinforce Social Inequality'. *Journal of Adolescent Research* 33 (2): 187–208. doi.org/10.1177/074355841 6684957.

Bell, D. 1983. *Daughters of the Dreaming*. Melbourne: McPhee Gribble/George Allen and Unwin.

Bern, J. 1970. *Field Report on Social Anthropological Research At Ngukurr, Northern Territory, December 1979 to June 1970*. Canberra: Australian Institute of Aboriginal Studies.

Bern. J. 1976. 'Reaction to Attrition: The Ngukurr Strike of 1970'. *Mankind* 10: 213–24. doi.org/10.1111/j.1835-9310.1999.tb01449.x.

Bern, J. 1979a. 'Ideology and Domination, Towards a Reconstruction of Australian Aboriginal Social Formation'. *Oceania* 50 (2): 118–32. doi.org/10.1002/ j.1834-4461.1979.tb01948.x.

Bern J. 1979b. 'Politics in the Conduct of a Secret Male Ceremony'. *Journal of Anthropological Research* 35 (1): 47–60. doi.org/10.1086/jar.35.1.3629496.

Berndt, R. M. and C. H. Berndt. 1969. *The First Australians*. Sydney: Ure Smith.

Bessant, J. 2004. 'Mixed Messages: Youth Participation and Democratic Practice'. *Australian Journal of Political Science* 39 (2): 387–04. doi.org/10.1080/1036 114042000238573.

Chenhall, R. and K. Senior. 2009. 'Those Young People All Crankybella': Indigenous Youth, Mental Health and Globalisation'. *International Journal of Mental Health* 38 (3): 28–43. doi.org/10.2753/IMH0020-7411380302.

Clarsen, G. 2019. 'Black As: Performing Indigenous Difference'. In *Mobilities, Mobility Justice and Social Justice,* edited by N. Cook and D. Butz, 159–72. London: Routledge. doi.org/10.4324/9780815377047-11.

Dempster, N. and A. Lizzio. 2007. 'Student Leadership: Necessary Research'. *Journal of Education* 51 (3): 276–85. doi.org/10.1177/000494410705100305.

Elkin, A. P. 1938. *The Australian Aborigines: How to Understand Them.* Sydney: Angus and Robertson.

France, A. 1998. 'Why Should We Care?: Young People, Citizenship and Questions of Social Responsibility. *Journal of Youth Studies* 1 (1): 97–111. doi.org/10.1080/13676261.1998.10592997.

Haber, P. 2011. 'Peer Education in Student Leadership Program: Responding to Cocurricular Challenges'. *New Direction for Student Services* 133: 65–76. doi.org/10.1002/ss.385.

Hiatt, L. 1965. *Kinship and Conflict: A Study of Aboriginal Community in Northern Arnhem Land.* Canberra: Australian National University Press.

Hinkson, M. 2017. 'Aftermath', editorial, *Arena Magazine.* 148.

Houwer, R. 2016. *Changing Leaders, Leading Change: A Leadership Development Model for Marginalized Youth in Urban Communities.* Toronto: Youth Research and Evaluation eXchange (YouthREX). doi.org/10.15868/socialsector.34106.

Ivory, B. 2009. 'Kunmanggur, Legend and Leadership, a Study of Indigenous Leadership and Succession, Focusing on the Northwest Region of the Northern Territory of Australia'. PhD thesis, Charles Darwin University.

Keen, I. 1994. *Knowledge and Secrecy in an Aboriginal Religion.* Oxford: Clarendon Press.

Meggitt, M. 1962. *Desert People: A Study of Walbiri Aborigines of Central Australia.* Sydney: Angus and Robertson.

Myers, F. R. 1976. 'To Have and to Hold: A Study of Persistence and Change in Pintupi Social Life'. PhD thesis, University of Michigan.

O'Donnell, R. 2007. 'The Value of Autonomy: Christianity, Organisation and Performance in an Aboriginal Community'. PhD thesis, University of Sydney.

Sanders, W. 2013. 'Losing Localism, Constraining Councillors: Why the Northern Territory Supershires are Struggling'. *Policy Studies* 34 (4): 473–90. doi.org/10.1080/01442872.2013.822704.

Senior, K. 2003. 'A Gudbala Laif? Health and Wellbeing in a Remote Aboriginal Community—What Are the Problems and Where Lies the Responsibility?' PhD thesis, The Australian National University, Canberra.

Senior, K. and R. Chenhall. 2007. '"Stopping Sniffing is Our Responsibility": Community Ownership of a Petrol Sniffing Program in Arnhem Land'. *Health Sociology Review* 16 (3–4): 315–27. doi.org/10.5172/hesr.2007.16.3-4.315.

Strehlow, T. G. H. 1947. *Aranda Traditions*. Melbourne: Melbourne University Press.

Trigger, D. S. 1992. *Whitefella Comin' Aboriginal Responses to Colonialism in Northern Australia*. Cambridge: Cambridge University Press.

Wang, C. and M. A. Burris. 1997. 'Photovoice: Concept, Methodology, and Use for Participatory Needs Assessment'. *Health Education and Behavior* 24 (3): 369–87. doi.org/10.1177/109019819702400309.

Wang, C. C., W. K. Yi, Z. W. Tao and K. Carovano. 1998. 'Photovoice as a Participatory Health Promotion Strategy'. *Health Promotion International* 13 (1): 75–86. doi.org/10.1093/heapro/13.1.75.

Youniss, J., S. Bales, V. Christmas-Best, M. Diversi, M. LcLaughlin and R. Silbereisen. 2002. 'Youth Civic Engagement in the Twenty-First Century'. *Journal of Research on Adolescence* 12 (1): 121–48. doi.org/10.1111/1532-7795.00027.

4

Food Practices of Young People in a Remote Aboriginal Community

Danielle Aquino

Introduction

A common trope is that Aboriginal and Torres Strait Islander people are 'lost', 'trapped' or 'caught' between two worlds: that of Aboriginal and Torres Strait Islander culture and that of mainstream Australian society:

> Aboriginal people are sometimes lost between the two realities, trying to preserve their traditional culinary heritage and culture and at the same time trying to adopt new food practices and eating habits. (Sebastian and Donelly 2013, 70)

Conceptualising people as being lost between two cultures is, however, a 'thoroughly constrained notion of intercultural engagement' (Hinkson and Smith 2005, 161) and one that is limiting as an explanation for Aboriginal people's food practices in contemporary life. The contemporary food system in most remote Aboriginal communities is an intercultural space, comprising commercial, customary, locally grown, and state or welfare elements (Brimblecombe et al. 2014; Buchanan 2014). While there are differences between the Aboriginal and introduced or whitefella 'domains' of the food system, they are interrelated through people, organisations and institutions. It is within this intercultural space that the 'new food practices and eating habits' referred to above are evolving. Aboriginal and Torres Strait Islander people and non-Aboriginal people may have 'different forms of experience, knowing and practice' (Merlan 2005, 174) of each of the food systems. Understanding how Aboriginal and Torres Strait Islander people understand and engage with the contemporary food system, and valuing their knowledges and perspectives, presents opportunities for addressing complex issues such as nutrition and diet (Wilson et al. 2020).

Young people are particularly subject to being portrayed as 'caught between' contemporary Australian society and a reified notion of traditional Aboriginal and Torres Strait Islander culture (McCoy 2009, s20). Their food practices are often cause for concern to health practitioners and within families and communities. Reliance on junk food and a perceived 'loss' of taste for traditional foods are common concerns (Brimblecombe et al. 2014; Saethre 2013). Unfortunately, the perspectives of Aboriginal young people themselves in relation to their food and eating practices are very much lacking. As Eickelkamp (2011) notes, there is little research in general on how Aboriginal children and young people experience life, shape their social world and imagine the future: all aspects of life that may affect dietary practices. This chapter, along with others in this volume, attempts to glimpse into the perspectives and life circumstances of some Aboriginal young people. First, I provide a brief snapshot of epidemiological evidence to set the scene as to why a focus on young people's food and eating practices is of interest in the wider effort to reduce Aboriginal and Torres Strait Islander disadvantage. Then, drawing on ethnographic material from Ngukurr, a remote Aboriginal community in the Northern Territory, I explore young people's subjective and embodied experiences of food and eating.

Aboriginal and Torres Strait Islander Food and Nutrition

National and regional surveys consistently find that many Aboriginal and Torres Strait Islander children and young people, particularly those living in rural and remote areas, are consuming low amounts of vegetables and high amounts of soft drinks and processed foods (Australian Bureau of Statistics 2015a; 2015b; Gwynn et al. 2012). Such dietary patterns are reflective of community-level diets in remote Aboriginal settings, which tend to be high in refined cereals (e.g. white flour and white bread) and added sugars (particularly from soft drinks) and low in fruits and vegetables (Brimblecombe et al. 2013; Brimblecombe and O'Dea 2009; Lee et al. 2016; Lee, O'Dea and Mathews 1994). These dietary patterns are implicated in the excess burden of disease experienced by Aboriginal and Torres Strait Islander peoples (Australian Institute of Health and Welfare 2015; 2016, 86; Vos et al. 2009).

Influences on Food Practices in Aboriginal and Torres Strait Islander Communities

A consistently safe and secure food supply is unattainable for many families and individuals in remote Aboriginal communities due to several factors: the high cost of foods; reliance, in most remote communities, on a single food store; and remoteness itself. Nationally, it is estimated that just under one-third of Aboriginal and Torres Strait Islander people living in remote communities run out of food and are unable to buy more (Australian Bureau of Statistics 2015a). A range of factors that contribute to food insecurity in remote communities have been described, including low individual and household incomes, high food prices, store infrastructure and management practices, household infrastructure, substance misuse, cultural expectations to share food and other resources, and a limited range of foods (Brimblecombe et al. 2014; Leonard 2003).

While poverty and economic constraints are clearly important determinants of food and nutrition in remote Aboriginal and Torres Strait Islander communities, food insecurity alone does not wholly explain food and eating practices in food insecure environments (Paul et al. 2011). Cultural preferences, group identity, social interactions and psychological needs all shape food behaviour regardless of income (Ikeda 1999). What people eat is shaped by their social, familial, environmental, cultural and political contexts, as well as their own individual tastes and preferences. To what extent people's food choices are determined by social structures and to what extent they are attributable to individual agency is an ongoing tension in nutrition and food research that tends to frame people as 'unwitting dupes of the food system' or argue that 'food consumer demand is largely responsible for shaping the food supply' (Schubert 2008, 263).

In the case of food practices, the improved affordability and availability of healthier foods should result in people eating a healthier diet. There is evidence to suggest that economic levers have a modest effect on consumption of vegetables and fruit (Brimblecombe et al. 2017). There is also evidence that suggests that diet quality has decreased in some communities despite sustained efforts to improve the availability of nutritious foods (Lee et al. 2016). Further, self-efficacy and social context remain largely unchanged despite education and economic interventions (Brimblecombe et al. 2017). Meaningful improvements in the diets of Aboriginal people in remote communities will not be possible 'without addressing the underlying constraints that reinforce unhealthy dietary behaviours' (Brimblecombe et al. 2017). However, these constraints do not necessarily work in linear ways (Chenhall and Senior 2017). Considering food choice as mostly a material matter without also attending to the social, cultural and personal aspects of food and eating means that understandings of why people eat the way they do will only ever be partial. Ethnographic research can assist in expanding understandings about sociocultural aspects of food choice.

Setting and Methods

Ngukurr[1] is a township with a population of around 1,000 situated just over 300 km south-east of Katherine, Northern Territory. It was established as a mission by the Anglican Church, which continues to have a strong presence in the community. The services available to residents at Ngukurr include a single grocery and general store, a school with primary and secondary classes, and a health centre managed by a community-controlled health organisation. Other social and wellbeing services, including a new integrated child and family centre incorporating early years education and family support programs, are also available. Municipal, youth, and sport and recreation programs are managed by the shire council. Economic development, including construction, and a cattle enterprise is led by a local development corporation. Despite new and renovated housing, accommodation remains in short supply and overcrowding and poor conditions are common.

I first started work at Ngukurr in 2010 as a public health nutritionist coordinating a child nutrition project. In 2014, I took on a new role, as a PhD candidate, and undertook intensive fieldwork between 2014–15. This was a new role for me, both epistemologically, moving away from

1 See Chapters 1–3 in this volume for more details about Ngukurr.

the empiricism of nutrition science towards a more constructivist view of food and eating, and methodologically, engaging with the community as a participant observer rather than service provider. Field visits were conducted for periods of one to four weeks,[2] mostly during the accessible 'dry season' (May–October). I used a range of methods, including participant observation, individual and group interviews with young people and adults, photo elicitation with young people and young mothers, and workshops with groups of two to 10 young women. In these workshops, the young women listed foods they 'liked' and 'disliked' (Table 4.1). They also created body maps (Chenhall et al. 2013) of fictitious young women (Appendix Figures 4.1 and 4.2). We discussed the living circumstances, diet, relationships and daily activities of the characters created in the body maps. The body map characters had diets that were perhaps more aspirational than the daily diets of the young women participating in the activity.

The main informants for this work were mostly young mothers who attend the supported playgroup and some of their extended family, some other young people and some older women and men. Both the male and female informants were biological and/or classificatory grandmothers, grandfathers, mothers, fathers, uncles and aunts in the Aboriginal kinship system, and all have roles in the socialisation of babies, children and young people. Ethical clearance for this research was granted by the Human Research Ethics Committee of the Northern Territory Department of Health and Menzies School of Health Research (HREC 2014-2291).

Young People's Preferred Foods

Young people's declared food preferences incorporate a range of foods from the store, 'tuckshop' and bush[3] (Table 4.1, Appendix Figures 4.1 and 4.2). Food preferences are fairly conservative with little variation between foods listed in the free-listing activity, body maps and during interviews. The foods were largely reflective of what is stocked in the local store and takeaway. Meal patterns at Ngukurr are rarely structured, people

2 Personal circumstances and housing availability precluded me from living in Ngukurr for an extended period as is the norm for ethnographic research. I remained living in Katherine (where I had lived since 2000) and made regular visits to Ngukurr.

3 Young women use bush foods. Bush foods also include fish. Some referred to 'killer' (beef) bush food.

eat when they are hungry and when the opportunity presents itself. Young people might eat when there is food available at home, usually prepared by older members of the household; if they or their friends had some money and were able to get to the shop or takeaway to buy something; through school meals programs; or if they were attending a community activity (e.g. a barbeque at the youth centre).

Table 4.1: Results from free-listing activity

Likes			**Dislikes**		
Turkey	Banana	Hotdog	Witchetty grub[4]	Watermelon	Liquorice
Jupi (blackcurrant)	Peanut	Tea	Goanna	Frozen vegies	Hot foods (only sometimes)
Green plum	Orange	Coke	Kangaroo	Tuna	Salty plum
Magpie goose	Mango	Juicy fruit (chewing gum)	Camel[5]	Liver	Chocolate
Catfish	Corn	Hungry Jacks			Ice cream
Turtle	Water	Salty plum			Pizza
	Green peas	Cake			Tamarind
	Broccoli	Hot chips			
	Avocado	Red Rooster			
	Rice crackers	Sprite			
	Apple	Nutri-Grain			
	Cherries	KFC			
	Milk	McDonalds			
	Mushroom	Ice cream			
	Damper	Pizza			
	Beef	Popcorn			
	Eggs	Coco Pops			
	Red grapes	Chocolate			
	Onion (cooked)				
	Banana				
	Carrot				
	Strawberries				
	Weetbix				
	Watermelon				

The consumption of takeaway foods, as well as other snack-type foods, is a recognisable feature of young people's food practices at Ngukurr. When young people have access to money, these are what they prefer to spend it on. As young people are not usually responsible for purchasing and cooking for the household, and often eat food at school, the foods they

4 Witchetty grubs are not a traditional food in the Ngukurr area. The young woman who identified this as a dislike attends school in Central Australia where witchetty grubs are a common (and often highly prized) traditional food.

5 It was noted by the young women that although they'd never tried camel, they thought they would dislike it.

have most control over are those sold at the 'tuckshop'. 'Hot foods' from the takeaway, such as chips, meat pies and burgers, were prominent in the diets of the body map characters (Appendix Figures 4.1 and 4.2), and both young and older people observed these choices:

> You see young people they carry bag with Coke, lollies, chips, salty plum, tamarind. (Young woman, 15–19 years)

> Tuckshop food is the main food for every young people. Hot food and bottle of Coke. All those greasy stuff from the tuckshop. No young people can't say they don't eat tuckshop foods. (Grandmother, 50+ years)

Food can be an important symbol of identity and people may use their food choices and dietary practices to define themselves (Bisogni et al. 2002; Stead et al. 2011). A young woman (15–19 years) described how it is common for young people to mix salty plums[6] and/or dried tamarind with lemonade or lemon juice into a thick paste (Appendix Figure 4.3). This is a 'young people's food'. Young women at Ngukurr describe foods in relation to themselves, as one young woman told me 'Nutri-Grain is my cereal, not Weetbix'.

Interested in their perspectives about accessibility, I asked the young women to identify which foods were easily available and which were more difficult to obtain. They said that 'easy to get' foods were some fruit, soft drink, damper, tea, cake, hot chips and a few vegetables (Table 4.1). 'Hard to get' foods were either bush foods, highly seasonal fruits or takeaway foods available only from outlets in Katherine, Darwin or Alice Springs (e.g. Hungry Jacks, KFC and McDonalds) (Table 4.1).

Foods that were more difficult to access were coveted. A passion for seasonal bush foods is seen during *jupi* (blackcurrant) season, when people of all ages, but particularly young people, are frequently off foraging and congregating with large containers filled with the small, sweet, astringent deep purple berries. There is great desire for *jupi*, although towards the end of the season, as the novelty wanes, young people refer to being 'tired of *jupi*' and adults say they are sick of hearing about '*jupi, jupi*'.

6 Salty plums are a dried plum coated in a salty powder. Originally from China, they are a commonly eaten snack food in the Northern Territory.

It is not just seasonality that places some coveted foods out of reach. While young people might desire magpie goose, catfish and green plums, they are constrained by their knowledge and that of their family: 'When they (parents) go away and the kids have to stay with other aunties and uncles, probably them other mob don't have that experience of fishing' (Mother, 20–29 years). Access to bush foods also requires resources such as transport, firearms, ammunition and digging tools, as well as accessible land and waterways. As Saethre (2005, 164) says of hunting and collecting of traditional foods in Lajamanu (another remote Aboriginal community in the Northern Territory):

> Hunting and gathering actually require a greater level of monetary and other resources, and greater amounts of time, too. Moreover, because of kin obligations, they usually yield only a single meal to the hunter or gatherer.

At Ngukurr, families with access to transport, particularly through ranger programs, royalties or tourism ventures, visit their outstations more regularly and could return with an abundance of traditional foods such as crab, mussels and *yarlbun* (lily seedpods). Others, however, struggle to find transport, have issues with land access and/or have everyday life challenges (e.g. caring for very sick, elderly relatives or alcoholism) that prevent them from fulfilling their want for traditional foods.

Young people view foods purchased from outlets outside of Ngukurr as more delicious, cheaper and better. Eating branded takeaway foods such as KFC, McDonalds and Hungry Jacks, which are only available in Katherine, Darwin or Alice Springs, is a special treat even though fried chicken, burgers and chips are a constant at Ngukurr's local store. As this grandmother observed of young people: 'You know, even in town everybody get spoiled going out McDonald's and Kentucky Fried Chicken and whatever, buying that' (Grandmother, 50+ years).

The preference and desire to 'go out' to fast food outlets represents one of the many ways that Aboriginal young people's lives are 'enmeshed in the globalised world' (Hinkson and Smith 2005, 157). These outlets are inexpensive and informal places where Aboriginal young people from Ngukurr feel comfortable. Going out to McDonalds in Katherine or Darwin[7] is a way to fulfil aspirations for variety (Bridle-Fitzpatrick 2016) within the constraints of cost and familiarity. Fast food outlets, in Katherine at least, are spaces used by both non-Aboriginal and Aboriginal people, unlike some other spaces that are markedly 'white' (Merlan 2005).

Young people at Ngukurr appear to have a shared food *habitus* of simple foods, soft drinks and takeaway. They prefer a range—albeit limited—of foods both healthy and unhealthy, and their food preferences include foods that are store bought as well as sourced by fishing, hunting and gathering. There are constraints to young people's food practices, and it seems that opportunities to access preferred foods are not necessarily available to all young people equally.

Hunger and Not Having Enough Food

In addition to constraints on accessing their preferred foods, young people at Ngukurr also face the issue of accessing *enough* food. Not having food to eat or worrying about getting enough food was a common experience for young people at Ngukurr. They are keenly aware of the physical sensations of hunger, which they describe as feeling shaky, getting 'desperate for food', having a sore or growling stomach, and feeling sick to the point of vomiting (Appendix Figures 4.1 and 4.2). These sensations are expected and frequent. Young people seemed resigned to the fact that there will be times when they must go without food: 'Sometime, when we hungry at home and it's night we just—and we really hungry—we can just sleep without food' (Young man, 15–19 years).

Young people at Ngukurr generally did not raise specific concerns about food costs,[8] despite higher food costs and low incomes being well established as drivers of food insecurity in remote communities. They did, however, point out that gambling and drug and alcohol use diverted money away from food and other goods. For example, the young woman

7 The desirability of these fast food outlets may be different for Aboriginal young people who live in urban and regional centres for whom McDonalds is mundane and who are seeking a wider variety of foods in different ways (see Chapter 6).

8 The few young people who did raise the cost of food with me were also parents; therefore, it may be that, once they had caring responsibilities and an income through child benefits and were expected to be responsible for food purchasing, they became more acutely aware of the cost of food.

created in the body map (Appendix Figure 4.2) 'doesn't worry for money because she never plays cards'. People often suggested that it is 'others' in the community who do not responsibly prioritise buying food:

> And the problem is at family camp, some families don't buy food. When they got that drug and alcohol problem. Well like me and Steven[9] we're drinkers but we still buy food. But some don't think to buy food first. (Mother, 20–29 years)

> When I get my pay I buy food first, then powercard, every main thing I buy it. Then I just go gamble with the leftovers. (Young man, 15–19 years)

Asking for food, or money to obtain food, from other family members is the usual strategy that people at Ngukurr, both young and old, use whenever they run out of food. In turn, they are expected to reciprocate when their kin require assistance. This reciprocity can both positively and negatively influence food access and nutrition. Obligations to share food and resources between kin can provide a safety net but may also place excessive pressures on certain households and household members (Brimblecombe 2007; Smith et al. 2003). Sharing obligations also influence the types of foods that people at Ngukurr purchase. Some foods, such as single-serve takeaway foods are less amenable to sharing, and hence may be preferred (Senior 2003). In the context of fluid and uncertain eating opportunities, there is a preference for foods that require minimal preparation such as tinned spaghetti, or can be consumed 'as is', such as takeaway, fruit or chocolate bars.

Being *Munanga*?

Aboriginal and Torres Strait Islander people often refer to foods as being whitefella foods or bush foods, related to the experience of traversing 'two worlds' (see e.g. Brimblecombe et al. 2014; Colles, Maypilama and Brimblecombe 2014; Saethre 2013; Senior 2003). This separation of foods and food practices as *munanga* (whitefella or non-Aboriginal) foods or *blekbala* (Aboriginal) was also evident at Ngukurr. Interestingly, it was generally deployed *about* young people's practices rather than *by* young

9 All names used are pseudonyms.

people. Young people, as observed above, had a preference for a range of foods rather than being concerned specifically as to whether they were *blekbala* or *munanga*.

Despite traditional foods ranking highly in young people's food likes, older adults at Ngukurr often lament that young people are no longer interested in traditional foods and have been lured into eating only *munanga* food from the store. They assert that young people's preference for takeaway foods drives them to return early from fishing trips, which are usually highly prized occasions, to get to the takeaway before it closes:

> We went for *sugarbag* [bush honey]. We tried to get the kids to have a taste, but they didn't like it, because it was a long time, there was a space. It was first time they were eating that *sugarbag*. Cause they never had that taste, they never got brought up with that taste. There was a gap there. Never had it. (Mother, 20–29 years)

> We go out fishing, Jason always make damper, no the kids don't want damper they always want bread. And even when we cook when we get fish or turtle they don't want it, they want tinned meat. That's the difference. (Adult male, 40–49 years)

The narrative that young people have 'lost the taste' and are disinterested in traditional foods is common in other Aboriginal communities (Brimblecombe et al. 2014; Saethre 2013). Such disconnect between older and younger generations with respect to food and other aspects of life is not confined to Aboriginal families. Migrant families trying to preserve traditional food cultures within their new home country similarly lament that younger generations are acquiring a preference for Western-style foods (Momin, Chung and Olson 2014), and there is much anxiety about the demise of the 'family meal' in Western societies (Murcott 1998).

The 'space' between opportunities to taste the *sugarbag* that the young mother points to above is often attributed to the requirement to participate in the Western education system. Traditionally, children and young people would learn about foods while accompanying their parents hunting and gathering (Brimblecombe et al. 2014). Even if they wanted to, families perceive that they are unable to pass on such knowledge because of the amount of time children must spend at school:

> They all just going *munanga* way now. When they go to school, they learn *munanga*. Holiday times we teach them but not during the week because they have to go to school. (Young mother, 20–29 years)

Many of the older people interviewed attended school while it was under mission control. As such, parents and grandparents of children and young people today who were schooled during that period may continue to perceive that school is a place to learn Western cultural and social norms—a place of assimilation. While the quotation above is from a younger woman, it suggests that school is still understood as a non-Aboriginal space, where non-Aboriginal values and practices dominate (Burbank 2006). Despite this perception, school also offers some opportunities for children to learn about traditional foods and culture. Young people at Ngukurr noted that, as well as learning from their family, 'culture classes' at school were the source of some of their information about traditional foods. 'Culture classes' and customary activities incorporated into school programs helped to make school a more enjoyable institution for some children (Burbank 2006).

The concern about Aboriginal children not liking traditional foods is also about more than their real or imagined distaste for such foods. It is a statement about whitefella invasion and dominance in Aboriginal family life. Food is being used as a tactical device to draw attention to Aboriginal and non-Aboriginal relations. Colonisation disrupted intergenerational transmission of knowledge about traditional foods, creating the 'gap' that the young mother describes above.

Having social networks from which to access food is perceived as a positive, protective part of life for Aboriginal people at Ngukurr, and a marker of significant difference between Aboriginal and non-Aboriginal cultures: 'Only black Aboriginal people who share food, not white people … It's hard for white people eh? But black people it's more easier' (Mother, 20–29 years). Sharing and young people's reliance on family was viewed as another difference between Aboriginal and non-Aboriginal young people. The latter were perceived as independent of their families and as having to carve out lives for themselves: 'Non-Indigenous people when they're that age (teenagers) they don't depend on their parents' (Grandmother, 50+ years).

Parents and grandparents at Ngukurr are concerned that if children and young people adopt a more individualistic way of thinking about food and eating they may lose their social connections:

> But if you try and teaching the kids to live independently now, they won't be, they'll be nobody when they grow up you know. They'll be on their own. And the other family will say 'He or she is selfish' and you know … Where that family wants to try and change their ways, but they can't change, 'cause the other family will judge. (Mother, 20–29 years old)

Emphasising the individual's wants and needs without consideration of social relationships and sharing obligations forms part of Aboriginal explanations of imbalances in health and wellbeing (Brimblecombe et al. 2014; Smith et al. 2003).

At Ngukurr, and elsewhere, Aboriginal people associate attempts to diet or change their eating habits with being non-Aboriginal (Foley 2005; Thompson, Gifford and Thorpe 2000). There is some ambivalence about adopting practices that are framed as *munanga*, as while such practices might be understood as healthier, they are also seen as unattainable and disconnected from the everyday experience of living at Ngukurr (Senior 2003). The moral imperative is to care for others, ensuring that foods purchased are acceptable to all who will partake, rather than concern for the individual's nutrition. Food, even food that is bad for one's physical health, can be morally good if it is shared and used to demonstrate care of others (Chenhall and Senior 2017; Schwarz 2018).

At Ngukurr, food choice is constrained by money and household resources, as one young mother described to me:

> I don't know how to put it, well, you *sabi blekbala mind* [understand Aboriginal people's way of thinking], some don't have the money all the time, they just eat what's there. We don't have that fridge or something like that, but you can't buy vegetables with no fridge. (Mother, 20–29 years)

Eating if and when food was available without preoccupation for ascetics or aesthetics was considered among many informants a particularly *blekbala* way of eating, in contrast to the use of food for innovation and differentiation as seen in many Western societies (Lupton 1996). Planning what and when one would eat, and being concerned with eating the 'right' kinds of foods at the 'right time', was considered by Aboriginal people at Ngukurr to be the purview of *munanga* (see also Brimblecombe 2007).

Discussion

This chapter has explored some of the ways that Aboriginal young people at Ngukurr understand and engage with food. Food practices of young people at Ngukurr are very much situated in the 'intercultural'. The contemporary diet of Aboriginal young people comprises a mix of introduced and traditional foods, and both categories of food are preferred. The meanings that Aboriginal young people attach to food arise from interactions between material disadvantage, discourses of identity and embodied experience.

The discourses of cultural difference, inequality and marginalisation that underlie tensions for many practitioners in Aboriginal affairs are also evident in the accounts of Aboriginal young people's food practices presented in this chapter. Kowal and Paradies (2010) highlight tension between maintaining cultural difference while achieving statistical equality as an underlying dilemma in policy and programs aimed at improving Aboriginal health.[10] An unsettling prospect, at least for some working in Aboriginal health, is that intervening to close the gap in health and life expectancy will further erode Aboriginal culture, an echo of past assimilationist policies (Kowal and Paradies 2005). The food types and eating patterns that are part of everyday life for young people at Ngukurr are often positioned as antithetical to *munanga* ways. There is ambivalence about practices such as individualistic purchasing and distribution of food in so far as they appear disconnected from Aboriginal worldviews and may be damaging to intergenerational relationships and community solidarity.

Responsivity to hunger, as well as uncertainty about whether there will be anything to eat, underlies young people's food practices at Ngukurr. Their food choices are complicated by an environment of limited choice and a legacy of colonialism and disempowerment. In such circumstances,

10 Statistical equality in life expectancy, health, education and economic attainment with non-Aboriginal Australians is the primary goal of most policy in Aboriginal health and development. There are various critiques of this policy approach. Most relevant to this chapter is the argument that the drive for statistical socioeconomic equality undervalues diversity and difference (Altman 2009).

making the 'healthy choice' may not be the logical or practical choice. Young people's food practices are also constrained by the extent to which they can control their food choices. Foods sold at the tuckshop, and foods packaged for instant consumption (such as salty plums and soft drinks) are some of the foods over which young people have most control. They are available for instant consumption and are familiar and satisfying.

Young people's preference for takeaway foods, soft drinks and salty plums might be seen as evidence that they are unable to make rational choices and, therefore, need more education about store-bought foods and to be taught why choosing healthy foods is important for their health. Classifying young people's preferred foods as 'bad' perpetuates a picture that all young people are unhealthy eaters, which, in turn, becomes a barrier to change (Stevenson et al. 2007). This is particularly salient to Aboriginal young people, as Aboriginal identities are often bound with the inevitability of ill health (Kowal and Paradies 2010). Moreover, like young people more broadly, an argument for minimising consumption of such foods on the grounds of health is unlikely to persuade young people at Ngukurr (Neumark-Sztainer et al. 1999; Stead et al. 2011). There is a logic to eating opportunistically when everyday life involves asking around for money and food from other family members, family and friends who gamble away their money, and fridges that don't work.

There is also a logic to conservative food choices: people are reluctant to step too far from the collective food *habitus*. For young people at Ngukurr, food is always socially embedded. As has been found in urban Aboriginal communities, foods that others liked and could easily be shared were valued over aesthetics and ascetics (Foley 2005; Thompson and Gifford 2000; Thompson, Gifford and Thorpe 2000). Social obligations in food distribution were perceived by young people at Ngukurr in both positive and negative lights. Having family to depend on was considered uniquely Aboriginal and something to be proud of. However, having an extensive family network with whom food needed to be shared strained household resources and restricted the types of foods people were willing (or encouraged) to purchase.

Young people at Ngukurr preferred a variety of bush and store-bought foods. Access to their preferred foods was constrained by geography, seasonality and material resources. In some ways, it was the constraint that made these foods more special: the joy of *jupi* and the privilege of 'going out' to McDonalds in Katherine. Being able to access these preferred foods required different forms of social and cultural capital, which it seems were not equally distributed within Ngukurr. Further, young people's declared desire for traditional foods may be as much about their preference for eating such foods as about 'declaring cultural allegiance to Aboriginality' (Saethre 2005, 166). Even though they may not have much opportunity to consume these foods, knowing about and desiring traditional foods may be important to young people, as it is seen to connect them with their Aboriginal identity. Creating opportunities for young people to learn about and gain access to traditional foods might well be valued by both young and older people (Senior et al. 2012). Participation in harvesting of traditional foods may also have positive benefits on physical activity and mental health. As young people themselves rarely have access to the resources needed for hunting and gathering, organised activities through community-based programs may be helpful, as well as family-based outings (Douglas 2015).

Conclusion

This chapter has presented an account of Aboriginal young people's engagement in the intercultural space of the contemporary food system. Food provisioning in this space is thoroughly constrained. The sorts of material and social constraints described by young people in this research align with those highlighted in various epidemiological studies and articulations of the social determinants of health. This research, however, offers 'a picture of the lived engagement people have with broader structures' and the unpredictable ways that social determinants interact in young people's lives (Chenhall and Senior 2017).

Appendix

Nickeisha is a 24-year-old woman (Figure 4.1). She has two children, aged four and seven years. She has no husband and lives with her family—mum, dad, abuja (father's mother), gagu (mother's mother), 17-year-old sister and 14-year-old brother. Her parents help her to look after her kids. At the house she lives in there is a fridge and a stove and each room has an air conditioner. She's got a Troopy (Toyota Landcruiser). The kids have toys. There is a TV, Playstation and Xbox 360.

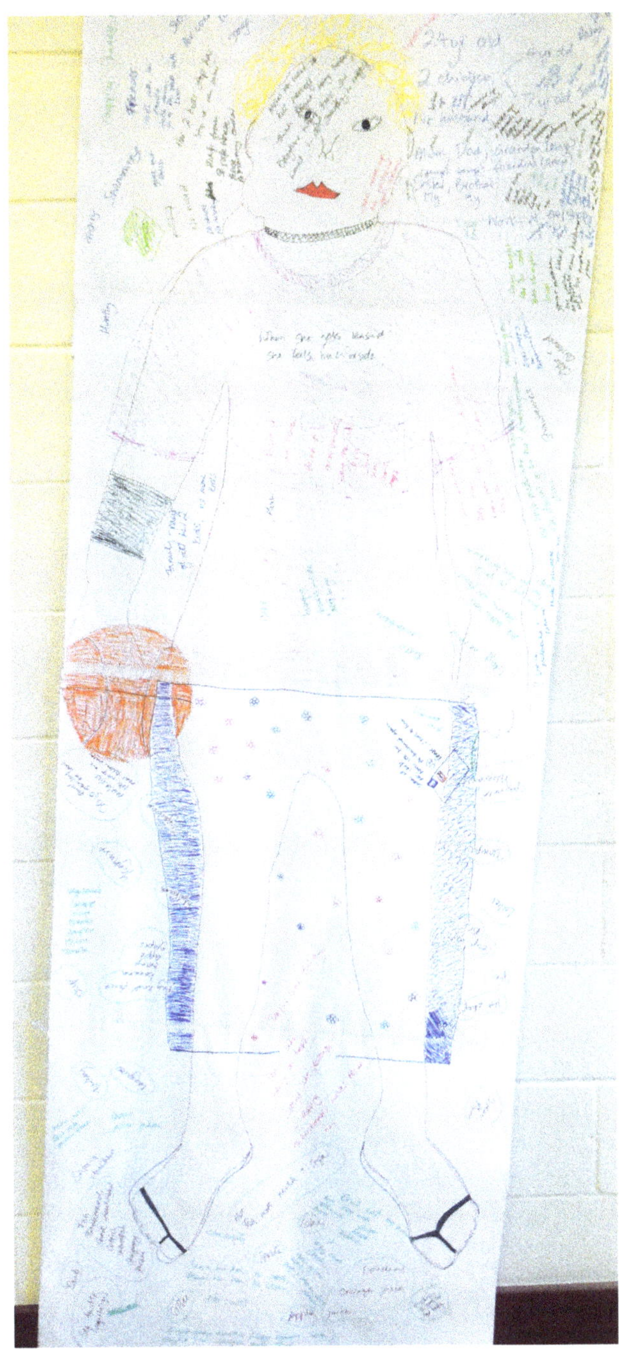

Figure 4.1: Body map Nickeisha.

Source: Phototograph by Danielle Aquino, 2016.

She works at the shop. She goes to work every day. She doesn't worry for money because she never plays cards. She smokes, but not weed (cannabis), and she doesn't drink (alcohol). Her mum and dad also smoke. Her sister smokes weed. Her abuja and gagu don't smoke.

She likes to eat damper, spaghetti bolognaise, soup with rice, hot chips, pie, cake and custard, yoghurt, any kind of fruit (e.g. bananas, apples, oranges, grapes, green plums), bush food (e.g. turkey, kangaroo, *jupi*), chicken, tea, hot coffee, sea turtle (*nalaligi*), *debil debil* (shark), swordfish, catfish, stingray and bream. She knows how to cook. Her gagu taught her how to bake damper and make soup. Sometimes she cooks for her family; sometimes her mum or dad does the cooking. Her grandma and grandpa are too old. Nickeisha, as well as her mum and dad, do the shopping.

She likes feeding her kids bush tucker—barramundi, shark, catfish, swordfish, stingray, bream, sea turtle, crab, turkey and kangaroo. Foods that she thinks are good are vegetables— like cabbage, carrots, pumpkin, potatoes and onions—tomatoes, Coke, pie, chips, *jupi*, yoghurt, *sugarbag*, *yarlbun* (tummy ache), fruit, green plum, lollies, damper, spaghetti bolognaise, fried rice, cordial, orange juice, apple juice, Sprite, coffee, hot tea with milk and sugar, *jojo* and *mularlu*.

Sometimes she runs out of food. Sometimes she goes and asks her babies' father's family. When she can't eat all day, she feels hungry and her stomach hurts '*ardi binji*'. She sleeps sometimes when she doesn't have food. Sometimes, when she doesn't have food, she'll go out along the river to look for fish. She thinks food gives her energy. When she eats spaghetti bolognaise, she feels much better.

Brenae is a 13-year-old girl (Figure 4.2). She likes to eat apples, oranges and bananas. For breakfast she likes to eat bacon and eggs, spaghetti, Weetbix and baked beans. She likes to drink Coke, Sprite, lemonade, Fanta and Sunkist. At lunch she likes toasted ham and cheese sandwiches. At dinner she has spaghetti bolognaise. And fish too. Sometimes she has beef with capsicum and carrot. She doesn't eat vegetables on their own, only with meat. Her mum gives her money to go to the tuckshop. She buys chips, Dairy Milk and Cherry Ripe (chocolate), salty plums, tamarind, hamburgers and cheese burgers, fried rice and ice cream. She gets her money by doing chores for her mum like cleaning up and sweeping up. Her mum, grandpa, grandmother and aunty taught her to cook. Usually her mum cooks for her but sometimes she tells Brenae to cook. She knows how to cook damper. Sometimes she cooks noodles with tinned beef for breakfast. Her *amuri* (father's father) taught her about bush food. She likes the taste of bush food.

Figure 4.2: Body map Brenae.

Source: Phototograph by Danielle Aquino, 2016.

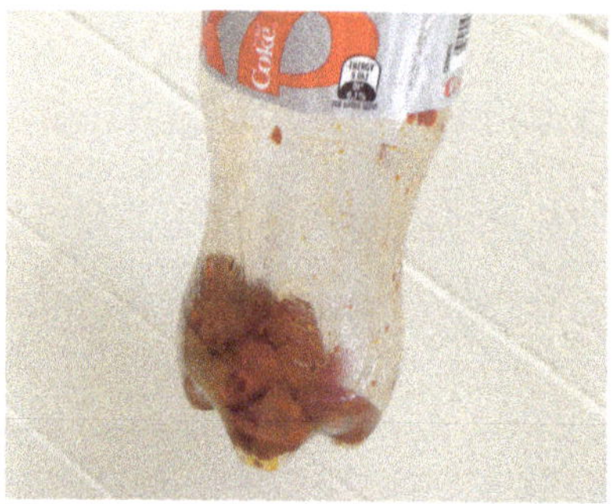

Figure 4.3: Salty plums in a soft drink bottle.

Source: Phototograph by Danielle Aquino, 2016.

Sometimes she hasn't got any food. She feels sick in the stomach and gets diarrhoea. Her tummy's growling and sometimes she feels like vomiting. In her head she feels nervous. Stressing. Maybe she goes angry or quiet. Lazy. Some of the other kids smoke too. She can go to her grandmother, grandfather or other family to eat.

References

Altman, J. C. 2009. *Beyond Closing the Gap: Valuing Diversity in Indigenous Australia*. Canberra: CAEPR.

Australian Bureau of Statistics. 2015a. 'Australian Aboriginal and Torres Strait Islander Health Survey: Nutrition Results—Food and Nutrients, 2012–13'. Last modified 17 December 2015. www.abs.gov.au/ausstats/abs@.nsf/mf/4727.0.55.005.

Australian Bureau of Statistics. 2015b. 'Australian Health Survey: Consumption of Food Groups from the Australian Dietary Guidelines 2011–12'. Last modified 6 June 2018. www.abs.gov.au/ausstats/abs@.nsf/Lookup/4364.0.55.012main+features12011-12.

Australian Institute of Health and Welfare. 2015. *The Health and Welfare of Australia's Aboriginal and Torres Strait Islander Peoples 2015*. Cat. no. IHW 147. Canberra: AIHW.

Australian Institute of Health and Welfare. 2016. *Australian Burden Of Disease Study: Impact and Causes of Illness and Death in Australia 2011*. Canberra: AIHW.

Bisogni, C. A., M. Connors, C. M. Devine and J. Sobal. 2002. 'Who We Are and How We Eat: A Qualitative Study of Identities in Food Choice'. *Journal of Nutrition Education and Behavior* 34 (3): 128–39. doi.org/10.1016/S1499-4046(06)60082-1.

Bridle-Fitzpatrick, S. 2016. 'Tortillas, Pizza and Brocoli, Social Class and Dietary Aspirations in a Mexican City'. *Food Culture and Society* 19 (1): 93–128. doi.org/10.1080/15528014.2016.1147871.

Brimblecombe, J. 2007. 'Enough for Rations and a Little Bit Extra: Challenges of Nutrition Improvement in an Aboriginal Community in North East Arnhem Land'. PhD thesis, Charles Darwin University.

Brimblecombe, J., M. Ferguson, M. D. Chatfield, S. C. Liberato, A. Gunther, K. Ball, M. Moodie, E. Miles, A. Magnus, C. N. Mhurchu, A. J. Leach and R. Bailie. 2017. 'Effect of a Price Discount and Consumer Education Strategy on Food and Beverage Purchases in Remote Indigenous Australia: A Stepped-Wedge Randomised Controlled Trial'. *Lancet Public Health* 2 (2): e82–e95. doi.org/10.1016/S2468-2667(16)30043-3.

Brimblecombe, J. K., M. M. Ferguson, S. C. Liberato and K. O'Dea. 2013. 'Characteristics of the Community-Level Diet of Aboriginal People in Remote Northern Australia', *Medical Journal of Australia* 198 (7): 380–84. doi.org/10.5694/mja12.11407.

Brimblecombe, J., E. Maypilama, S. Colles, M. Scarlett, J. G. Dhurrkay, J. Ritchie and K. O'Dea. 2014. 'Factors Influencing Food Choice in an Australian Aboriginal Community'. *Qualitative Health Research* 24 (3): 387–400. doi.org/10.1177/1049732314521901.

Brimblecombe, J. K. and K. O'Dea. 2009. 'The Role of Energy Cost in Food Choices for an Aboriginal Population in Northern Australia'. *Medical Journal of Australia* 190 (10): 549–51. doi.org/10.5694/j.1326-5377.2009.tb02560.x.

Buchanan, G. 2014. 'Hybrid Economy Research in Remote Indigenous Australia: Seeing and Supporting the Customary in Community Food Economies'. *Local Environment* 19 (1): 10–32. doi.org/10.1080/13549839.2013.787973.

Burbank, V. 2006. 'From Bedtime to On Time: Why Many Aboriginal People Don't Especially Like Participating in Western Institutions'. *Anthropological Forum* 16 (1): 3–20. doi.org/10.1080/00664670600572330.

Chenhall, R., B. Davison, J. Fitz, T. Pearse and K. Senior. 2013. 'Engaging Youth in Sexual Health Research: Refining a "Youth Friendly" Method in the Northern Territory, Australia'. *Visual Anthropology Review* 29 (2): 123–32.

Chenhall, R. and K. Senior. 2017. 'Living the Social Determinants of Health: Assemblages in a Remote Aboriginal Community'. *Medical Anthropology Quarterly* 32 (2): 177–95.

Colles, S. L., E. Maypilama and J. Brimblecombe. 2014. 'Food, Food Choice and Nutrition Promotion in a Remote Australian Aboriginal Community'. *Australian Journal of Primary Health* 20 (4): 365–72. doi.org/10.1071/PY14033.

Douglas. J. 2015. 'Kin and Knowledge: The Meaning and Acquisition of Indigenous Ecological Knowledge in the Lives of Young Aboriginal People in Central Australia'. PhD thesis, Charles Darwin University.

Eickelkamp, U. 2011. 'Agency and Structure in the Life-World of Aboriginal Children in Central Australia'. *Children and Youth Services Review* 33 (4): 502–08. doi.org/10.1016/j.childyouth.2010.05.014.

Foley. W. 2005. 'Tradition and Change in Urban Indigenous Food Practices'. *Postcolonial Studies* 8 (1): 25–44.

Gwynn, J. D., V. M. Flood, C. A. D'Este, J. R. Attia, N. Turner, J. Cochrane, J. C. Louie and J. H. Wiggers. 2012. 'Poor Food and Nutrient Intake among Indigenous and Non-Indigenous Rural Australian Children'. *BMC Pediatrics* 12: 12. doi.org/10.1186/1471-2431-12-12.

Hinkson, M. and B. Smith. 2005. 'Introduction: Conceptual Moves towards an Intercultural Analysis'. *Oceania* 75 (3): 157–66. doi.org/10.1002/j.1834-4461.2005.tb02877.x.

Ikeda. J. P. 1999. 'Culture, Food and Nutrition in Increasingly Culturally Diverse Societies'. In A *Sociology Of Food And Nutrition: The Social Appetite*, edited by J. Germov and L. William, 149–68. Oxford: Oxford University Press.

Kowal, E. and Y. Paradies. 2005. 'Ambivalent Helpers and Unhealthy Choices: Public Health Practitioners' Narratives of Indigenous Ill-Health'. *Social Science & Medicine* 60 (6): 1347–57. doi.org/10.1016/j.socscimed.2004.07.009.

Kowal, E. E. and Y. C. Paradies. 2010. 'Enduring Dilemmas of Indigenous Health. "You're Always Hearing about the Stats … Death Happens So Often": New Perspectives on Barriers to Aboriginal Participation'. *Cardiac Rehabilitation. Comment. Medical Journal of Australia* 192 (10): 599–600. doi.org/10.5694/j.1326-5377.2010.tb03647.x.

Lee, A. J., K. O'Dea and J. D. Mathews. 1994. 'Apparent Dietary Intake in Remote Aboriginal Communities'. *Australian Journal of Public Health* (18) 2: 190–97. doi.org/10.1111/j.1753-6405.1994.tb00224.x.

Lee, A., S. Rainow, J. Tregenza, L. Tregenza, L. Balmer, S. Bryce, M. Paddy, J. Sheard and D. Schomburgk. 2016. 'Nutrition in Remote Aboriginal Communities: Lessons From Mai Wiru and the Anangu Pitjantjatjara Yankunytjatjara Lands'. *Australia New Zealand Journal of Public Health* 40 (1): S81–88. doi.org/10.1111/1753-6405.12419.

Leonard, D. 2003. *Foodnorth: Food for Health in North Australia*. Western Australia: Department of Health.

Lupton, D. 1996. *Food, the Body and the Self.* London: Sage Publications.

McCoy, B. 2009. 'Living between Two Worlds': Who Is Living in Whose Worlds?' *Australasian Psychiatry* 17: S20–S23. doi.org/10.1080/10398560902948647.

Merlan, F. 2005. 'Explorations towards Intercultural Accounts of Socio-Cultural Reproduction and Change'. *Oceania* 75 (3): 167–82. doi.org/10.1002/j.1834-4461.2005.tb02878.x.

Momin, S., K. Chung and B. Olson. 2014. 'A Qualitative Study to Understand Positive and Negative Child Feeding Behaviors of Immigrant Asian Indian Mothers in the US'. *Maternal & Child Health Journal* 18 (7): 1699–710. doi.org/10.1007/s10995-013-1412-9.

Murcott, S. 1998. 'Sociological and Social Anthropological Approaches to Food and Eating'. *World Review of Nutrition and Dietetics* 55 (1): 1–40. doi.org/10.1159/000415556.

Neumark-Sztainer, D., M. Story, C. Perry and M. A. Casey. 1999. 'Factors Influencing Food Choices of Adolescents: Findings from Focus-Group Discussions with Adolescents'. *Journal of the American Dietetic Association* 99 (8): 929–37. doi.org/10.1016/S0002-8223(99)00222-9.

Paul, K. H., M. Muti, S. S. Khalfan, J. H. Humphrey, R. Caffarella and R. J. Stoltzfus. 2011. 'Beyond Food Insecurity: How Context Can Improve Complementary Feeding Interventions'. *Food Nutrition Bulletin* 32 (3): 244–53. doi.org/10.1177/156482651103200308.

Saethre, E. 2005. 'Nutrition, Economics and Food Distribution in an Australian Aboriginal Community'. *Anthropological Forum* 15 (2): 151–69. doi.org/10.1080/00664670500135212.

Saethre, E. 2013. *Illness Is a Weapon : Indigenous Identity and Enduring Afflictions*. Vanderbilt: Vanderbilt University Press. doi.org/10.2307/j.ctv16758m5.

Schubert, L. 2008. 'Household Food Strategies and the Reframing of Ways of Understanding Dietary Practices'. *Ecology of Food and Nutrition* 47 (3): 254–79.

Schwarz, C. 2018. 'Eating Morality: Food and the Goodness of Care in Northern Aboriginal Australia'. *Asia Pacific Journal of Anthropology* 19 (1): 19–34. doi.org/10.1080/14442213.2017.1394363.

Sebastian, T. and M. Donelly. 2013. 'Policy Influences Affecting the Food Practices of Indigenous Australians Since Colonisation'. *Australian Aboriginal Studies* 2: 59–75.

Senior, K. 2003. 'A Gudbala Laif? Health and Wellbeing in a Remote Aboriginal Community—What Are the Problems and Where Lies The Responsibility?' PhD thesis, The Australian National University, Canberra.

Senior, K., W. Ivory, R. Chenhall, T. Cunningham, T. Nagel, R. Lloyd and R. McMahon. 2012. *Developing Successful Diversionary Schemes for Youth from Remote Aboriginal Communities*. Canberra: CRA Council.

Smith, D., L. Mununggurr, D. Bamundurruwuy, K. Edmund, P. Wununmurra and H. Nyomba. 2003. *How Children Grow: Indigenous and Health Professional Perceptions*. Darwin: Cooperative Research Centre for Aboriginal and Tropical Health.

Stead, M., L. McDermott, A. M. Mackintosh and A. Adamson. 2011. 'Why Healthy Eating Is Bad for Young People's Health: Identity, Belonging and Food'. *Social Science and Medicine* 72 (7): 1131–39. doi.org/10.1016/j.socscimed.2010.12.029.

Stevenson, C., G. Doherty, J. Barnett, O. T. Muldoon and K. Trew. 2007. 'Adolescents' Views of Food and Eating: Identifying Barriers to Healthy Eating'. *Journal of Adolescence* 30 (3): 417–34. doi.org/10.1016/j.adolescence.2006.04.005.

Thompson, S. J. and S. M. Gifford. 2000. 'Trying to Keep a Balance: The Meaning of Health and Diabetes in an Urban Aboriginal Community'. *Social Science and Medicine* 51 (10): 1457–72. doi.org/10.1016/S0277-9536(00)00046-0.

Thompson, S. J., S. M. Gifford and L. Thorpe. 2000. 'The Social and Cultural Context of Risk and Prevention: Food and Physical Activity in an Urban Aboriginal Community'. *Health Education Behaviour* 27 (6): 725–43. doi.org/10.1177/109019810002700608.

Vos, T., B. Barker, S. Begg, L. Stanley and A. D. Lopez. 2009. 'Burden of Disease and Injury in Aboriginal and Torres Strait Islander Peoples: The Indigenous Health Gap'. *International Journal of Epidemiology* 38 (2): 470–77. doi.org/10.1093/ije/dyn240.

Wilson, A., R. Wilson, R. Delbridge, E. Tonkin, C. Palermo, J. Coveney, C. Hayes and T. Mackean. 2020. 'Resetting the Narrative in Australia Aboriginal and Torres Strait Islander Nutrition Research'. *Current Developments in Nutrition* 4 (5): nzaa080. doi.org/10.1093/cdn/nzaa080.

5

Bush Medicine Knowledge and Use among Young Kriol Speakers in Ngukurr

Greg Dickson

In 2013, in a Ngukurr backyard, I was preparing to interview a young mother about her knowledge and use of bush medicine. It was a familiar remote community scene—outdoor social space populated by ebbing and flowing tides of various relatives. Present at the time was me, the young Kriol-speaking mum who had agreed to be interviewed, some kids, the parents of the interviewee and a visiting elder of some stature in the community. Each generation had distinctive upbringings: the visiting elder had been born in the bush and the parents of the interviewee were mission raised. Their daughter—the target of my interview—was old enough to have spent considerable time on local outstations when they were funded, while the children were a southern Arnhem Land version of 'urbanised' in Ngukurr. We all spoke in Kriol, as is the norm in Ngukurr, despite the older people present having knowledge of traditional languages. I was explaining the premise of my little study—in Kriol. Hearing that I was investigating what young people know about bush medicine, the visiting elder declared, with some disdain, 'they don't know nothing'. This chapter focuses on the issue of language retention among youth in this community. The research was conducted at the same time as the Ngukurr research that generated the other chapters in this book and so is situated within an exchange of ideas about health and wellbeing, particularly in regard to traditional knowledge and bush medicine.

Stated beliefs that younger generations are not retaining cultural knowledge and practices of their forebears are common. They can be heard coming from elders, from non-local/non-Indigenous commentators and even among young people themselves. These perceptions are unsurprising given the sharp shifts in lifestyles that remote Aboriginal societies have experienced in so few generations. Language shift—in which younger generations speak a different language from preceding generations—is a salient phenomenon, inescapably noticeable given the obvious primacy of verbal communication in daily life. Loss of language (or, more accurately, language shift) becomes an easy hook on which to hang feelings of loss when a group or society is stressed and ways of life are threatened. In its crudest form, this manifests as the sentiment: 'got no language, got no culture'.

There is certainly good anecdotal evidence to affirm ideas of disappearing cultural knowledge and practices. In Ngukurr, no one has made or paddled a dugout canoe for decades and there are now two generations who have never seen or hunted goanna.[1] But, as a blanket statement, beliefs that young people are not retaining cultural knowledge are rarely investigated.

Is the Practice of Bush Medicine at Ngukurr Diminishing?

The loss of knowledge and use of traditional or 'bush' medicine is typically deemed to exemplify the loss of knowledge and diminished cultural practices more generally among Kriol-speaking adults in Ngukurr and elsewhere. Take, for example, an early claim (in antiquated language) that, 'as civilization spreads into primitive areas, the first aspect of primitive culture to be lost is knowledge of the use of plants as medicine' (Farnsworth 1966, 229). When linguist Jeffrey Heath (1980, 445) documented Nunggubuyu (traditionally spoken to the immediate north-east of Ngukurr) in the 1970s, he claimed that 'bush medicine is … practiced to a limited extent, chiefly by older people'. More recently, a study into health beliefs in Ngukurr supported this, finding 'little evidence that people were currently using bush medicines on a regular basis' (Senior 2003, 115). Another manifestation of ideas that bush medicine knowledge and usage

1 Editor's note: There was considerable excitement in Ngukurr, when, in 2018, goannas were seen (and hunted) near the community.

is endangered knowledge are compensatory efforts to document ethnobotanical knowledge held by senior custodians (e.g. Levitt 1981; Scarlett, White and Reid 1982; Latz 1995; Winydjorrodj et al. 2005; Roberts et al. 2011; Hector et al. 2012; Bordulk et al. 2012).

Upon commencing my research, I too adhered to the ideas mentioned above. I assumed that an investigation into bush medicine would exemplify loss of cultural practices, rather than maintenance. The bush medicine sub-study was to contrast with an exploration of kinship—a domain believed to more robustly exhibit cultural continuities across language shift. As readers will see, beliefs about diminishing bush medicine practices turned out to be somewhat of a misconception.

Working with Old People and the Ubiquity of Bush Medicine

My involvement with Ngukurr goes back to 2004 when I was employed by Diwurruwurru-Jaru Aboriginal Corporation (aka Katherine Regional Aboriginal Language Centre) as the Ngukurr-based community linguist, a position I held for three years before moving to Katherine. Since then, I have continued to work with senior community members who are speakers of various endangered traditional languages and supported their endeavours to prolong the longevity of their critically endangered languages. Given the intrinsic link between land and language (Merlan 1981), a fundamental aspect to language revitalisation and documentation work is travel to various sites. Sometimes, the travel reconnects elders with a particular geographic landmark (e.g. sacred site) important to their language group. Other times, it reconnects them with speakers or stakeholders of the given language living in another location. Sometimes, our trips would just be to spend time fishing, hunting or procuring materials from the bush (food, medicine or stuff needed to make artefacts)—travel combining leisure, economic and cultural maintenance purposes.

Across dozens of journeys of these types, the importance of bush medicine to senior people in Ngukurr became obvious. Even when remaining in Ngukurr, spending time with older people regularly includes a request, longing for or appreciation of bush medicine. When journeying out of Ngukurr, more often than not, I'd be told to stop (if I was driving) and, typically, someone would spring from the vehicle, with or without explanation, and return a few minutes later with several branches of a common medicine type. One elder in particular, Betty Roberts (to whom I dedicated my PhD thesis for her decades-long commitment to language work), would usually be able to produce some form of bush medicine from her bag—whether it was some recently nabbed leaves or a decoction of some variety.

Further evidence of senior people maintaining bush medicine traditions came from community projects. In the 1980s, the local Nganiyurlma Media Association (1990) prioritised bush medicine and made it the topic of a 72-minute edited video.[2] In the 1990s, Marra elders working with Diwurruwurru-Jaru Aboriginal Corporation produced a three-volume in-house publication on *Marra plants and Their Uses* (Huddleston et al. n.d.-a, n.d.-b, n.d.-c) and, during my time as the corporation's Ngukurr-based linguist, Betty and her sister assisted in developing more bush medicine materials. In 2007, they composed a series of short monolingual texts in Marra describing 14 taxa, providing a unique example of written documentation of bush medicine knowledge composed by Marra speakers themselves.

My observations, coupled with what McClatchey (2012) calls 'secondary or documentary evidence' (e.g. written documentation, new and existing audio recordings, and photographs), demonstrates that, for older generations who grew up speaking and hearing the traditional languages of Ngukurr, bush medicine is an important part of expressed and practiced cultural life.

Young People and Bush Medicine: Some Observations

But what of younger people in Ngukurr, young adults who—along with their parents, peers and children—all speak Kriol and are rarely immersed in traditional languages? In the early stages of my doctoral fieldwork in 2010, I was at *Yawurrwarda* billabong, only a few kilometres from Ngukurr, with a senior man of Marra heritage aged in his 60s and three women aged in their 20s who all call him 'father'. One of the women had

2 This video, *Bush Medicine from Ngukurr*, features prominent elders including Ginger Riley, Willie Gudabi, Sambo Barra Barra and Sam Thompson, describing and demonstrating 10 medicinal taxa, bookended by commentary from senior Aboriginal health worker Alex Thompson.

brought two of her kids, aged about five and eight at the time. We were making recordings in Kriol involving all except the young mum, who, having moved away a short distance to leave us in (relative) peace, took up the opportunity for a quick fish in the billabong while minding her children. At the time, her son (aged five) had some painful boils or skin sores. While we were doing our 'language work', the young mum took it upon herself to quietly and matter-of-factly cut bark from a nearby *ngalangga* (*Eucalyptus camaldulensis*) tree. Though she had taken her son to the local medical clinic for treatment, she had also self-prescribed treating her son's condition with *ngalangga* and had sufficient knowledge to independently acquire and prepare the medicine herself. This was a sign that not only are young people using bush medicine but also that it could fly under the radar, unnoticed by outsiders.

If this young mother's competent prescription and procurement was surprising, stated beliefs in the efficacy and value of bush medicine were not. Senior's (2001, 8) finding that 'a clear preference was stated for the use of bush medicines' certainly applied to the young adults I interviewed. Two women in their 30s demonstrate this quite emphatically, although note also that one also values Western medicine to a degree:[3]

(1)

GD: *wani yu laigi mo, munanga medisin o bush medisin?*
what do you like more, Western medicine
or bush medicine?

GD: [*o bouth?*
or both?

EN: [*bush medisin*
bush medicine

PD: *bush medisin=*
bush medicine

EN: =*bush medisin*
=bush medicine

EN: *det munanga medisin, im meigi yu wik*
Western medicine, it makes you weak

3 Some symbols and conventions used in conversation analysis are utilised in interview transcripts in this chapter. Square brackets indicates the talk overlaps with the neighbouring line of square bracketed speech. The = sign indicates the talk is latched on to prior talk with no gap or lapse in between.

PD: *sam ... [lilbit rait, help you*
some...(is) kind of okay, (it) helps you

EN: *[meigi yu slip, en,*
makes you sleep, and

PD: *ome I don't like, like, takin' it too much ... all different ones*

Accompanying this rhetoric, the women quoted above demonstrated declarative knowledge of numerous (around 10) bush medicine taxa. Others I interviewed did not. Yet, despite two young men in their 20s declaring that '*mela nomo sabi bush medisin*' (we don't know bush medicine), they maintained an aversion to Western medicine despite the self-identified knowledge gap, expressing a reliance on elders for bush medicine treatments:

(2)

GD: *bat wani yunbala regen, yunbala regen ... laik, yu jas tras la munanga medisin na?*
but what do you two think, do you two think ... like ... do you trust only Western medicine now?

KM: *na=*
no

DR: *=ai nomo dringgi', [ai nomo] oldei dringgim munanga medisin wen mi sik=*
I don't take, I don't take Western medicine when I'm sick

KM: *[not me]*

KM: *=not me, ai nomo gu-*
not me, I don't go-

DR: *me- mela nomo, mela nomo gu na, na, na, na hospel o na klinik ba dringgim medisin laik-... yuno, ba, ba peinkila, mela nomo yusu*
we-, we don't, we don't go to, to, to, to the hospital or to the clinic to take medicine, like- ... you know, for, for painkillers, we don't use it

GD: *ngi?*
don't you?

DR: *bikos mela nomo sabi wani (xx xx) them staf, yuno*
because we don't know what (is in) that stuff, you know

GD: *so if you sikwan, mo beda yu dringgim=*
so if you're sick, it's preferable that you drink=

DR: *=bush medisin=*
=bush medicine=

GD: *ngi?=*
is it?=

KM: *=mm=*

DR: *=so im natural, straight from, yuno, [plent en det-*
=so it is natural, straight from, you know, plants and that-

KM: *[so main klinik la det olgamen na*[4]
so my clinic is that old lady

GD: *yuwai*
yeah

DR: *ola olpipulmo' bala alabat didei!*
The poor elders, my heart goes out to them these days.[5]

During the interviews, young people typically shared stories of applying certain medicines and gave testimonials supporting their efficacy. One 31-year-old man described treating his son's sores with bush medicine during a visit to another community. Speaking of the results of the treatment, he said:

(3)

Neksdei, alibala na, imin jis klin na. En detmo la Beswick bin gedimbat shok.

Then next day, early, it was really clear (i.e. his skin). And those guys at Beswick were really surprised.

Another interviewee, a 33-year-old female, spoke of using the bark of *Buchanania obovata* to treat toothache, saying emphatically: '*Im wek. Streitawei im wek*' (It works. It works immediately).

4 KM is referring to Betty Roberts, mentioned above, who had been referred to previously in the interview as an expert in bush medicine.

5 Here *bala* (a shortened form of *bobala* from 'poor fellow') is an exclamation of bittersweet sorrow. It is not necessarily a negative feeling as indicated by the etymon 'poor fellow' but rather indicates a feeling of fondness, longing, pity, nostalgia or a feeling of missing somebody or something, hence the translation: 'heart goes out to'.

Young People and Bush Medicine

In May 2013, I interviewed 14 adults at Ngukurr, utilising methods described by Hoffman and Gallagher (2007). The participants were recruited through personal contacts and through promoting the study on social media. The participants were an equal gender split and aged between 22 and 35 (mean: 29 years). The group was diverse across various social demographics including education, employment status and occupations types. Most (but not all) had children and all had lived in the region for most of their lives. In terms of language abilities, they all spoke Kriol as a first language and had competencies in English varying from fair to excellent. Knowledge of traditional languages was generally low: five reported no knowledge, seven reported little knowledge, and two reported being fluent speakers (one of Wägilak and one of Anindilyakwa) due to heritage and time spent in other locations where those languages are in regular use.

I am a fluent speaker and accredited Kriol–English interpreter. I conducted the interviews in Kriol at various locations in Ngukurr. The interviews lasted 25–30 minutes and were structured accordingly:

1. personal information
2. free-listing exercise (i.e. list as many types of bush medicine as you can)
3. recent use: describe the most recent occasion you used bush medicine (time, ailment, treatment, procurement, result, etc.)
4. checklist exercise: a reference list of 38 bush medicine names in Kriol and Indigenous languages, checking for recognition and declarative knowledge, adding to taxa listed in Part 2
5. preference exercise: list 'top 5' bush medicines
6. free-listing exercise on lizard taxa (data on an additional ethno-biological domain for comparability).

Results

The free-listing exercise asked participants to list as many types of bush medicine as they could. Variation in identification methods were accommodated: participants were free to identify taxa by an Indigenous-derived name, a Kriol or English-derived name, or by description or pointing/indicating.

The number of taxa the 14 participants could list ranged from between 3 and 9 (mean: 6). There was some gender differentiation, with the seven male participants' range being 3 to 7 (mean: 4.9) and female participants ranging from 5 to 9 (mean: 7.1).

A further consideration was the sum total of taxa enumerated across the group. Across the 14 participants, 21 taxa were listed. Gender differentiation was negligible when examining the results this way, with men listing 15 taxa in total and women listing 16. However, age was a factor, with the seven participants aged under 30 (aged 22–29) describing a total of 12 taxa and the seven older participants aged 30–35 collectively describing 20 taxa.[6]

As an indication of the figures that might be expected from senior people, my research on evidence documented from Ngukurr elders shows collective knowledge of at least 26 bush medicine taxa. A recent study of knowledge held by Mangarrayi and Yangman elders (in the neighbouring upper Roper River region) listed 37 plant species as having reported medicinal properties (Roberts et al. 2011).

Following the free-listing task, I referred to a checklist of 38 attested local bush medicine names (a mix of Indigenous-language derived and English-derived names) and read them to participants, allowing them to recall further knowledge. All but one participant increased the number of bush medicine taxa they reported knowledge of. Following the checklist, the average number of taxa known to each participant increased from 6 to 8.6 and the range shifted from 3 to 9 to 4 to 13. Male participants had more of their memory jogged than the women, with the average number of taxa known to men shifting from 4.9 after only the free-listing task to 7.7 after the checklist. For women, the mean increased from 7.1 to 9.5. Age differentiation became more prominent following the checklist, with the under 30s' mean increasing by 1.3 to 6.3; however, the cohort aged between 30 and 35 recalled an additional 3.9 taxa on average, increasing the mean to 10.9.

6 These quantitative data need to be interpreted with caution due to the very small sample size. It should be noted, though, that age was not a clear predictor: the youngest person interviewed (22) listed more than the average at 8 taxa while one of the two oldest (35) listed a less-than-average 5 taxa.

Table 5.1: Frequency and salience measures of all taxa listed in free-listing exercise

Bush medicine (most common name/s in Kriol)	English name (where available)	Species name	% of informants who listed the taxon (N = 14)	Salience measure
Dumbuyumbu	Sandalwood	*Santalum lanceolatum*	100 (14/14)	0.7
Mayarranja	Sandpaper fig	*Ficus opposita*	57 (8/14)	0.3
Ngalangga, waitbak tri	River gum	*Eucalyptus camaldulensis*	64 (9/14)	0.3
Guyiya, dogbul	Emu bush	*Grewia retusifolia*	36 (5/14)	0.2
Warlan, warlantri	-	*Eucalyptus tectifica*	50 (7/14)	0.2
Smeligras, smelilif	-	*Pterocaulon serrulatum*	50 (7/14)	0.2
Plamtri	Green plum	*Buchanania obovata*	43 (6/14)	0.1
Gulban, titri	Ti-tree	*Melaleuca stenostachya*	29 (4/14)	0.1
Barnarr, mabultri	-	*Owenia vernicosa*	29 (4/14)	0.1
Jupi	Blackcurrant	*Antidesma ghesaembilla*	14 (2/14)	0.0
Gardayka	Stringybark	*Eucalyptus tetrodonta*	7 (1/14)	0.0
Pinifek	Spinifex	*Triodia microstachya*	7 (1/14)	0.0
Marlabangu	Freshwater mussel	*Velesunio wilsonii*	7 (1/14)	0.0
Neilfish medisin	?	?	14 (2/14)	0.0
Garnaya	Lily root	*Nymphaea violacea, N. gigantea?*	7 (1/14)	0.0
Burduga	-	*Clerodundrum floribundum*	7 (1/14)	0.0
Burrunburrun	-	*Cassytha filiformis?*	7 (1/14)	0.0
Souptri	Soap tree	*Acacia holosericea*	7 (1/14)	0.0
Lemingras	Lemongrass	*Cymbopogon procerus*	7 (1/14)	0.0
Wisiling tri	She-oak	*Casuarina equisetifolia*	7 (1/14)	0.0
Maypiny	Ironwood	*Erythrophleum chlorostachys?*	7 (1/14)	0.0

Information derived from recalling the most recent time each participant had used bush medicine provided various data. Information regarding the recency of usage is shown in Table 5.2.

Table 5.2: Most recent instance of using bush medicine: time

Most recent usage	Number of participants (N=14)	% of participants
Within a week	1	7
Within a month	4	29
Within six months	6	43
Within a year	9	64
Within three years	11	79
Anytime	14	100

Six different types of bush medicine were used 'most recently', as shown in Table 5.3.

Table 5.3: Most recent instance of using bush medicine: type of medicine used

Bush medicine type (most common name/s in Kriol)	Scientific name	Number of participants (N=14)
Ngalangga	*Eucalyptus camaldulensis*	4
Dumbuyumbu	*Santalum lanceolatum*	3
Smeligras/smelilif	*Pterocaulon serralatum*	3
Warlan	*Eucalyptus tectifica*	2
Maypiny	*Erythrophleum chlorastachys*	1
Plamtri	*Buchanania obovata*	1

Similarly variable were the ailments or reasons given for the most recent application of bush medicine, as shown in Table 5.4.

Table 5.4: Most recent instance of using bush medicine: ailment treated/reason for use

Ailment	Number of participants (N=14)
Toothache	4
Flu/sinus	3
Sores	3
Boils	1
Hangover	1
Diarrhoea	1
High blood pressure	1
Used as a tonic/preventative	1

When the 14 participants were asked to nominate their top five bush medicines, 12 attempted the task: seven nominated between two and four preferred medicines and five completed a top five list. The results are shown in Table 5.5.

Table 5.5: 'Top 5 bush medicine' survey results

Bush medicine type (name/s given by participants)	Scientific name	Position on 'top 5' list				
		1	2	3	4	5
Dumbuyumbu	*Santalum lanceolatum*	4.5	2.5	2	1	
Warlan	*Eucalyptus tectifica*	3	1		1	
Ngalangga	*Eucalyptus camaldulensis*	1.5	2.5	2	1	
Maypiny	*Erythrophleum chlorastachys*	1				
Smeligras/Smelilif	*Pterocaulon serralatum*	1			1	2
Plamtri	*Buchanania obovate*	1			1	1
Mayarranja	*Ficus opposite*		4	1		
Gulban/Titri	*Melaleuca stenostachya*		1	1		
Guyiya	*Grewia retusifolia*		1			
Barnarr/Mabultri	*Owenia vernicosa*			1	1	
Pinifek	*Triodia microstachya*			1		
Neilfish medisin	?				1	
Garnaya	*Nymphaea violacea (bulb)*					1
Gardayka (Stringybark)	*Eucalyptus tetrodonta*					1

Discussion: Gaps and Continuities across Language Shift

Table 5.1 shows that only one taxon, *dumbuyumbu* (*Santalum lanceolatum*), was self-identified by all participants and is clearly the most salient bush medicine. A further three taxa were self-identified by over half the participants and another five taxa were named by four or more. Most of the taxa—12 out of 21—were self-identified by only one or two participants.

The average number of taxa Kriol-speaking young adults listed in the free-listing task was six: this is low compared to traditional language speaking elders (see e.g. the 14 bush medicine texts in Marra composed by elders Betty and Freda Roberts [2007]). But, collectively, the younger group described 21 taxa and, with prompting via a checklist, individuals demonstrated knowledge of up to 13 taxa. This indicates that, while young people's individual taxonomic knowledge of bush medicine is generally lower than that of senior people, collectively they demonstrate a comparable level of knowledge (albeit still diminished). Yet, most taxa that were identified by young people were only known to a few. This may indicate that much of the knowledge that young Kriol speakers collectively hold is fragile and in danger of being lost. Conversely, it may mean that individual knowledge will over time be disseminated to others, leading to some of the currently lesser known taxa increasing their cultural and cognitive salience as the young age. A longitudinal study with the same participants would illuminate this further.

In terms of actual usage, over one-quarter (four of 14) of the participants said they had used bush medicine in the month prior to being interviewed. One male (aged 35) had used *ngalangga* (*Eucalyptus camaldulensis*) so recently that he pointed to a just-healed boil on his leg during the interview. In another interview, a female respondent (aged 22) discussing *dumbuyumbu* (*Santalum lanceolatum*) casually reported that:

(4)

Main mami en dedi bin jis gaji yestadei sambala.

My mum and dad just got some yesterday.

This material, along with other material in this study, contradicts earlier suggestions that bush medicine is practised to a 'limited extent' (Heath 1980, 445). In addition to the recent use reported by a number of young people, the diverse range of applications they reported further indicates a continuation of complex bush medicine practices. As shown in Table 5.4, eight different reasons or ailments were cited by the 14 participants as to why they had used bush medicine, despite referring only to their most recent usage. The most common treatment was toothache, likely to be attributable to the lack of dental care available in remote regions. Additional reasons for the most recent application of bush medicine included sores, flu/sinus, treating boils, diarrhoea, high blood pressure, hangovers or simply as a tonic or preventative measure. This range of applications is broader than Senior's (2001, 8) suggestion that bush medicine was used 'predominantly to treat of colds, flus and headaches', indicating that the knowledge and usage of bush medicine among young people in Ngukurr is more prevalent and sophisticated than previously thought.

Building upon the evidence that bush medicine has diverse applications, several interviewees revealed prescriptions more sophisticated than single use. One respondent reported treating high blood pressure with a self-administered two-week course of *warlan* (*Eucalyptus tectifica*), with the outcome that it '*kili im olagija*' (killed in permanently). Another described a three-day process of treating her youngest son's sores with *ngalangga* (*Eucalyptus camaldulensis*):

> (5)
>
> *Ai bin boilimbat ba dis beibiwan las taim. Ngalangga tri. Yea imin sik garra ... daiyariya en ... bedkol plas imin abu det esma du. Aibin jis breigi det ngalangga ba im na en ... breigi from ja gu boili ba im. Neksdei mela bin gu breigi biyain na, det olmen Gumbuli kemp ... neksdei mela bin gu breigi la ... riba.*
>
> I boiled it for this baby last time (I used it). *Ngalangga* tree. Yeah, he was sick with … diarrhoea and … sinus, plus he had asthma too. I just broke off some *ngalangga* for him then and … broke it off and then went and boiled it for him. The next day we went and broke off some beyond the old man Gumbuli's house … the next day we went and broke some off at the river.

There are, however, also indications of diminished knowledge and use compared to previous generations. Even after listening to a checklist of bush medicine names, four of the 14 participants could still only identify five or fewer taxa. Likewise, with reported usage, three participants said they had not used bush medicine in three years prior. The taxonomic knowledge displayed by the participants as a cohort resulted in 21 taxa described, yet over half of those taxa were only identified by one or two of the study participants.

For many, bush medicine appears to retain ongoing importance, both as a core component of health belief systems and in its practical application. As social media proliferates in remote communities (that have mobile coverage), bush medicine rates a mention. Facebook status updates (Figures 5.1–5.3) from three adults aged between 25 and 35 show young people are bringing the pre–contact derived domain of bush medicine into new domains that are particular to young people.

Figure 5.1: Facebook status from a young man in Ngukurr (11 May 2011).

Figure 5.2: Facebook status from a young mother from Minyerri (16 June 2013).

Figure 5.3: Facebook status from a young mother from Ngukurr (16 July 2013).

Evidence of young adults demonstrating innovation in the domain of bush medicine was attested twice during interviews. One participant described mixing medicines to treat an illness—a practice rarely attested in descriptions of Aboriginal bush medicine practice:

> (6)
>
> *Det taim wen ai bin abu det swainflu, ai bin gu la klinik, en thei bin jis oni gimi penadol. Thei bin jis oni gimi penadol en den, thei bin dalim mi thei kuden du enijing <u>about it</u>. Thei bin dalim mi <u>there's no, any medicine</u> ba det ting, so ai bin lafta yusu det ngalangga na en det ... pinifek gras... en dem, keldapwan na smeligras. Boilim oldot togetha, en bogibogibat na, fo wan wik.*

> The time I had swine flu, I went to the clinic, and they only gave me Panadol. They only gave me Panadol, and then, they told me they couldn't do anything about it. They told me there's no medicine for it, so I had to use *ngalangga* then, and that spinifex grass, and those, curled up things—smelly grass. Boil them all together and then wash with it, for a week.

Another young man reported the use of *dumbuyumbu* (*Santalum lanceolatum*) by football players to assist with performance:

> (7)
>
> *Samtaim wi yusu wen wi plei futbul. Bifo wi plei, mela oldot dringgi olda bois, ba meigi lait insaidwei.*
>
> Sometimes we use it when we play football. Before we play, we all drink it, all the boys, to make us 'light' on the inside.

Conclusion

In the 1970s, a Nunggubuyu elder told linguist Jeffrey Heath that bush medicine practices were being abandoned:

> *Arraga wu-warragurag adanu waari naambuyijimdhang, naambu-warnbang, naambu-warralharrgang, naambu-warramaarndhang anubu-junyung nurri-nyinyung ana-baniyinyjinyung, warra-miiiiny-ngambara-wajinyung.*
>
> Now it (bush medicine) is no longer in use, we do not use it, we do not do that to it, swallow it, make it. That sort of thing, it is ours, of long ago, of the time of the elders. (Maadi, quoted in Heath 1980, 462, translation has been altered)

Despite assertions such as these—which are generally made more convincing when language shift is an added factor—young people's actual knowledge or use of bush medicine (or lack thereof) has rarely been investigated. The study described in this chapter is possibly the first ethno-botanical study in Australia that focuses specifically on a non-expert group who do not have a traditional language as their first language. Such groups are often perceived by insiders and outsiders alike to a) hold less knowledge and b) engage in bush medicine practices less frequently than older people who are considered experts in such domains and/or are native speakers of an Indigenous language. Previous research in 2003 had argued that Kriol speakers in Ngukurr maintain in their health belief systems a high regard for bush medicine commensurate to that of their forebears (Senior 2003). I have found that, while young people generally are less knowledgeable that more senior residents in Ngukurr, they do hold a degree of knowledge about bush medicine and are applying that knowledge to a greater degree than was previously thought. I also might note that Aquino (see Chapter 4, this volume) has made a similar observation with regard to young people's preferences for, and consumption of, native or imported food. The young people who informed this study described and identified over 20 taxa, many described and reported recent instances of usage and application, and a diversity of preferences and practices were revealed. For bush medicine to be mentioned and 'liked' on young people's Facebook feeds and consumed prior to football training indicates that not only are bush medicine practices being maintained in Ngukurr, but also a degree of dynamism is ensuring such practices are riding the waves of rapid cultural change and language shift.

References

Bordulk, D., M. T. Nikipini Dalak, L. Bennett, R. Tingey, M. Katherine, S. Cutfield, M. Pamkal and G. Wightman. 2012. *Dalabon Plants and Animals*. Darwin: Department of Land Resource Management.

Farnsworth, N. R. 1966. 'Biological and Phytochemical Screening of Plants'. *Journal of Pharmaceutical Sciences* 55 (3): 225–76. doi.org/10.1002/jps.2600550302.

Heath, J. 1980. *Nunggubuyu Myths and Ethnographic Texts*. Canberra: Australian Institute of Aboriginal Studies.

Hector, I. K., G. J. Kalabidi, S. Banjo, T. N. N. Dodd, R. J. W. Wavehill, D. Danbayarri, V. N. Wadrill, B. Puntiyarri, I. B. Malyik, B. Wavehill, H. Morris, L. Campbell, F. Meakins and G. Wightman. 2012. *Bilinarra, Gurindji and Malngin Plants and Animals*. Katherine/Darwin: Department of Land Resource Management.

Hoffman, B. and T. Gallagher. 2007. 'Relative Cultural Importance Indices in Quantitative Ethnobotany'. *Ethnobotany Research & Applications* 5: 201–18. doi.org/10.17348/era.5.0.201-218.

Huddleston, G., G. Dinah, B. Roberts and A. George. n.d.-a. *Marra Plants and Their Uses*, vol. 1. Katherine: Katherine Regional Aboriginal Language Centre.

Huddleston, G., D. Garadji, B. Roberts and A. George. n.d.-b. *Marra Plants and Their Uses*, vol. 2. Katherine: Katherine Regional Aboriginal Language Centre.

Huddleston, G., D. Garadji, B. Roberts and A. George. n.d.-c. *Marra Plants and Their Uses*, vol. 3. Katherine: Katherine Regional Aboriginal Language Centre.

Latz, P. 1995. *Bushfires and Bushtucker: Aboriginal Plant Use in Central Australia*. Alice Springs, NT: IAD Press.

Levitt, Du. 1981. *Plants and People: Aboriginal Uses of Plants on Groote Eylandt*. Canberra: Australian Institute of Aboriginal Studies.

McClatchey, W. 2012. 'Basic Methods for Documenting Biological Knowledge Represented in Languages'. In *The Oxford Handbook of Linguistic Fieldwork*, edited by N. Thieberger, 281–97. Oxford: Oxford University Press.

Merlan, F. 1981. 'Land, Language and Social Identity in Aboriginal Australia'. *Mankind* 13 (2): 133–48. doi.org/10.1111/j.1835-9310.1981.tb00716.x.

Nganiyurlma Media Association. 1990. *Bush Medicine from Ngukurr* [Video]. Ngukurr: Nganiyurlma Media Association. 72 mins.

Roberts, B. and F. Roberts. 2007. *Bush Medicine Texts*. Unpublished manuscript. Ngukurr: Diwurruwurru-Jaru Aboriginal Corporation.

Roberts, J. G., S. Y. Conway, R. Morgan, A. Dirn.gayg, S. Harris, E. Farrar, F. B. Roberts, F. Merlan, E. Collyer, T. Calnan and G. Wightman. 2011. *Mangarrayi and Yangman Plants and Animals*. Darwin: Department of Land Resource Management.

Scarlett, N., N. White and J. Reid. 1982. 'Bush Medicines: The Pharmacopoeia of the Yolngu of Arnhem Land'. In *Body, Land and Spirit: Health and Healing in Aboriginal Society*, edited by J. Reid, 154–91. St Lucia, Queensland: University of Queensland Press.

Senior, K. 2001. *Health Beliefs and Behaviour : The Opportunities And Practicalities Of 'Looking After Yourself' in Ngukurr*. Wollongong, NSW: South East Arnhem Land Collaborative Research Project, University of Wollongong.

Senior, K. 2003. 'A Gudbala Laif ? Health and Wellbeing in a Remote Aboriginal Community—What Are the Problems and Where Lies Responsibility?' PhD thesis, The Australian National University, Canberra.

Winydjorrodj, P., S. Flora, N. Brown, P, Jatbula, J. Galmur, F. Merlan and G. Wightman. 2005. *Jawoyn Plants and Animals*. Darwin: Northern Territory Department of Natural Resources, Environment and the Arts.

6

'They *Do* Think about Health': Young Indigenous Women's Ideas about Health and Their Interaction with the Health System

Mascha Friderichs

Introduction

One day I was talking with a non-Indigenous service provider who asked me what my research was about. I told her I wanted to know how often young Indigenous women in Katherine thought about health and how they engaged with health and social services. Her response was that it would be 0 per cent because Indigenous people do not think about 'health' because health it is a Western concept. This service provider's idea was in line with much of the literature, which states that there is no Aboriginal word for health (Atkinson 2002, 44; National Aboriginal Health Strategy Working Party 1989). However, to say that Indigenous young women in Katherine have no conception of the term health or ideas about health is to overlook the reality they live in. The young women in my research were living in a town where non-Indigenous people were in the majority; they attended school, engaged with Western media and used the Western health care system. As such, they cannot be regarded as isolated and independent from their surroundings (Merlan 1998). Moreover, the fact that there is no word in Aboriginal languages that means health in the Western sense does not mean that people do not think about issues that are generally regarded as being in the domain of health and sickness.

Research on Aboriginal health often falls into one of two categories. Research from a biomedical perspective only looks at health from that perspective and is generally based on statistical indicators of mortality and morbidity, without acknowledging the existence of traditional beliefs. Conversely, much research on Aboriginal health beliefs focuses on traditional beliefs (Maher 1999), with anthropologists emphasising sorcery and traditional healing (see also Senior 2003). Both perspectives run the risk of overlooking the reality and complexity of people's views and behaviour. Indigenous health is an issue of concern for governments, service providers and researchers, which makes it imperative to consider whose perspectives are prioritised. Research findings need to reflect Indigenous people's own lived experiences.

The majority of anthropological research on Indigenous health has focused on the general population or on small children (see e.g. Carson et al. 2007; Reid 1983; Saggers and Gray 1991a). Research focused on Indigenous youth, on the other hand, is not always focused on health specifically (Burbank 1988; Eickelkamp 2011).[1] However, research with young people is important, as many health-compromising behaviours, as well as patterns of health service utilisation, are developed during adolescence (Vingilis, Wade and Seeley 2007). It is at this age that people become aware of their bodies and start making active decisions regarding their health (World Health Organization 2003, 7–9). If public health policies and the work of service providers are to contribute to improved health outcomes for Indigenous young women, it is necessary first to understand their views on health and what is important to them.

Many ethnographic studies on Indigenous health focus on remote locations rather than town contexts. Yet, young Indigenous women in towns are exposed to different influences on their health beliefs and behaviours than those in remote areas. Although there is increasing recognition that the living circumstances of Indigenous people in remote communities should be seen as intercultural (Burbank 2011), there is a stronger boundary between Aboriginal and non-Aboriginal contexts in remote communities

1 Exceptions include Chenhall and Senior (2009), and Senior et al. (2014), who looked at remote Indigenous youth mental health and sexual health.

than in towns. Whereas in the former, non-Indigenous people are always outsiders (i.e. never permanent), towns form home for both Indigenous and non-Indigenous people. In towns, Indigenous and non-Indigenous people mutually influence each other, and strict distinctions between Aboriginal and non-Aboriginal domains—between tradition and modernity—cannot be made (Merlan 1998, 4).[2] This is especially relevant when considering young people may have multicultural friendships and who attend school and activities such as sports together. Another difference related to location is that, although the populations of remote communities generally consist of people from various language groups, this variety is even more pronounced in towns.

In this chapter, I show the multitude of health beliefs held by Indigenous young women in Katherine. The chapter starts with a description of Katherine and the 12 main informants in this study. This includes an explanation of how their Indigenous identity can be understood, as well as a consideration of Katherine as an intercultural place. This is followed by a short overview of the methods used, then an exploration of definitions of health, including how services influence young women's views, as well as ideas around taking responsibility for health. Subsequently, I discuss the use of health services, focusing on the role of Aboriginal Community Controlled Health Organisations (ACCHOs). The final section before the discussion considers the changing role of bush medicine and traditional healing.

Indigenous Young Women in Katherine

This study was conducted in Katherine, a small town with a population of about 6,300 people in the Northern Territory, about 300 km south of Darwin on the Katherine River (Australian Bureau of Statistics 2018; Merlan 1998). Katherine has an elongated shape, with Northside and Southside situated along the river and Eastside a little further away along the Stuart Highway. Several Aboriginal communities surround Katherine, such as Kalano on the western side of the river, and Rockhole, which is located 15 km to the south-east. Katherine's climate is subtropical with a wet and a dry season and average daily temperatures from 25°C–35°C,

2 It is important to recognise, however, that the relationships are characterised by inequality, resulting in the experience of marginality by Aboriginal people (Merlan 1998, 2005).

although 40°C days are not uncommon. Due to the town's location at the intersection of two main highways, and the presence of several national parks and cultural centres and galleries, many tourists visit each year during the dry season. Katherine is also a hub for many agencies that service communities in a large surrounding area, as well as for Aboriginal people from communities who visit to see family and to access shops, bars and other facilities.

Around 25 per cent of the population of Katherine is Indigenous (Australian Bureau of Statistics 2018). The Jawoyn people are recognised as the Traditional Owners of an area that includes Nitmiluk National Park north of the town (Kearney 1988). Currently, there are competing and disputed native title claim applications for the town of Katherine. The other main language groups of the region are Wardaman and Dagoman, who are from areas south-west of Katherine, and Mayali from the north-east (Merlan 1998, 14, 23). People from many other language groups also live in Katherine.

Katherine has a public and a private high school. There are two boarding houses for students from towns and communities elsewhere in the Northern Territory. Wurli-Wurlinjang Health Service (hereafter Wurli) is the ACCHO servicing Katherine (Wurli n.d.). In addition, there are other health clinics, a hospital and many social services. The service provider population tends to be transient, with many young service providers coming from 'down south' to work in Katherine for a year or two.

This chapter primarily focuses on the views and experiences of 12 Indigenous young women, varying in age from 16 to 24 years. At the time of my research, four were still attending high school; five were employed, two of whom were enrolled in a Certificate III or Certificate IV course;[3] one had a job lined up; and two were not working or enrolled in education, one of whom had a baby. Their living circumstances varied from living at a boarding house to living alone to living with a partner to living with family members. Four of the young women were born in Katherine, two had moved with their families from elsewhere in the Territory, two were boarding students from elsewhere in the Territory and two were from interstate. All had access to, and interest in, Western items and activities, such as mobile phones, music, television and sports (Burbank 2011,

3 These are vocational educational qualifications.

128–30; Chenhall and Senior 2009, 36–40). Most participants were religious and stated that they believed in God and Jesus, with the majority being Catholic.

As noted above, Katherine should be understood as an intercultural space. This understanding is linked with how culture is conceptualised. Hinkson (2010, 5) has noted that anthropologists working with Indigenous people in Australia generally understand culture in two different ways: classicism and interculturalism. The former focuses on classical anthropological topics such as kinship and cosmology, regards Indigenous culture as relatively independent and stresses cultural continuity over change. The latter focuses more on processes and change. Merlan (2005, 169–70) describes two ways in which the concept of intercultural can be understood. The first emphasises separateness, highlighting the differences between Indigenous and non-Indigenous people. Culture is then understood as 'high culture': an essentialised and past-based view that focuses on the concrete and visible aspects of a culture that is imagined as unchanging (Merlan 1998, 227–28). The second way shows how beliefs and practices are shaped in the interaction between Indigenous and non-Indigenous people, and considers culture as expressed in everyday sociality and experience. However, these understandings are not mutually exclusive. An intercultural analysis should draw on both approaches as outlined by Merlan (2005), showing how an understanding of culture interacts with people's lived experiences (Hinkson and Smith 2005).

Both approaches are relevant to my research in Katherine. The young women I interviewed in Katherine described culture as including language, art, respect, hunting and fishing, 'knowledge about my tribe', songlines, their Dreaming, the Law, kinship, bush medicine and traditional healing. Culture was talked about as something that could be 'lost' and as something that could be 'strong or weak'. This is similar to Merlan's (2005, 169–70) first sense of the term intercultural. At the same time, Indigenous young women's sense of identity, as well as their health beliefs, are a product of everyday interactions within a multicultural context.

Rather than following the three-pronged approach to Indigeneity outlined by the National Aboriginal Health Strategy Working Party (1989), in this study I use self-identification only.[4] Some of the young women in this study were of mixed Aboriginal and European descent, but, for a variety of reasons, all but one always identified as Indigenous.[5] With regard to Indigenous identity, the young women could broadly be divided into two groups. In the first group, Indigenous identity was unquestioned; they had mainly Indigenous ancestors and they grew up around their Aboriginal family; they had a skin name[6] and had learned culture from their own language group. In the second group were young women for whom Indigenous identity was more ambivalent. These women had lost touch with their culture because their mothers or grandmothers were part of the Stolen Generations,[7] or because they had not grown up around their Aboriginal family. They made explicit efforts to learn about Aboriginal culture, acquiring knowledge in a similar way as outsiders would.[8] Some of them did not have a skin name. They felt that they needed to know about their culture to strengthen their Indigenous identity.

Methods

The findings in this chapter are based on one year of ethnographic fieldwork in Katherine.[9] Prior to starting my research, I had already lived there for eight months, which enabled me to start building relationships

4 This allows a focus on the insider perspective of Indigeneity. Certain conjunctions of speech, comportment, phenotype and so on influence what some non-Indigenous locals perceive as typically Indigenous. Some of my informants would not be perceived as typically Indigenous, yet others would be, and, as such, they included a range of young women with regard to identity.

5 One young woman was, in her owns words, 'a quarter Aboriginal', but she frequently identified as non-Indigenous. Indigeneity is only a small part of her biological heritage and, as she is fair skinned, people often assume that she is non-Indigenous. Her story provides an interesting case regarding identity and culture, as she grew up in a largely Aboriginal town and was mostly raised by several Aboriginal women who she calls her nannas. Compared to many of the other young women in this study, she is very familiar with traditional Aboriginal knowledge.

6 Skin names indicate the section or subsection that a person belongs to. Non-Indigenous people who spend time in communities are often given skin names as a way of managing and referring to them.

7 'Stolen Generations' refers to Indigenous children, often those of Western appearance, who were taken from their families to be adopted into non-Indigenous families or placed in orphanages.

8 For example, they did this on camps during which Indigenous youth go out bush for one or two weeks and learn about clan groups, weaving, bush tucker, traditional healing and other aspects of traditional culture.

9 This chapter is based on my PhD research. Ethical approval for this study was provided by the Human Research Ethics Committee of the Northern Territory Department of Health and Menzies School of Health Research (Reference Number 2013-2112).

and get to know the town. Although my focus was on Indigenous young women who were 16–24 years of age and service providers who worked with them, through my participation at various organisations and my daily life in town, many more people became involved.

During my time in Katherine, I volunteered with the YMCA at their Drop-in Night and Girls Program,[10] and at the Good Beginnings' Supported Playgroups[11] in Katherine, Kalano and Rockhole. I had a casual job as a tutor at Callistemon, a boarding house for high school students, where I mainly worked with the senior girls. I also joined two service provider networks and participated in various events in and around town, such as NAIDOC[12] Week, Youth Week, a Stolen Generations Healing Camp[13] and the Barunga Festival.[14] For seven months, one of my housemates was an Aboriginal health practitioner and, over time, I had several housemates who worked for social services in town.

In addition to the informal and unstructured interviews that were a common occurrence during my fieldwork, I conducted semi-structured interviews using an interview guide with Indigenous young women and service providers (Bernard 2011, 158; Heath et al. 2009, 80–83). All semi-structured interviews were recorded and transcribed. Many of the young women I interviewed, if they did not know something, commented that they could ask someone else, such as their aunt or grandmother. I found myself repeatedly clarifying that I was interested in their *own* experiences and ideas. I explained that, rather than creating a pharmacopeia of bush medicine, for example, knowing that someone did not know much about something and the reasons for that lack of knowledge was the information I was after.

10 Drop-in Night was held every Friday from 7 pm to 10 pm. It was attended weekly by 100–400 children and young people. The Girls Program was held on Tuesday nights during school terms for girls aged 10–18.

11 The playgroups were aimed at parents with children from birth to five years old, providing an opportunity for children to play and develop school readiness. I attended each playgroup once a week.

12 NAIDOC stands for National Aborigines and Islanders Day Observance Committee.

13 This camp was organised by the Northern Territory Stolen Generations Aboriginal Corporation, a not-for-profit organisation that attends to the needs and concerns of members of the Stolen Generations and their families and communities, including family tracing and counselling (Northern Territory Stolen Generations Aboriginal Corporation 2019). The camp, which was targeted at women who are part of the Stolen Generations, was held one weekend at the rural campus of Charles Darwin University, Katherine.

14 This festival in the community of Barunga has been held yearly since 1985, featuring musical performances, sporting competitions and cultural performances and workshops.

During my research, I worked with two peer researchers, Tamara[15] and Channy, who, when I first met them, were 16 and 20 years old, respectively. They were involved in different stages of the research.[16] I also worked closely with Sonia, a traditional healer in her 50s. She 'adopted' me as her daughter and gave me the skin name Kotjan. Besides her role as mother, she also took on the role of mentor and teacher. She taught me about the kinship system and other facets of culture. She allowed me to help make bush medicine on several occasions and to watch her do traditional massages, both in the hospital and in other settings.

Defining Health

In literature exploring definitions of health, a distinction is generally made between the biomedical perspective, which focuses on health as the absence of disease, and a more holistic perspective, which is positively framed in terms of wellbeing in different domains, including socially (Johansson, Weinehall and Emmelin 2009). In 1948, the World Health Organization created the following holistic definition of health: 'Health is a state of complete physical, mental and social wellbeing and not merely the absence of disease or infirmity' (World Health Organization 1986). Many indigenous people in the world have built upon this definition of health. In public health documents, the most commonly used definition of health for Aboriginal people is:

> Not just the physical well-being of the individual but the social, emotional, and cultural well-being of the whole community. This is a whole of life view and it also includes the cyclical concept of life-death-life. (National Aboriginal Health Strategy Working Party 1989, x)

15 All names used are pseudonyms.

16 We discussed my research proposal and interview guide to make sure that the questions were relevant and suitable for young people. I conducted multiple interviews so that we were able to explore important topics in-depth; during subsequent interviews, I often heard new information about topics we had discussed before. This was especially common when talking about sensitive or personal topics. Channy introduced me to other young women for interviews and we conducted these interviews together. Although I knew many young women before interviewing them, when I did not, the presence of Channy, who knew some of them well, helped to garner more in-depth information than I would have been able to get by myself. All interviews were conducted in English, with Channy sometimes clarifying my questions in terms that were more familiar to informants. Finally, I discussed my findings and my interpretations of the interviews with both peer researchers.

Constructed in 1989, this definition provides a justification for Aboriginal-specific health services and draws attention to the social and cultural factors relevant to Aboriginal people's health (Brady 1995). The working party that created it consisted of 10 government representatives and nine Aboriginal community representatives. Therefore, the definition may not reflect the variety of health beliefs of Indigenous groups and individuals across the country, and is likely to have more currency in the political realm than in most ordinary people's everyday lives (Boddington and Räisänen 2009; Brady 1995; Friderichs 2018). Currently, the definition is used in policy documents that address disease prevention and health care management. It is also taught in cross-cultural awareness programs to people who are going to work in Aboriginal health (Lea 2008, 99).

Rather than using terms and phrases such as 'holistic wellbeing' or 'not being sick', the young people I spoke to framed health in terms of behaviour. Health was generally described as healthy eating and keeping fit, and hygiene was sometimes also mentioned. There was a focus on physical health, although one of my interviewees, Kimberley, said: 'It's not just the body, it's the mind as well'. Some women added that being happy was important for being healthy. When asked if they felt healthy and why, most young people said they felt healthy, and their answers illustrated their views of health as a behaviour. For example, Tamara said: 'Yes. I eat salads and fruit every day'. This view of health as behaviour can also be seen in this excerpt:

> MF: And do you feel healthy?
>
> Bridget: Sometimes.
>
> MF: Sometimes?
>
> Bridget: Depends on what I have and stuff. After I do my—like I do sports and stuff or go for a run, I feel good. And eating good I feel good—if I've eaten something good—like healthy.

When talking about whether people felt healthy, physical health problems were rarely named. Bridget had a broken arm but she did not mention this when talking about feeling healthy. The young women often mentioned health issues at different times during the interview that they had not mentioned earlier, but these did not seem to affect their perception of their health.

The young women had learned about health from a variety of sources, including school, clinics, family members, their jobs[17] and the internet. A significant way in which standard health messages of healthy eating and exercising were distributed in Katherine was through social services. Service providers said that they incorporated health in their work through providing healthy food, taking care of hygiene, encouraging active behaviour and doing activities that reinforced self-esteem, such as letting the girls who attended the YMCA Girls Program do modelling at the Women of the World Festival.[18] My observations confirmed these statements; for example, at Good Beginnings, the children attending playgroups always had to wash their hands before having morning tea, and they were given sandwiches and fresh fruit to eat. The YMCA was another place where the standard health message was clearly present. One project of the Girls Program was organising a 'Rainbow Run'. Together with a local participant of the Indigenous Marathon Project, the girls started a walking/running group. They decided to organise a run and to open it up to the entire community.

In addition to exercise, health was emphasised in terms of food and further changes were made to ensure this: cordial was replaced by water, and the dessert, if there was any, was fresh fruit. The message about health was taken in by the girls who attended the program such as Ashley:

> MF: So, what do you think of the YMCA?
>
> Ashley: I think it's really good. It keeps kids busy … They have good food, like healthy food and stuff, which is really good and gives the girls like an idea how, or what they can eat at home.

Despite providing narrow definitions of health as healthy eating and exercise, the young women I interviewed held much broader ideas about what constituted the domain of health, including ideas about spiritual sickness, mental wellbeing, medical care and biomedical diseases. One possible explanation for the narrow definitions of health they provided is that, particularly in the early stages of my research, they perceived me as

17 This includes the work of the peer researchers. On several occasions, they asked me questions about specific health issues, such as how you can tell when you have cancer, and what happens when you get an abortion.

18 The international Women of the World Festival has taken place at Katherine several times. It celebrates women and girls, and features a variety of speakers, exhibitions, performances and workshops.

a non-Indigenous service provider, knowledgeable about health, and the interview as a kind of exam. This is evident in the notes I made following a conversation I had with Felicity, a woman in her 30s:

> Can you tell me what health means to you? What is health? Felicity seemed to find this a difficult question. Looked away and laughed a bit. I explained that there is no right or wrong answer, I just want to know what people think. She then said (still sounding a bit unsure): 'I guess it's healthy eating, getting a bit of exercise in'. And then 'that's what they say at the clinic anyway, you need to change your diet'. (Field notes, 29 May 2015)

Even if my informants knew that I was looking at health in a broader way, their answers remained the same. Several interviews started with a discussion of bush medicine, traditional healing, domestic violence, alcohol and drug use, being connected to country and other aspects that may be understood as part of health. However, when Channy or I asked the concrete question 'what is health?', the answers were always the same: 'eat healthy food, drink lots of water, run, do weights' (Aleisha). It was as if this question automatically brought out this response, no matter what other dimensions of health the young women identified when asked different questions. It made no difference whether it was Channy or me who asked the question.

Another explanation for why all the young women defined health in the same way was given by Tamara. When I asked her what she had learned about health at school, she replied, 'they pretty much tell me what I think', referring to our earlier discussions about health. She explained that others, if they were taking the same class, would provide the same answers. I explored with her the possibility of using a more encompassing term, which would make it clear during subsequent interviews that I was aiming to get broader definitions than those provided so far:

> MF: Do you think it's right to say 'health' like most people would think, it's just that sort of Western idea?
>
> Tamara: Yeah. They think going for a run and they'll think all that. The way I think.

Although Tamara agreed that health is much broader than this, she did not have any term that encompassed all that fits into this domain.

Health: An Individual Responsibility?

For a long time, health policies have been based on the idea that health is an individual responsibility (McCarthy 2006, 275). However, nowadays there is increasing recognition of the social determinants of health. Following a gradient, differences in socioeconomic status, education, employment, housing, social capital and other factors are understood to contribute to differences in health at the population level (Marmot 2011; Marmot and Wilkinson 2006).[19] Although government policies such as Closing the Gap increasingly reflect this recognition (Department of Families Housing Community Services and Indigenous Affairs 2012, 69; 2013, 67), public health programs continue to emphasise behavioural change.[20] Underlying this is the assumption that people value their health, want to improve it and feel a sense of control over it. However, perceptions about the importance of health differ between health professionals and everyone else. Health researchers and public health professionals are focused on health by default; whereas, for lay people, health is just one of many aspects of their life (Bukman et al. 2014). People have differing health needs and experience numerous and different barriers to healthy behaviour. Similarly, feelings of control over health differ between groups of people.

Senior (2003, 229–31) found that many Aboriginal people in Ngukurr had a utilitarian or functional view of health: health was seen as a necessity that enabled people to perform everyday tasks, such as work. However, people in Ngukurr did not need jobs to have an income—there were few jobs available in the community and the majority of residents received social security payments. Therefore, there was a low need for health, as all they needed it for was to walk around the community to be social. In contrast, for most young women in Katherine, the value of health was more implicit. They said it was 'important' but did not elaborate or explain why, as seen in Katie's roundabout explanation: 'Cause it's important … It's the way to go, keep your body healthy'. Only Robyn related the need to be healthy to her job.[21] Although health was mostly considered to be important in itself, some

19 Social and structural factors that specifically influence the Indigenous population include the history of colonisation, dispossession, marginalisation, racism and 'country' (Burgess and Morrison 2007; Calma 2008; Carson et al. 2007; Nazroo and Williams 2006).

20 A critical discussion of Closing the Gap and how it relates to Indigenous identities can be found in Friderichs (2018).

21 Nevertheless, she did not talk about this when I asked her about the importance of health. It came up when talking about medications. She said that she did not like to take medications, but if she did not take them and got sick, then someone else who may have already worked that day might have to cover a shift for her.

of the young women talked about wanting to live longer. In relation to having a hospital in town, Katie said: 'it's good … I don't wanna die. I'm still young'. Robyn said that living to an old age was important to her because she wanted to be around for her family. She never met her grandmother, who died at a young age, and the desire to meet her own grandchildren and great-grandchildren motivated her to stay healthy.

Most of the young women in this study, when asked about their expectations for future health, said that they expected their health to be good. They usually answered this question in terms of healthy behaviour. For example:

> MF: Do you think you'll be healthy in the future?
>
> Tamara: I try to keep fit. Keep training, playing sports, go to the gym.

In a sense, the way the young women defined health implied control over it. If health is defined as 'you stay fit, keep strong, eat healthy' (Tamara) or 'health is looking after your health' (Bridget), and a healthy person is defined as 'someone that looks after themselves' (Channy), this is something that people can (choose to) do. If health *is* behaviour, then it can be controlled. However, my informants also talked about the effect that this behaviour would have. Sometimes they did this in a general way and sometimes in terms of specific diseases. For instance, although diabetes and heart disease were common in Tamara's family history, she thought she would not get them 'if I don't eat much sugar'.

The extent to which people exhibit healthy behaviour depends on their assessment of the risk of ill health. On the one hand, it is generally thought that young people believe they are invincible, leading to risky behaviours and inactivity regarding their health (Wickman, Anderson and Greenberg 2008).[22] On the other hand, fatalistic attitudes to health, such as those described by Senior (2003, 157–58, 175–76),[23] can also inhibit people from taking good care of their health, as they do not

22 However, there is some evidence that adolescents are concerned about their health, health risk factors and health-related needs (Ott et al. 2011; Waters, Stewart-Brown and Fitzpatrick 2003). Additionally, rates of smoking and risky drinking among young people have decreased, and the age of first drinking and smoking has increased (Australian Institute of Health and Welfare 2017, 11–12, 24), indicating a shift away from unhealthy behaviours.

23 Many people in Ngukurr had a fatalistic attitude to health because of lay epidemiologies and a sense of a lack of control over health.

expect their behaviour to make a difference. Neither appeared to be the case among the young women in Katherine. Discussions around their future health showed that they were aware of the high risk of contracting certain diseases because they were prevalent in their families. Although this made some young women unsure about their future health, they still believed that healthy behaviour would positively affect their health, and their attitudes appeared more realistic than fatalistic. In general, family histories of specific diseases made informants take more action regarding their health rather than becoming passive:

> The fact that I have high cholesterol and I have such a big family history of poor health, I think that's what sort of motivated me a little bit more to keep my health a little more on the positive side because at the end of the day, everything that I do to my body is going to affect me in the future. It doesn't matter how small. Whatever I put into my body today is going to affect me in twenty years down the track. So it does worry me in the sense that I've already got everything against me. (Robyn, 20 years old)

The young women in this study showed a strong view of individual responsibility for health. Statements such as 'We can help, but in the end it's your body' from May, who worked as a service provider, and 'If you really wanted to get healthy, you'll do it' (Channy), show the view that the final responsibility lies with the individual person. This idea was not only applied to other people but also extended to themselves, as they all expressed the view that they should keep eating healthy foods and exercising for their future health. This emphasis on individual behaviour assumes that choices are made on an individualistic basis in a social vacuum, not recognising the structural impacts on people's behaviour (Cockerham 2005). Further questioning revealed that the young women's behaviour was influenced by their circumstances—for example, when their family or the boarding house determined what food was available to them. On a broader level, Robyn declared her disgust for fast food outlets, especially McDonalds, on several occasions. She asserted that the government needed to step in to make them less available and to have more fresh fruit and vegetables available in Katherine. Other young women agreed with this, but they struggled to come up with anything else that could change at the community level, reflecting the emphasis on individual behaviour.

Use of Health Care Services

An often used model for analysing health care systems, Kleinman's (1980) distinguishes between popular, professional and folk sectors. Each sector has its own aetiology, treatment methods and practitioners. In this model, health care providers and services are labelled as belonging to either the traditional/folk sector or the Western biomedical/professional sector. The underlying assumption is that what people perceive as the cause of their illness determines their choice of treatment, with the treatment residing in the same sector as the perceived cause of the illness. In line with this thinking, Aboriginal and biomedical health systems have been viewed as conflicting and mutually exclusive by both researchers and Aboriginal people (see Saethre 2007). However, research in remote communities has shown that the choice of health practitioner is often not based on the presumed diagnosis, but on other factors such as the practitioner's gender, whether the patient is familiar with the practitioner (i.e. has a connection), cost and convenience (McCoy 2008; Saethre 2007). This section discusses the health care–seeking behaviour of the Indigenous young women in Katherine who participated in this study, focusing on their use of Wurli, the ACCHO in Katherine.

All of the young women I interviewed had been to a doctor in the previous few months. The main reasons were for general and sexual health check-ups, cold and flu, and feeling sick in general. Other reasons included tonsillitis, pregnancy tests, boils, migraines, a check-up for a broken arm, runny ears, having collapsed and feeling very tired, and having a swollen leg and being unable to walk. Some young women elaborated that a check-up can include a diabetes check, and that check-ups are done 'to see if my heart and kidneys and all that are all right' (Channy).

The young women all attended Wurli. Although some had accessed other clinics in town (e.g. Kintore Clinic and Gorge Health), the majority went to Wurli when they needed to see a general practitioner. Most had been to the local hospital.[24] The hospital was accessed for more serious conditions, such as pneumonia, meliodosis[25] and broken bones, or on

24 Indigenous people from remote communities are often reluctant to go to hospital due to loneliness, perceiving hospitals as places where people die, and also because of communication problems with medical staff (Brady 2003; Senior 2003, 127–28; Shahid, Finn and Thompson 2009). These factors did not play a significant role in Katherine (Friderichs 2018).

25 Meliodosis is a bacterial disease transmitted through contact with soil that is widespread in tropical northern Australia.

weekends when Wurli was closed. Some informants had been to a dentist when younger, but they did not go anymore. Other health services were also used, including a chiropractor, physiotherapist, podiatrist, dietician and the Royal Darwin Hospital, but use of these services was rare.

Drawing a distinction between Aboriginal and Western health systems is useful when comparing traditional healers with Western doctors and clinics. However, ACCHOs do not neatly fit in this model. ACCHOs have been operating since the 1970s, providing health care to Indigenous people who may not access mainstream services due to factors such as cost and racism (Marles, Frame and Royce 2012). Their acceptance among Indigenous people varies. In several remote communities, the local clinic is perceived as an outside, non-Indigenous institution (Saethre 2007; Chenhall and Senior 2017). In Katherine, young women identified the care at Wurli as biomedical and, as such, not different from the care delivered at other clinics. The difference lay in the fact that Wurli was an Indigenous-specific service, providing a culturally safe environment. Although there are no clear-cut criteria for measuring the 'Indigenous friendliness' of services, such criteria can include having Indigenous staff, an Indigenous board of directors and CEO, and a reconciliation action plan; providing cultural awareness training to all staff; using culturally appropriate materials; the physical layout of the service; how many Indigenous people they serve; and being non-judgemental and community focused (Fredericks 2014; Whop et al. 2012; interviews conducted with service providers). Young women in Katherine mainly went to Wurli because they were 'used to going there'. Other reasons for preferring Wurli included having family that worked there, the fact that Wurli had Indigenous staff, the ample time taken to discuss health concerns, the lack of cost, the provision of transport, the ability to walk in without an appointment, short waiting times, and the presence of helpful and friendly staff.

Confidentiality is often mentioned as a barrier to accessing ACCHOs, especially for sensitive issues such as testing for sexually transmitted infections (STIs) and pregnancy. Aboriginal health practitioners are often known to patients as they may be community members and relatives (Hengel et al. 2015; James, Cameron and Usherwood 2009). This was clearly the case in Katherine, where many young women had relatives working at Wurli. Whereas I only heard of one instance of an actual breach in confidentiality, most of the young women worried about confidentiality when accessing Wurli. When asked why, they all replied in a similar way: 'because I know them, I know how they are, I know how they talk'. Regardless of whether confidentiality was actually a problem at Wurli, the fact that young women perceived it as a risk when going there could influence their willingness to seek health care. Young people run significant risks in damaging their reputations among their peers if they find out they have an STI (Senior et al. 2014).

Worldwide, indigenous health services have been found to be the most suitable to address the barriers that indigenous people experience accessing primary health care (Davy et al. 2016). Nevertheless, criticism of ACCHOs on the grounds that they duplicate already existing medical services have been expressed (see Saggers and Gray 1991b, 405). Some of the young women in this study, as well as some older women of their mothers' and grandmothers' generations, did not go to Wurli when they needed health care, but they nonetheless thought it was good that the service was there. They felt that Wurli was good for 'Indigenous people', but did not consider that they needed this type of support themselves. They were positive about Wurli's practice of employing Aboriginal health practitioners who speak Kriol,[26] use of promotional material that is more visual and in simpler language than other clinics, and connections with communities. One woman, who was more comfortable using other health services, showed strong support for Wurli, not because of how it operated, but because of its symbolic role. She considered the existence of ACCHOs as a healing pathway and an acknowledgement of the history of Aboriginal people.

Despite valuing Wurli as an Indigenous-friendly service, there was a strong tendency among the young women in the study to feel that health and social services should be for everyone. This was supported by statements such as: 'I really don't like to see black and white separate. We're all humans. We should respect each other for what we really are' (Channy) and 'Wurli needs to be for more than just Indigenous people. It doesn't matter what race you are, your health is always still important' (Robyn). In addition, many Indigenous young women felt that having special services for them could create jealousy and racism from non-Indigenous people.

Some informants said that, for them, it did not matter whether they went to Wurli or a *munanga*[27] clinic, and that for mental health they would rather talk with an unknown, non-Indigenous person. However, these

26 Kriol is the creole language spoken by Indigenous people in the Top End of Australia.

27 *Munanga* is the regional word for non-Indigenous person.

statements were not supported by their actual behaviour, as they always went to Wurli. The culturally safe feeling they experienced at Wurli may have been implicit; they may not have realised or considered that other clinics might feel different. Familiarity with a service was an important consideration when accessing health care, and this would be lacking at other services. I also noticed that it often took the young women several conversations to open up to me, and that they only discussed their worries at places that felt supportive and safe, such as the church and the camps that some of them attended, and with friends and cousins. Notwithstanding the fact that many did not agree with Wurli excluding non-Indigenous people, having an Indigenous-friendly health service was crucial to many of them, even if they did not always realise or appreciate this.

Bush Medicine and Traditional Healing

One of the things that struck me during my research was that bush medicine and traditional healing were more common than I had expected. It was difficult to find out much about bush medicine and traditional healing before I started my fieldwork. Government reports about the health of Indigenous people in Katherine did not include any information about it (e.g. Li et al. 2011; Tay, Li and Guthridge 2013), and little research overall has been done on bush medicine and traditional healing in towns.[28] During my initial conversations in Katherine, no one talked about it. This type of healing was not part of the rhetoric around health. When I asked about it specifically, most people told me that it was rare in Katherine and emphasised that it was more common in remote communities (see Chapter 5) and in Central Australia, specifically noting that medical professionals in Alice Springs were more accepting of traditional healing. Some people expressed secrecy surrounding it: 'If it's going on, I don't hear of it, like. I know it could be hush-hush. It could be like a hush-hush thing'. The health organisation that serviced communities east of Katherine claimed on its website that 'incorporating traditional healing and the use of bush medicines' was one of their goals

28 One study that looked at the use of bush medicine and traditional healers in Katherine included only Indigenous people 40 years and older, thus excluding the views and experiences of young people. Although reported familiarity with, and occasional use of, bush medicines and traditional healers were 52 per cent and 35 per cent, respectively, only 4.9 per cent of participants had used bush medicines in the two weeks preceding the interview. In contrast, 82.2 per cent of people had used prescribed or over the counter medicines (Sevo 2003).

(Sunrise Health Service 2018), yet Wurli (n.d.), which claimed to be culturally appropriate, did not mention bush medicine or traditional healing on their website.

Later interviews and observations revealed that bush medicine and traditional healing were still being used in Katherine. Nevertheless, people's experiences with it varied. Although most young women claimed to have some familiarity with bush medicine, their knowledge about it was limited.[29] They could rarely tell me the name, look and use of certain plants. They gave descriptions such as 'there's this yellow flower. I can't remember the name' (Tamara) and 'use for bathing' (Julia), but rarely anything more concrete than that. Only a few of the young women had experience with traditional healing, and these experiences did not take place in Katherine.

There are two main ways in which Indigenous young women in Katherine learn about bush medicine and these mirror the ways of learning that Merlan (1998, 102) documented over two decades ago. The first was by 'observation, imitation, and internalisation of ways of doing things'. The second, which was more common among younger people in Merlan's (1998) research, treated Aboriginal culture in a more objectified, explicitly teachable, way. Reflections of these two ways of learning could still be seen and were mostly linked to how young women identified. Those for whom Indigenous identity was unquestioned learned about bush medicine from their family and elders as a part of everyday life. It was used for sickness; for example, Sarah told me her 'nanna' made her soak in a bath with *dumbuyumbu* (see Chapter 5) when she had chicken pox as a child. Learning occurred when family members took the young women out bush to collect bush medicine. Most informants who had learned about bush medicine in this way did not express any specific reasons for wanting to learn about it.

Those young women whose Indigenous identity was more ambiguous did not use bush medicine primarily for sickness and nor was it a part of their everyday life. They understood bush medicine as part of their culture and, therefore, as part of their identity as an Indigenous person. These young women expressed an explicit desire to learn about bush medicine

29 At least partly, this can be explained by the fact that acquiring this knowledge and the authority to speak about it comes with age (Dickson 2015, 37).

and other aspects of Aboriginal culture. In contrast to those for whom bush medicine was a part of daily life, they learned about it from various language groups, not family members.

One way in which the practise of bush medicine was becoming more formalised and less the domain of families was through the Banatjarl Strongbala Wumin Grup (hereafter Banatjarl), which was formed in 2003 (Jawoyn Association Aboriginal Corporation 2016). Banatjarl aims to save and bring back cultural knowledge, collaborate with other organisations in the Katherine region, and reduce violence and substance dependency among Aboriginal people. Several adult women mentioned Banatjarl as the place where they obtained bush medicine. This included women living in Katherine itself as well as in surrounding communities. These women referred to Banatjarl as soon as I brought up bush medicine and did not refer to any collection or preparation of bush medicine in the community itself. In addition to obtaining bush medicines through Banatjarl, some also stated that their children learned about bush medicine through this organisation. Besides providing bush medicine to people for whom acquiring it might otherwise be difficult, Banatjarl endeavoured to reintroduce and spread knowledge about bush medicine. They were teaching about bush medicine in primary and high schools and to medical students. They held bush medicine workshops at public events open to Indigenous and non-Indigenous people, such as the Women of the World Festival, a National Sorry Day event, NAIDOC week and the Barunga Festival, where they also sold containers with bush medicine. Bush medicine made during a private healing camp of Stolen Generations women was used specifically as a healing tool.

In all these instances, the plant that was used was *Marangmarang*. Dickson (2015, 284–85) and Senior (2003, 303) have described its traditional preparation at Ngukurr, which involves crushing and inhaling the leaves for colds, boiling the leaves and drinking the extract like a tea, or using it as a wash for colds, flu, sinus congestion, diarrhoea, sores and skin infections. Taking a distinctly modern approach, Banatjarl mixed *Marangmarang* 'with some contemporary ingredients'. When I observed and assisted in making this bush medicine, it was made with olive oil and bees wax. The women from Banatjarl told me that they used to use emu or goanna oil, but they changed to using olive oil from the supermarket. They used a mortar and pestle, and modern equipment such as plastic containers, measuring cups, kitchen scales and a gas stove. This was the only preparation of bush medicine I encountered during my fieldwork, although I have been told of other uses such as boiling the plant to make tea.

Some participants understood the Aboriginal and the biomedical health system to be mutually exclusive and subscribed to the idea that the cause of the illness determined the choice of treatment (Kleinman 1980, 90). For example, several young women said that, if women went to a men's dreaming site and got sick, they had to go to a traditional healer. During one interview, Channy and Brianna imagined what a Western doctor would say if someone came to them with an illness with a supernatural cause. In a tone suggestive of hearing an impossible idea, they said: 'Sorry? Sorry what's the trouble you wanna get help for?' This view was also conveyed the other way around: most of the young women I interviewed thought that, with a disease such as cancer or diabetes, people needed to visit a Western doctor, not a traditional healer. In fact, though the young women were not aware of this, Sonia had started using traditional medicine for what are regarded as biomedical diseases. This included giving a traditional massage to a stroke patient, and using bush medicine made from green ants, a lemongrass treatment, and massage on a cancer patient.

As mentioned above, numerous factors can influence the choice of practitioner (McCoy 2008; Saethre 2007). Location proved to be a major determinant in this study, with people saying that healing ceremonies happened out bush, whereas in town sick people went to Wurli or the hospital. Bush medicines are region specific, so, for the young women who came from other areas in Australia, the medicine that their language group used was not always available in Katherine. Having the time and knowledge to prepare medications is another inhibiting factor (Senior 2003); however, the provision of bush medicine in Katherine by Banatjarl partly solves this issue.

In terms of Kleinman's (1980) model, the Aboriginal health system cannot just be opposed to the biomedical model. It consists of two separate parts that need to be understood differently. Traditional healing can be seen as part of Kleinman's folk system: there are specialised healers with knowledge and skills that are not widely shared in the community. Bush medicine, on the other hand, is part of the popular sector: it comprises non-specialised knowledge of home remedies by lay people. In Katherine, a noticeable shift is occurring. In the past, knowledge about bush medicine was held by everyone; it was transmitted within the family and its preparation and use occurred in the popular sector as self-treatment. However, at the time of my research, bush medicine was becoming more institutionalised and increasingly part of the folk sector through Banatjarl. Comprehensive knowledge about it was only held by some people, and it was being transferred in a professional manner, such as during workshops. This study's intercultural context, in which the expression of Indigenous identity and culture is salient, as well as non-Indigenous people's growing interest in traditional medicine, were factors affecting these changes.

Discussion

Contrary to the views of non-Indigenous health workers in Katherine who suggest that Aboriginal people do not think about health because health is a 'Western concept', this study clearly demonstrates that some Aboriginal girls and young women *do* think about health. Humans are adept at learning new things and new ideas. In an intercultural space (Merlan 2005) such as Katherine, learning across cultures is to be expected. Certainly, the young Aboriginal women I was privileged to spend time with have absorbed Western health messages regarding the benefits of eating healthy food and regular exercise.

The provision of information is an important first step in a public health effort to change individual behaviour, but other factors, both psychological and sociocultural, require attention. People have to want to change; they also have to believe that it is possible to change. The young people involved in this study valued their health and many expressed the desire for a long life. They had learnt that their behaviour affected their future wellbeing. However, additional factors must be identified before substantial changes in health behaviours can be achieved. These include factors that limit control over health behaviour arising from the intercultural environment.

Often, ethnographic studies of Indigenous health focus on remote Australia. Yet, many young Indigenous women live in towns where they are likely exposed to a more diverse array of social and cultural arrangements, many of which may influence their health beliefs and behaviour. There is increasing recognition that the circumstances of Indigenous people in remote communities can be understood as intercultural (e.g. Merlan 2005; Burbank 2011). However, there may be more defined cultural boundaries between Aboriginal and non-Aboriginal people in remote communities; in remote communities, non-Indigenous people are almost always outsiders and are rarely permanent residents. Towns, in contrast, may be the lifelong homes of both Indigenous and non-Indigenous populations. Distinct groups of people, who may have different ways of making sense of the world, live in Katherine (Merlan 2005,169). Mutual influence is apparent and strict distinctions between Aboriginal and non-Aboriginal domains—between tradition and modernity—are often difficult to identify (Merlan 1998, 4). This observation is especially relevant for understanding young people who attend school, have multicultural friendships and engage in activities, such as sports, that are open to both Aboriginal and non-Aboriginal youth. Of course, cultures can and do change and there are always differences within cultures. There are also differences within individuals (Agar 1996) and an array of ideas about health can exist within one person.

The fact that the young women in this study defined health as eating good food and keeping fit does not mean they are completely Westernised. At the same time, their Indigenous identity should not be essentialised; being Indigenous does not mean that they will *only* use Indigenous-specific services or that they do not think about the concept of 'health'. Bush medicine and traditional healing can continue to be important for them (as a part of their identity if not as a health remedy) even if it is not important to their peers. Change is apparent everywhere; change is especially important to recognise in intercultural settings such as Katherine where the distribution of new beliefs and practices many be uneven. For example, the young Aboriginal women and girls I spoke to emphasised similarities with non-Indigenous people, but it is difficult to imagine older people doing this.[30] Thus, Indigenous young women's health beliefs and behaviour, as well as their sense of identity, should be seen as a product of everyday interactions within a dynamic and intercultural context.

30 For example, in Bourke (New South Wales), a town with a population composition similar to that of Katherine, people emphasised the perceived boundaries between the two groups rather than the overlap (Cowlishaw 2004, Ch. 5).

References

Agar, M. 1996. *The Professional Stranger: An Informal Introduction to Ethnography*. 2nd ed. San Diego: Academic Press.

Atkinson, J. 2002. *Trauma Trails, Recreating Song Lines: The Transgenerational Effects of Trauma in Indigenous Australia*. North Melbourne: Spinifex Press.

Australian Bureau of Statistics. 2018. '2016 Census QuickStats: Katherine'. Last modified 19 September 2020. www.censusdata.abs.gov.au/census_services/getproduct/census/2016/quickstat/UCL714001?opendocument.

Australian Institute of Health and Welfare. 2017. *National Drug Strategy Household Survey 2016: Detailed Findings*. Drug Statistics Series, no. 31. Cat. no. PHE 214. Canberra: AIHW. doi.org/10.258/5ec5bc1bed176.

Bernard, H. R. 2011. *Research Methods in Anthropology: Qualitative and Quantitative Approaches*. Lanham, MD: AltaMira Press.

Boddington, P. and U. Räisänen, U. 2009. 'Theoretical and Practical Issues in the Definition of Health: Insights from Aboriginal Australia'. *Journal of Medicine and Philosophy* 34 (1): 49–67. doi.org/10.1093/jmp/jhn035.

Brady, M. 1995. 'WHO Defines Health? Implications of Differing Definitions on Discourse and Practice in Aboriginal Health'. In *Aboriginal Health: Social and Cultural Transitions*, edited by G. Robinson, 187–92. Darwin: NTU Press.

Brady, M. 2003. 'Health Care in Remote Australian Indigenous Communities'. *Lancet* 362 (s1): 36–37. doi.org/10.1016/S0140-6736(03)15069-6.

Bukman, A. J., D. Teuscher, E. J. M. Feskens, M. A. v. Baak, A. Meershoek and R. J. Renes. 2014. 'Perceptions on Healthy Eating, Physical Activity and Lifestyle Advice: Opportunities for Adapting Lifestyle Interventions to Individuals with Low Socioeconomic Status'. *BMC Public Health* 14 (1): 1036. doi.org/10.1186/1471-2458-14-1036.

Burbank, V. K. 1988. *Aboriginal Adolescence: Maidenhood in an Aboriginal Community*. New Brunswick: Rutgers University Press.

Burbank, V. K. 2011. *An Ethnography of Stress: The Social Determinants of Health in Aboriginal Australia*. New York: Palgrave Macmillan. doi.org/10.1057/9780230117228.

Burgess, P. and J. Morrison. 2007. 'Country'. In *Social Determinants of Indigenous Health*, edited by B. Carson, T. Dunbar, R. Chenhall and R. Bailie, 177–202. Crows Nest, NSW: Allen & Unwin.

Calma, T. 2008. 'Indigenous Health and Human Rights'. *Australian Journal of Human Rights* 14 (1), 21–39. doi.org/10.1080/1323238X.2008.11910844.

Carson, B., T. Dunbar, R. D. Chenhall and R. Bailie. 2007. *Social Determinants of Indigenous Health*. Crows Nest, NSW: Allen & Unwin.

Chenhall, R. and K. Senior. 2009. '"Those Young People All Crankybella": Indigenous Youth Mental Health and Globalization'. *International Journal of Mental Health* 38 (3), 28–43. doi.org/10.2753/IMH0020-7411380302.

Chenhall R. D. and K. Senior. 2017. 'Living the Social Determinants of Health: Assemblages in a Remote Aboriginal Community'. *Medical Anthropology Quarterly* 32 (2): 177–95. doi.org/10.1111/maq.12418.

Cockerham, W. C. 2005. 'Health Lifestyle Theory and the Convergence of Agency and Structure'. *Journal of Health and Social Behavior* 46 (1): 51–67. doi.org/10.1177/002214650504600105.

Cowlishaw, G. 2004. *Blackfellas, Whitefellas, and The Hidden Injuries of Race*. Malden, MA: Blackwell Publishing.

Davy, C., S. Harfield, A. McArthur, Z. Munn and A. Brown. 2016. 'Access to Primary Health Care Services for Indigenous Peoples: A Framework Synthesis'. *International Journal for Equity in Health* 15: 163. doi.org/10.1186/s12939-016-0450-5.

Department of Families Housing Community Services and Indigenous Affairs. 2012. *Closing the Gap: Prime Minister's Report 2012*. Canberra: Department of Families, Housing, Community Services and Indigenous Affairs.

Department of Families Housing Community Services and Indigenous Affairs. 2013. *Closing the Gap: Prime Minister's Report 2013*. Canberra: Department of Families, Housing, Community Services and Indigenous Affairs.

Dickson, G. F. 2015. *Marra and Kriol: The Loss and Maintenance of Knowledge across a Language Shift Boundary*. Canberra: The Australian National University.

Eickelkamp, U. 2011. *Growing Up in Central Australia: New Anthropological Studies of Aboriginal Childhood and Adolescence*. New York: Berghahn Books.

Fredericks, B. 2014. 'There is Nothing That Identifies Me to That Place': Indigenous Women's Perceptions of Health Spaces and Places'. In *History, Power, Text: Cultural Studies and Indigenous Studies*, edited by T. Neals, C. McKinnon and E. Vincent, 291–309. Sydney: UTS ePress. doi.org/10.5130/978-0-9872369-1-3.r.

Friderichs, M. S. 2018. '"They Do Think about Health"—Health, Culture and Identity in Katherine'. PhD thesis, Charles Darwin University.

Heath, S., R. Brooks, E. Cleaver and E. Ireland. 2009. *Researching Young People's Lives*. London: SAGE Publications. doi.org/10.4135/9781446249420.

Hengel, B., R. Guy, L. Garton, J. Ward, A. Rumbold, D. Taylor-Thomson and L. Maher. 2015. 'Barriers and Facilitators of Sexually Transmissible Infection Testing in Remote Australian Aboriginal Communities: Results from the Sexually Transmitted Infections in Remote Communities, Improved and Enhanced Primary Health Care (STRIVE) Study'. *Sexual Health* 12 (1): 4–12. doi.org/10.1071/SH14080.

Hinkson, M. 2010. 'Introduction: Anthropology and the Culture Wars'. In *Culture Crisis: Anthropology and Politics in Aboriginal Australia*, edited by J. C. Altman and M. Hinkson. Sydney: University of New South Wales Press.

Hinkson, M. and B. Smith. 2005. 'Introduction: Conceptual Moves towards an Intercultural Analysis'. *Oceania* 75 (3): 157–66. doi.org/10.1002/j.1834-4461.2005.tb02877.x.

James, J., S. Cameron and T. Usherwood. 2009. 'The Practice of Confidentiality in an Aboriginal Medical Service: What Do GPs Need to Know?' *Australian Family Physician* 38 (10): 837–42.

Jawoyn Association Aboriginal Corporation. 2016. 'Banatjarl Women and Centre'. Accessed 21 September 2020, www.jawoyn.org.au/community/banatjarl.

Johansson, H., L. Weinehall and M. Emmelin. 2009. '"It Depends on What You Mean": A Qualitative Study of Swedish Health Professionals' Views on Health and Health Promotion'. *BMC Health Services Research* 9 (1): 191. doi.org/10.1186/1472-6963-9-191.

Kearney, W. J. 1988. *Jawoyn (Katherine Area) Land Claim: Report by the Aboriginal Land Commissioner to the Minister for Aboriginal Affairs and to the Administrator of the Northern Territory*. Canberra: Australian Government Publishing Service.

Kleinman, A. 1980. *Patients and Healers in the Context of Culture: An Exploration of the Borderland between Anthropology, Medicine, and Psychiatry*. Berkeley: University of California Press. doi.org/10.1525/9780520340848.

Lea, T. 2008. *Bureaucrats and Bleeding Hearts: Indigenous Health in Northern Australia*. Sydney: University of NSW Press.

Li, S. Q., S. Guthridge, E. Tursan d'Espaignet and B. Paterson. 2006. *From Infancy to Young Adulthood: Health Status in the Northern Territory 2006.* Darwin: Department of Health and Community Services. Accessed 8 June 2021, digitallibrary.health.nt.gov.au/dspace/bitstream/10137/84/1/infancy_to_young_adulthood_2006.pdf.

Li, S. Q., S. Pircher, S. Guthridge, J. Condon and J. Wright. 2011. *Hospital Admissions in the Northern Territory, 1976 to 2008.* Darwin: Department of Health.

Maher, P. 1999. 'A Review of 'Traditional' Aboriginal Health Beliefs'. *Australian Journal of Rural Health* 7 (4): 229–36. doi.org/10.1046/j.1440-1584.1999.00264.x.

Marles, E., C. Frame and M. Royce. 2012. 'The Aboriginal Medical Service Redfern: Improving Access to Primary Care for Over 40 Years'. *Australian Family Physician* 41 (6): 433–36.

Marmot, M. 2011. 'Social Determinants and the Health of Indigenous Australians'. *Medical Journal of Australia* 194 (10): 512–13. doi.org/10.5694/j.1326-5377.2011.tb03086.x.

Marmot, M. and R. Wilkinson. 2006. *Social Determinants of Health.* 2nd ed. Oxford: Oxford University Press. doi.org/10.1093/acprof:oso/9780198565895.001.0001.

McCarthy, M. 2006. 'Transport and health'. In *Social Determinants of Health*, edited by M. Marmot and R. Wilkinson. Oxford: Oxford University Press.

McCoy, B. F. 2008. 'Outside the Ward and Clinic: Healing the Aboriginal Body'. *Journal of Contemporary Ethnography* 37 (2): 226–45. doi.org/10.1177/0891241607312486.

Merlan, F. 1998. *Caging the Rainbow: Places, Politics, and Aborigines in a North Australian Town.* Honolulu: University of Hawai'i Press. doi.org/10.1515/9780824861742.

Merlan, F. 2005. 'Explorations towards Intercultural Accounts of Socio-Cultural Reproduction and Change'. *Oceania* 75 (3): 167–82. doi.org/10.1002/j.1834-4461.2005.tb02878.x.

National Aboriginal Health Strategy Working Party. 1989. *A National Aboriginal Health Strategy.* Canberra: Department of Aboriginal Affairs.

Nazroo, J. Y. and D. R. Williams. 2006. 'The Social Determination of Ethnic/Racial Inequalities in Health'. In *Social Determinants of Health*, edited by M. Marmot and R. Wilkinson. Oxford: Oxford University Press.

Northern Territory Stolen Generations Aboriginal Corporation. 2019. [Home page]. Accessed 21 September 2020, www.ntsgac.org.au/.

Ott, M. A., J. G. Rosenberger, K. R. McBride and S. G. Woodcox. 2011. 'How Do Adolescents View Health? Implications for State Health Policy'. *Journal of Adolescent Health* 48 (4): 398–403. doi.org/10.1016/j.jadohealth.2010.07.019.

Reid, J. 1983. *Sorcerers and Healing Spirits.* Canberra: Australian National University Press.

Saethre, E. J. 2007. 'Conflicting Traditions, Concurrent Treatment: Medical Pluralism in Remote Aboriginal Australia'. *Oceania* 77 (1): 95–110. doi.org/10.1002/j.1834-4461.2007.tb00007.x.

Saggers, S. and D. Gray. 1991a. *Aboriginal Health and Society: The Traditional and Contemporary Aboriginal Struggle for Better Health*. North Sydney: Allen & Unwin.

Saggers, S. and D. Gray. 1991b. 'Policy and Practice in Aboriginal Health'. In *The Health of Aboriginal Australia*, edited by J. Reid and P. Trompf, 381–420. Sydney: Harcourt Brace.

Senior, K. 2003. 'A Gudbala Laif? Health and Wellbeing in a Remote Aboriginal Community—What Are the Problems and Where Lies The Responsibility?' PhD thesis, The Australian National University, Canberra.

Senior, K., J. Helmer, R. Chenhall and V. K. Burbank. 2014. '"Young Clean and Safe?" Young People's Perceptions of Risk from Sexually Transmitted Infections in Regional, Rural and Remote Australia'. *Culture, Health & Sexuality* 16 (4): 453–66. doi.org/10.1080/13691058.2014.888096.

Sevo, G. 2003. *A Multidimensional Assessment of Health and Functional Status in Older Aboriginal Australians from Katherine and Lajamanu, Northern Territory.* Canberra: The Australian National University.

Shahid, S., L. D. Finn and S. C. Thompson. 2009. 'Barriers to Participation of Aboriginal People in Cancer Care: Communication in the Hospital Setting'. *Medical Journal of Australia* 190 (10): 574–79. doi.org/10.5694/j.1326-5377.2009.tb02569.x.

Sunrise Health Service. 2018. [Home page]. Accessed 21 September 2020, www.sunrise.org.au/sunrise/sunrisestory.htm.

Tay, E. L., S. Q. Li and S. Guthridge. 2013. *Mortality in the Northern Territory, 1967–2006.* Darwin: Department of Health.

Vingilis, E., T. Wade and J. Seeley. 2007. 'Predictors of Adolescent Health Care Utilization'. *Journal of Adolescence* 30: 773–800. doi.org/10.1016/j.adolescence.2006.10.001.

Waters, E., S. Stewart-Brown and R. Fitzpatrick. 2003. 'Agreement between Adolescent Self Report and Parent Reports of Health and Well-Being: Results of an Epidemiological Study'. *Child: Care, Health and Development* 29 (6): 501–09. doi.org/10.1046/j.1365-2214.2003.00370.x.

Whop, L., G. Garvey, K. Lokuge, K. Mallitt and P. Valery. 2012. 'Cancer Support Services: Are They Appropriate and Accessible for Indigenous Cancer Patients in Queensland, Australia?' *Rural and Remote Health* 12 (3): 2018.

Wickman, M. E., N. L. R. Anderson and C. S. Greenberg. 2008. 'The Adolescent Perception of Invincibility and Its Influence on Teen Acceptance of Health Promotion Strategies'. *Journal of Pediatric Nursing* 23 (6): 460–68. doi.org/10.1016/j.pedn.2008.02.003.

World Health Organization. 1986. 'Ottawa Charter for Health Promotion', 21 November. Accessed 8 June 2021, www.who.int/healthpromotion/conferences/previous/ottawa/en/.

World Health Organization. 2003. *Adolescent Friendly Health Services: An Agenda for Change*. Accessed 8 June 2021, apps.who.int/iris/handle/10665/67923.

Wurli-Wurlinjang Health Service. n.d. [Home page]. Accessed 21 September 2020, www.wurli.org.au.

Yuan, N. P., J. Bartgis and D. Demers. 2014. 'Promoting Ethical Research with American Indian and Alaska Native People Living in Urban Areas'. *American Journal of Public Health* 104 (11): 2085–91. doi.org/10.2105/AJPH.2014.302027.

7

Growing Up Fast in Two Remote Aboriginal Communities

Sue McMullen

In this chapter, I focus on how young Aboriginal women find sexual partners, often with a view to marriage and child-bearing, in two communities. The first is a remote Aboriginal community that is restricted: non-residents must obtain a permit to enter (hereafter 'the community'). I lived and worked as a nurse in the community for several years. The second is a town, in the sense that there is unrestricted movement of both Indigenous and non-Indigenous people, but it is still a remote community (hereafter 'the town'). It is situated on the edge of Arnhem Land and is close to major mining developments. As such, the town has regular contact with non-Indigenous workers. A steady stream of non-Indigenous tourists also visit, attracted by fishing opportunities in the area. In contrast to the community, alcohol is readily available in the town. I visited the town regularly over a period of three years while researching my PhD thesis. Both places are connected through country and kinship relationships with family members travelling from one community to the other for funerals, ceremonies and social visits. In both, young Indigenous women appear to be growing up fast and forming sexual relationships in the early years of adolescence.

Two bodies of evidence inform this chapter. The first is based on my experience as a nurse in the community, with responsibility (among many other things) for the sexual health of young people. During this period, my view of young people's sexual relationships was narrow, confined to health education initiatives and point of care at the clinic. In terms of the numbers of teenage pregnancies and sexually transmitted infections, I was able to observe the scope of the issue, but I was not in a position to understand the motivation of young women and the decisions they made regarding their relationships. In 2012, I began my PhD research in the town of Boroloola. During this time, I lived in the town and was able to observe the lives and interactions of young women, as well as how their actions were perceived by older members of the community. My participant observation was supplemented by in-depth interviews with women and workshops exploring sexual decision-making. Many of the young women were reluctant to talk to me; therefore, explanations for some of the behaviours I observed were obtained from older women, whose perspectives may have been influenced both by their concern for, and propensity to critique, the younger generation.

Early sexual experience can have significant effects on the sexual and reproductive health of young Indigenous women, including higher rates of underage pregnancy and sexually transmitted infections. Such women and their children often experience negative long-term outcomes (Stark and Hope 2007). Early sexual relationships can also influence developmental outcomes, as those who are sexually active can disengage from education. This is due to the late nights in which young people carve out their personal space and time away from the eyes of adults (Senior and Chenhall 2008). They may have minimal knowledge about life choices that are not linked to relationships and reproduction (McMullen 2015). Premature reproduction, generally, is associated with negative or less than optimal outcomes for children (Brumbach, Figueredo and Ellis 2009). Very little is known about how Indigenous youths negotiate relationships, define risk, conceptualise their sexuality and sexual decision-making, or how their views may be influenced by the culture and society in which they live (Senior 2003). Indigenous sexual and reproductive health has long been a priority with successive governments. Many interventions (Guy et al. 2012) have been designed to address this issue but, despite some success, particularly in the reduction of sexually transmitted diseases, young Indigenous women continue to bear a significant burden.

Over the years, I have come to appreciate that young Indigenous women, living within a society at least partially governed by customary law, may experience a disconnection from the larger world and its social and cultural norms. Young Indigenous women living in the community and town examined in this chapter have many issues with which to contend. Remote Aboriginal communities have been severely tested by substance misuse and social disruption, a consequence of violent displacement from traditional lands and the introduction of welfare, alcohol and other drugs. Under such circumstances, young Aboriginal women trying to negotiate the perils of early adolescence appear to have no clear pathways (MacDonald and Boulton 2011; Burbank, Senior and McMullen 2015).

The Young Women

As a group, the young Aboriginal women in both the community and the town are difficult to reach. The mid-teenage group who are the focus of my study are intermittent attenders of school and tend to only become visible in the evening when they 'walk around' with groups of friends, usually sisters and cousins (see Senior and Chenhall 2008). Although the behaviours in both the community and town are similar, the appearance of the young women is markedly different. The young women in the community affect a very discrete form of dress, with long skirts (often with shorts underneath) or baggy shorts and tee-shirts. Shoulders and chest are well covered and there is little evidence of hairstyling or make-up. Chenhall et al. (Chapter 2, this volume) argue that, in Ngukurr, a closely related community, attention to dress and make-up constitutes a form of imagined defiance for young women, whose elders and partners exhort them to not stand out. A young woman in a relationship was expected to be as inconspicuous as possible so as not to provoke the jealousy of their partners (Senior and Chenhall 2008). In contrast, the young women in the town wore extremely short and revealing denim shorts and paid attention to their hair and make-up, especially when they were out walking with their friends.

Relationships and Sex

Although achieving a relationship is frequently a driving force in young women's lives, they are often deeply ambivalent about the realities of being in a relationship, especially one that involves babies. Many young women in both the community and the town commented that they had to stay at home all day looking after the house and children and food. Some young women told me that if they did not have food on the table when their husband awoke, they could be 'in for a thrashing' (see also Senior and Chenhall 2012, 380). Going to the shop to buy food and taking their children to the clinic were their main outings. They would also visit family members and, if they had enough money, they might join in a card game. Young women with children said that, although unmarried girls could access the youth centre and its activities, young mothers of the same age were stuck at home with their children. Their days of 'walking around at night' (Senior and Chenhall 2008), and all the fun and danger that represented, were now over (McMullen 2015).

Although most of the young women I spoke with said they would prefer a steady relationship with a loving partner, they were aware that this was not always possible. When they looked around, they saw relationships marred by heavy drinking, drug use and family violence, and many sought a way around this problem. One of the few ways that independence could be achieved was via welfare. Having children on their own allowed them to collect benefits that provided some measure of financial independence. However, this strategy was not without risk, as they were only able to maintain this state of affairs by resisting any form of permanent alliance/marriage with a male partner who may view their income, and indeed their life, as his own. Many women told me that they had endeavoured to keep their own money, but that they were not always successful (McMullen 2015).

Despite the risks, for some young women the 'single mother' life is a key aspiration as it is a means of achieving financial independence; therefore, some young women actively seek and form relationships that support this strategy (see also Chapter 2, this volume). A number of locals in both the community and the town told me that some young girls choose partners for their financial status and/or their ready access to alcohol and other drugs. Not being in a traditional relationship may also mean that young women are able to change partners or add additional partners if the relationship no longer meets their needs, especially in the areas of economic assistance or access to gifts or substances. Further, having casual partners may mean that young women are less likely to become victims of violence. For example, I once heard a young woman say that a woman with a few partners may find that young men fight among themselves for her favour instead of subjecting her to the forms of violence that can occur in more permanent relationships (McMullen 2015).

In order to attract partners, whether temporary or permanent, young women with few resources may rely on their powers of sexual attraction and go to great lengths to obtain appealing clothing, hair styles and jewellery, which is difficult due to their distance from large shops and the high price of such things in small, community shops. Although young women may hold the balance of power in deciding with whom to have sex, they may not have power in deciding how this encounter is managed and this is particularly the case when they try to negotiate condom use. It is well documented that men do not like to use condoms and will endeavour to persuade a woman by various means that a condom is not necessary (Mooney-Somers et al. 2012). Mooney-Somers et al. (2012) have noted that young disadvantaged Indigenous women are most at risk in this area of negotiation. The most obvious risks of unprotected sex are pregnancy and sexually transmitted infections. Although the risk of pregnancy may be managed by other methods such as Implanon (a skin implant that releases estrogen for a period of three years)[1] or the pill, the risk of sexually transmitted infections remains the same. How do young women manage these risks?

The obvious answer is condom usage, but this can depend on a number of factors beyond those just mentioned. Access to condoms can be a problem in both the community and town and can largely depend on the local health clinic's policy. Rather than requiring people to come to the clinic to ask for condoms, health personnel may leave condoms out in a specific area for people to take. There remain significant barriers to young people actually carrying condoms. In Borroloola, I was told by young women that it was a 'shame job' for a woman to carry around condoms. Even if it were not a shame job, young women rarely carry around a hand or shoulder bag, so they would have to stow condoms in their bra if they carried one at all.

Senior and Chenhall (2008, 2012; Chenhall and Senior 2017) have described the imbalance of power between males and females in negotiating sexual encounters, with females reluctant to do anything (such as suggest safe sex) that could potentially anger their partner and encourage them to move to another more willing one. Similarly, the young women in my study said that it could be difficult to get partners to use condoms and that they feared partners would get angry and accuse the young woman of thinking that they might have a disease. They anticipated that this could result in physical violence, which they wished to avoid and so they did

1 Implanon is the most common form of birth control used in remote communities. The Implanon capsule is injected into the upper arm by a doctor or a nurse and can be left in for three years. It is available for women aged 16 years and over.

not insist on condom usage. They also pointed out that, when a young woman is under the influence of alcohol or other substances, she may not even be able to think through the risks involved (McMullen 2015).

There is also the problem of unwelcome sex. Many young women complained to me that, although they did not want sex with a particular man, they might engage in it rather than risk violence (see Senior, Helmer and Chenhall 2017). Although they did not regard this as rape, they would not have had sex if they were not afraid of the potential for violence. Sexual activity under duress appeared to be a perennial problem. Parents were not always able to intervene on their daughters' behalf, even if they knew about the problem, for fear of repercussions from the young man's family. The young man's uncles, I was told, might come to the community with spears to defend his reputation (McMullen 2015).

From my observations and work in both the community and town, looking for a partner appears to follow the same course. At night, young women walk around or attend parties in an effort to find a partner. Once found, a prospective partner must be held onto and defended against the wiles of other young women and this involves sexual relations (Senior and Chenhall 2008; 2012; Burbank et al. 2015).

The use of alcohol and drugs is another part of the picture, and this is where my work differs from that of Senior and Chenhall, who worked in a dry (alcohol-free) community. Older women in the town told me that many young women were having sex when they were drunk and did not appear to care with whom they had it. This invariably causes problems when it comes to the identity of the father if a child is conceived. One young person told me that young men had been known to have sex with their 'sister/cousins' while drunk and were very concerned about the results of this act. Some girls also appeared to be attracted to the idea of receiving food, clothing or other items, which is hardly surprising given the poverty of their circumstances. I have been told by locals that casual liaisons may sometimes involve married Indigenous men or non-Indigenous men and, although some community members have tried to discourage this, people claim that it is now accepted practice (McMullen 2015). In the town, where permits are not required and where there are frequent opportunities for interactions with non-Indigenous men, young females considered that the transient population of contracted workers fulfilled several positive attributes as sexual partners. They were new and different, had access to alcohol and drugs, and were unlikely to require a permanent relationship. As I noted in my field observations in 2012:

> I observed groups of girls heading out of town just after dark. An informant finally told me that these young girls were heading out to the contractor's camp. She said that these young girls were going to the camp to party with the contractors and that it was the 'new and cool place to be'. Here young girls could get grog and gunja in return for sexual favours.

Sex Education

Local people say that Indigenous people do not talk about sexual health in the home as it is not considered appropriate and people express concern that this sort of discussion may lead to young women 'mucking around'. Local schools offer little sexual health information, which is only provided to secondary students. As school attendance among adolescent girls is very poor, many do not receive the information about sexual and reproductive health that other Australian youths receive (McMullen 2015).

Pregnancy and child-bearing are central issues in Indigenous life; however, according to my informants, some families do not educate their daughters about sexual activity and contraception and are accepting of a daughter who falls pregnant at a young age. While they may not approve of their daughter's sexual activity, may growl at the girl and view her behaviour as a 'shame job', they regard the pregnancy as a done deal and there does not appear to be any negative consequences for the young woman (see also Burbank 1988). An informant once told me that many young pregnant girls are frightened about going to the clinic to confirm a pregnancy and will ask their mothers to go with them. A common answer to this is: 'I wasn't standing next to you when you got pregnant was I?' Support, however, is usually forthcoming.

According to Northern Territory Government regulations, any young girl under the age of 16 who is having sex, especially with a man at least two years older than she is, must be reported to a government agency. This is a part of the *Northern Territory National Emergency Response Act 2007* (Australian Government 2007), known as 'the Intervention'. Mandatory reporting causes clinic staff much concern, both because the benefits to the wellbeing of the young woman are not clear and because they dislike violating confidentiality. There has been considerable protest from health professionals and many will not consider mandatory reporting (McMullen 2015).

Pregnancy and Birth

In my experiences as a nurse working in a clinic in Arnhem Land, young women did not come to the clinic for urine pregnancy tests as soon as a period had been missed. They would present at about three months for a confirmation of what they likely already knew. Many women did not present to the clinic at all and it was the eagle-eye of an Aboriginal health worker who would tell the clinic midwife that someone was probably pregnant. Testing and treatment regimens in remote clinics are much the same as in non-Indigenous society. The most common problem in early pregnancy for an Indigenous woman is anaemia, which is usually dealt with by supplying iron tablets and instituting monthly check-ups. Expectant mothers who have rheumatic heart disease are usually sent to Darwin for risk analysis, as are mothers with gestational diabetes. Most pregnancies, however, proceed normally, with check-ups becoming more frequent as the birth approaches (McMullen 2015).

As is noted in the literature, Indigenous women appear to get pregnant for the first time at a much younger age than in non-Indigenous society (Thompson, Zhang and Dempsey 2012). This is not to say that young Indigenous girls or women are necessarily more sexually active than their non-Indigenous counterparts, but that they do not have the same access to sex education, contraception and abortion as young non-Indigenous women. While I was working as a nurse in the Arnhem Land community, I found the lowest age of first pregnancies to be 16 years. More commonly, girls' first pregnancies occurred in their late teens and early 20s. In the town, I talked to girls as young as 12 who were pregnant and found, from the perspective of community members, that 14–16 years was not an uncommon age for first pregnancies. Many of these young girls were having a baby at the same time as their mother. Childbirth occasions fear in many of the young Indigenous women with whom I am familiar. Much of this fear involves the need for women to be removed from the community and from the supports of their families when their due date approaches (usually at 36 weeks).

Although all remote clinics are mandated to have a midwife on staff and antenatal equipment, clinics are not set up for complex medical emergencies. For this reason, women nearing the time of birth are flown out of the community to deliver in the nearest regional centre. For Arnhem Land, this is Gove, and for the MacArthur River area, it is Katherine. If the birth is expected to be difficult, women from both areas may be flown to Darwin.

These arrangements appear to create a stressful environment for new Indigenous mothers. I observed that most young women do not want to be separated from their family members at this time. Yet, they are flown out of the community, often without an escort, such as their partner or mother, to undergo labour in an unfamiliar urban hospital environment. Family members who have the money may seek to visit the urban centre to be with the birthing mother, but this is not always possible. Indigenous women living in urban centres and non-Indigenous women, including those living in remote areas, usually have their family members with them during this time, but remote-living young Indigenous women and girls who have little experience of the non-Indigenous world are sent off to have their babies with strangers (McMullen 2015). As Kildea, Barclay and Tracy (2010) point out in their argument for birthing on country, this removal not only creates stress for the woman and her baby, but also contributes to continuing poor reproductive outcomes by limiting the ability for continuing care in the community for mother and child.

Alcohol and Other Abused Substances

One of the main differences between the community and town is the ready availability of alcohol. I am not claiming that young women in the community do not drink, only that alcohol is not so readily available. By contrast, its presence in the town is all pervasive and often has a detrimental effect on the behaviour of young people. One woman said that young people 'find each other when they are drunk' and that alcohol loosens normal cultural inhibitions. Many older women criticised younger ones, saying that they were only interested in a man as long as he had money and access to substances such as grog and ganja (cannabis). These older women observed that some of the young ones were not interested in marriage and babies at all but preferred to party with anyone who could provide them with alcohol and ganja. They said that some girls did not marry young but lived with their parents or other relatives and had children and liaisons with different men.

Although alcohol and other factors appeared to have eroded community norms, most young women sought a steady partner with whom to raise a family. In the town, a 'young girl', about 14 years old, was pointed out to me and I was told: 'Ahhh, she all married up now'. The speaker then pointed to a young man, around 16 years of age, walking nearby and said he was the young woman's partner. I asked what would happen now, and my interlocutor said that the young woman would move into the house of the young man's parents; they were now considered as married. I asked whether the young woman's parents were in agreement with the arrangement. The reply was: 'Yare, he right skin for her'.[2] I asked if this was the way young people usually became 'married'. The reply was 'yes'—if the young people were of the right skin groups. This speaker said that young people who made a 'wrong way marriage' were not taken as seriously by older people and that support for the marriage, especially if the marriage was experiencing difficulties, was not always forthcoming (McMullen 2015).

Discussion and Conclusion

The life of young Indigenous women in both the community and the town is not easy. Their lives are characterised by very short periods of childhood and what Brumbach, Figueredo and Ellis (2009) describe as a 'fast life strategy'. It is unclear whether this strategy is an adaptive response to the harsh environments in which they grow up or a result of the very limited set of choices governing their lives (see Senior and Chenhall 2008, 2012).

From birth, this group of women face a set of circumstances unlike those of most non-Indigenous Australians. They are born into a society that was forced to abandon many of its laws and practices, but they are directed (often through fear of supernatural retribution [see Senior and Chenhall 2013]) to conform to those that remain. They also are encouraged to exist in the non-Indigenous world and to conform to many of its norms and practices, language and values. Historical forces have influenced the cultural and social norms of the community and town studied here (Baker 1999). The community was sheltered from the worst of the destructive influences of European contact under the Arnhem Land reserve (Cole 1979, 1985), but other nearby communities and towns have suffered greatly, the ready availability of alcohol and associated rates of violence further destroying Indigenous life ways. This exposure has led to poor outcomes in the sexual and reproductive health of young Indigenous women, as drinking may lead to early sexual initiation, resulting in

2 By this, the person meant that the two young people were in appropriate categories of kin to get married. In both the remote community and the town, society is divided into moieties and a fundamental rule is that one must marry someone from the opposite moity to oneself. Further divisions into semi moieties and skins refine the possible choices that individuals can make.

early pregnancy, increased rates of sexually transmitted infections, poor parenting standards and an increased risk of falling victim to family violence or assault. How young women cope with these outcomes appears to largely depend on the support they receive from family, community members and service providers. Importantly, the decisions these young women make regarding sexual and reproductive health will affect the remainder of their lives and the lives of the next generation.

References

Australian Government. 2007. *Northern Territory National Emergency Response Act 2007*. Canberra: Department of Families, Housing, Community Services and Indigenous Affairs.

Baker, R. 1999. *'Land is Life': From Bush to Town, the Story of the Yanyuwa People*. Sydney: Allen & Unwin.

Brumbach, B., A. Figueredo and B. Ellis. 2009. 'Effects of Harsh and Unpredictable Environments in Adolescence on Development of Life History Strategies—A Longitudinal Test of an Evolutionary Model'. *Human Nature* 20: 25–51. doi.org/10.1007/s12110-009-9059-3.

Burbank, V. K. 1988. *Aboriginal Adolescence—Maidenhood in an Australian Community*. New Brunswick: Rutgers University Press.

Burbank, V., K. Senior and S. McMullen. 2015. 'Precocious Pregnancy, Sexual Conflict, and Early Childbearing in Remote Aboriginal Australia'. *Anthropological Forum* 25 (3): 243–61. doi.org/10.1080/00664677.2015.1027657.

Chenhall, R. and K. Senior. 2017. 'Living the Social Determinants of Health: Assemblages in a Remote Aboriginal Community'. *Medical Anthropology Quarterly* 32 (2): 177–95.

Cole, K. 1979. *The Aborigines of Arnhem Land*. Adelaide: Rigby.

Cole, K. 1985. *From Mission to Church: The CMS Mission to the Aborigines of Arnhem Land 1908–1985*. Bendigo, Vic.: Keith Cole.

Guy, R., J. S. Ward, K. S. Smith, J. Su, R. L. Huang, A. Targey, S. Skov, A. Rumbold, A. Silver, B. Donovan and J. M. Kalder. 2012. 'The Impact of Sexually Transmissible Infection Programs in Remote Aboriginal Communities, a Systematic Review'. *Sexual Health* 9 (3): 205–12. doi.org/10.1071/SH11074.

Kildea, S. V., L. M. Barclay and S. Tracy, S. 2010. '"Closing the Gap", How Maternity Services Can Contribute to Reducing Poor Maternal and Infant Health Outcomes for Aboriginal and Torres Strait Islander Women'. *Rural and Remote Health* 10 (3): 1–18.

Macdonald, G. and J. Boulton. 2011. 'Reconceptualising Mothers: Mothers and Infants in Crisis in the Kimberley, Western Australia'. In *An Anthropology of Mothering*, edited by M. Walks and N. McPherson, 133–48. Toronto: Demeter Press.

McMullen, S. 2015. 'Growing Up Fast'. PhD thesis, Charles Darwin University.

Mooney-Somers J., A. Olsen, W. Erick, R. Scott, A. Akee and L. Maher. 2012. 'Young Indigenous Australians' Sexually Transmitted Infection Prevention Practices: A Community-Based Participatory Research Project'. *Journal of Community & Applied Social Psychology* 22 (6): 519–32. doi.org/10.1002/casp.1134.

Senior, K. 2003. 'A Gudbala Laif? Health and Wellbeing in a Remote Aboriginal Community—What Are the Problems and Where Lies Responsibility?' PhD thesis, The Australian National University, Canberra.

Senior, K. and R. Chenhall. 2008. '"Walkin' about at Night": The Background to Teenage Pregnancy in a Remote Aboriginal Community'. *Journal of Youth Studies* 11 (3): 269–81. doi.org/10.1080/13676260801946449.

Senior, K. and R. Chenhall. 2012. 'Boyfriends, Babies and Basketball: Present Lives and Future Aspirations of Young Women in a Remote Australian Aboriginal Community'. *Journal of Youth Studies* 15 (3): 369–88. doi.org/10.1080/13676261.2012.663890.

Senior, K. and R. Chenhall, R. 2013. 'Health Beliefs and Behaviour, the Practicalities of "Looking After Yourself" in an Australian Aboriginal Community'. *Medical Anthropology Quarterly* 27 (2): 155–74. doi.org/10.1111/maq.12021.

Senior, K., J. Helmer and R. Chenhall. 2017. '"As Long as He's Coming Home to Me", Vulnerability, Jealousy and Violence in Young People's Relationships in Remote, Rural and Regional Australia'. *Health Sociology Review* 26 (2): 204–15. doi.org/10.1080/14461242.2016.1157697.

Stark, A. and A. Hope. 2007. 'Aboriginal Women's Stories of Sexually Transmissible Infection Transmission and Condom Use in Remote Central Australia'. *Sexual Health* 4 (4): 237–42. doi.org/10.1071/SH07009.

Thompson F., X. Zhang and K. Dempsey. 2012. *Northern Territory Midwives' Collection. Mothers and Babies 2007.* Darwin: Department of Health.

8

The Aboriginal Spring? Youth, Mobile Phones and Social Media in a Remote Aboriginal Community

Kishan Kariippanon

Introduction: The Field Site and the Project

Awakened to the events of the Arab Spring, in which mobile phones and social media became the conduit for a revolution spearheaded by young people (Eltantawy and Wiest 2011), the potential for an 'Aboriginal Spring' sparked my interest in what I assumed were the temporal tools of an ever-changing technoscape (Appadurai 1988). The location of the research and its objectives emerged as a result of a social marketing project that attempted to address scabies with the help of emergent technology in a remote Aboriginal community. Rather than just regarding this technology as a convenient vehicle for public health messages, in the early stages of this project, I became interested in its meaning in this location. Similar to Hinkson's (2002, 2017) study of Walpiri new media, I was interested in how technology provides opportunities to extend and/or redefine sociality. This chapter explores the meanings embedded in mobile phones and social media for Yolngu youth in Yirkala in north-east Arnhem Land.

The aims of the study were crafted in consultation with multiple stakeholders. This involved a series of meetings with government agencies and the Aboriginal Medical Services Board and their public health team, and leaders of the families whose land I sought to enter to conduct my work. As a collective, we agreed that this research could be beneficial to the community by providing a clear understanding of the role of mobile phones and social media in Yolgnu society, and insight into the prevailing attitudes towards mobile phones and social media in the community, particularly among young people. To enable accessible and translatable findings for a broad audience, I would conduct ethnographic research exploring how emergent technologies belong in the community, and how they affect young people's kinship structure, social life and perceptions of community, including an account of how these technologies operate in their lives.

Through my attempts at learning the kinship system of the Yolngu people—that is, *Dhuwa* and *Yirritja* moieties and their respective clans—I arrived at an understanding that a randomised method of sampling would be culturally inappropriate. Through my interactions with cultural mentors, I became aware that my responsibility was to seek guidance from my maternal uncles (*ngapipi*), brothers (*wawa* and *gathu*) and fathers (*bapa*) regarding the networks and individuals I could access for the study. Knowledge in this community, and in Aboriginal Australia more broadly, is often held by specific individuals. My adopted status determined my relationship to these individuals and enabled them to share some of their knowledge. Female members of this Arnhem Land community to whom I was connected via kin relationships were also interviewed to achieve a balanced view. These included senior, young and non-Indigenous women; the last worked closely with Yolngu families and were accorded the cultural authority needed to share their knowledge with me on specific aspects of the community.

The study participants held multiple roles in the community, were of various ages and held various kinship relationships to me. My engagement with young people was guided by their personal interests and I was sensitive to their autonomy. I did not expect them to feel obliged to me, even though I was regarded as their 'kin'. As the study focused on emergent technologies, and not Yolngu traditional knowledge systems, there was little need to intrude in culturally sensitive or inappropriate areas. The young people negotiated an intercultural or two-way approach (Marika and Isaacs 1995) to our engagement, balancing Yolngu law and non-Yolgnu culture.

I quickly adapted to the new role of ethnographer, driving 'family' to and from funeral ceremonies or town, having the neighbours' children over for a play, being a water boy for one of the footy teams, setting up new mobile phone connections and producing music videos for teenagers. After three months in the community, I approached my next-door neighbour, a Traditional Owner, to ask if I could apply for the installation of wi-fi ADSL 2 broadband, which could be made available to the community. With his approval, the Telstra man arrived (there was only one contractor in the mining town) and my house was connected with 100 gigabyte ADSL 2+ broadband.

Soon thereafter, chairs showed up near my house, often on the veranda of my immediate neighbour, to access my wi-fi. Young people with mobile phones asked me for the wi-fi password and then added me as their friend on Facebook. They 'suggested' and 'introduced' other friends or family from different communities to extend their 'friend list' on Facebook. The wi-fi connection had anywhere between three and 10 users at a time. Depending on the ability of their phones' connection, and their proximity to my house, some young people were able to surf the internet from the comfort of their own homes.

Within two months, several mobile devices such as iPhones, Samsung flip phones and smartphones were joined by Android tablets as the arsenal of new technology in the community began to accumulate. Three months later, a brand new Hewlett Packard laptop was purchased by a neighbouring family who streamed movies and YouTube videos and downloaded music. As I began hearing different songs, I observed the transformative power of technology; however, it remained a technology that was wrapped in Yolngu culture, as I shall discuss throughout this chapter. The variety of expression and choices made via laptop, phone and the internet truly amazed me.

Learning to Observe Media and Emergent Technology in Context

Dark nights in the backyard were now lit by glowing computer or mobile phone screens, with shirtless men and children cooling off as they enjoyed a movie. Groups of young people started 'sitting about' instead of (or perhaps as well as) 'walkin about at night' (Senior and Chenall 2008) to find a boyfriend or girlfriend, a Yolngu version of the 'Netflix and chill' culture now prevalent among urban non-Indigenous youth (Griffith 2015). As my face became more familiar in the Gove Peninsula, I reached out through online and offline networks to connect with other youth. I looked forward to the biweekly footy training sessions in Yirrkala, of which I made a video clip using an iPhone 4 and iMovie on my MacBook Air computer. The head coach got all the players together and said: '[K] wants to take photos and videos to make a music video, if anyone doesn't like it just tell him straight up, *manymak* [good or ok]?!'

That was an excellent icebreaker. The men were somewhat shy in front of the camera and I was careful not to overstay my welcome. It had only to be a two-minute clip when finished, and about 20 minutes of raw footage was estimated to be sufficient. The finished product was not a music video with a health message about drink driving or domestic violence (which are some of the most common forms of externally produced films in the community). Instead, it was a lens of how I experienced the team—albeit a somewhat crude and simplistic one. The music video of footy players—some with boots, some barefoot, a few sockless—was a simple artistic portrayal that captured something of their lives in the context of the football game and their dedication to training and winning.

Just before our Thursday training at 5.30 pm, I brought my laptop to share the video and sought feedback for further editing. Johnny swiftly took over, showing me how to use bluetooth to send the video to his LG smartphone. The men were encouraging and supportive, showing their appreciation of my efforts through sharing the clip. Each bluetooth-enabled phone that downloaded the video showed up on my laptop's screen with its nickname or series of four numbers[1] as the players trickled in for practice and started putting on their boots.[2] Those who had a mobile phone 'bluetoothed' the video to each other, speeding up the process of sharing, behaviour that was expected in the community.

The challenges of life in a communal society with few resources and little employment made mobile phones transient. Despite their competent use of technology, the poverty of young people in this intercultural setting meant that continuing ownership of personal tools was imaginable only for a fortunate few. Demands for sharing meant that no one device stayed in the hands of one owner only.

1 Bluetooth ID.

2 Sports shoes with studs or 'stops' on the outer sole.

The Android tablets and mobile phones without protective covers eventually disintegrated in the hands of children who asked and received without hesitation. The new laptop met the concrete floor at an angle that told a story of anger and jealousy after an argument between a young woman and man. The technology was swiftly but tragically reduced to plastic and green wafers within three months.

Social Media or Social Trap?

In this remote intercultural setting, Facebook and YouTube revealed a different side of Aboriginal life. Only a few years ago, I had hoped that social media, especially Facebook and Twitter, would bring an 'Aboriginal Spring' (Eltantawy and Wiest 2011; Carlson and Frazer 2016), filling the vacuum of Western knowledge with information while simultaneously providing a means for Aboriginal people to voice their disapproval at the oppression wrought by the dominant culture in a way that might be broadly heard and used to shame unjust political structures (Bevir 1999).

Gradually, I began to find patterns in the social life of social media and mobile phones through discussions, interviews, observations and informal talks with a wide variety of individuals. My assumptions that these new technologies were the reincarnation of the *khayu* (message stick) or the *lippa* (dugout canoe), which had occurred in earlier centuries as a result of intercultural technological exchange between Indigenous nations and Macassan traders (Clark and May 2013), was nothing but a figment of my post-colonial imagination. Rather than being a major social innovation and encompassing radical change, social media in this remote Aboriginal community appeared to intensify pre-existing practices, both good and bad.

During my study, I systematically deconstructed and discarded the lens I arrived with and gradually developed a more accurate understanding of the effects of social media and mobile phones in this remote community. In this political and socioeconomic context, the 'spear' of technology used in the 'Arab Spring' (Eltantawy and Wiest 2011), and the blurring of colonial binaries as discussed by Tofighian (2013), seemed double-edged, distorting both the stability of the kinship system and the control of traditional law.

The kinship laws of *Gurrutu* and societal order are dictated to all living and inanimate beings (Keen 1990; Morphy and Morphy 1984). There is a place for everything and life is a prescribed existence in the Yolngu world. However, there was no place for social media and mobile phones: they arrived and gained a presence before laws and theories of their use could be formulated. Was this period of ebb and flow of negotiations between culture and the emergent technology producing a social trap? According to my interviewees, the path of prioritising individual 'ego' over the collective (clan hood) through the aid of technology risked creating discord among clans and families that could extend to individuals born from 'wrong way'[3] relationships (Burbank 1994)—in other words, a social trap.

Three o'clock in the morning was a typically youthful time to 'hang out' with peers. After the hustle and bustle of the local pub had dispersed into private homes or the poorly lit park, all was quiet for reflection. My brother and I placed ourselves cross-legged on a mat while our uncle (younger than I, chronologically) sat on a chair. My brother explained as my uncle nodded:

> Brother, this phone here is *Yirritja*, belongs to our uncle's moiety. Facebook is *Dhuwa*. The phone is *Yirritja* because it is a new tool and *Yirritja* have since *Mangatharra* (Macassan) times been the owner of new things. Facebook is *Dhuwa*; without it, the phone is only half.

This points to the complimentary nature of the kinship system: it could both accommodate the adoption of new technologies and recognise them as interrelated. Through the kinship system, the internet and social media could be used instrumentally to extend existing patterns of communication and kinship.

This extension was explained by Peter, an Indigenous footy coach. He found the use of Facebook highly appropriate and convenient to communicate with his players and their extended families. He said: 'The main role for the Facebook page [is] to announce training and match times, scores and draws'. He also said: 'it's the photos is what they love'.

A more complex scenario was presented by Josephine, who reflected on the use of Facebook as an online point of contact, a highly useful tool when vast distances stood between homelands and communities. However, she had seen videos of youths fighting that had been filmed by an onlooker.

3 Yolngu marriages that were contracted between romantic partners, suggesting 'incest' and a breaking of the traditional betrothal law.

She 'asked them, why do you have these videos? It's real'. She wanted the young boys to consider their actions: 'two people are fighting, they're hurting each other'. But, to her dismay, they seemed to lack empathy and respect. They said: 'Oh just for fun'. She looked at me and said, 'I think it is to tease the family of the boy who lost the fight', a form of cyberbullying amplified to discomfort a whole family unit or clan.

Susan, a mother of two teenage boys, spoke about the use of social media and mobile phones. Stressing the importance of brotherly acceptance, she said: 'For the boys it's proving yourself to your brothers, everybody, your group, your friends, especially your brothers'. The ability to defend yourself and intimidate peers, and to protect the honour of your family, was a pathway to self-discovery and identity formation for many young men. With the advent of new technologies, such conflict could continue on Facebook, YouTube or Divas Chat. Physical control of disputes by other relatives and allies no longer seemed necessary, or possible, and what often began as harmless teenage projects of self-exploration escalated into inter-clan arguments. And, as the new tool was used to communicate news in the community, it increased the spread of conflict through the reposting of screenshots of 'swearing' and 'jealousing' (Burbank 1994).

Subjected to the practice of 'demand sharing' (Peterson 1993; Altman 2011), the life cycle of mobile phones and phone numbers ranged from one month to less than a year. 'My workers go through phones as I go through clothes … regardless of cheaper phones or more expensive', said Sean, a non-Aboriginal health worker. (I had asked whether a more expensive phone would have a longer life and continuity with its owner.) Sean's Yolngu team endorsed the transient nature of mobile phones and concept of ownership in the community. Three men with families and leadership roles in the community, they glanced at me from time to time as a sign of agreement with Sean's comments.

During my study, I observed that only young people with a secondary education were able or empowered to avoid the pressure of sharing their phone or surrendering it to a more powerful or senior relative. 'That's right, they're stepping out', said Cindy, an Aboriginal mother who confirmed my thoughts. She continued:

> But they are not using it the way you do. They are looking for accolade within their peer group. They are not necessarily looking for accolade within the higher *Gurrutu* (kinship) structure, and that's just a normal teenage behaviour.

The Effects of Social Media Use on Youth

According to Subrahmanyam and Greenfield (2008), non-Indigenous youth use communication tools to reinforce existing relationships, both with friends and romantic partners. When compared to their offline worlds, social networking sites like Facebook mislead the young person into thinking that they can find privacy online. This encourages exploration and risk-taking: the young person believes their actions will not be discovered by their outside social networks and family. Yolngu youth share this misinformed perception of relative privacy and personal space in the online world. Regarding social media, boyd (2007) cautioned that 'words and photos can be copied or altered and shared with others who are not the intended audiences, thereby creating an avenue for cyberbullying'.

Subrahmanyam and Greenfield (2008, 124) draw on Hill's (1983, 124) claim that 'adolescent behaviour is best understood in terms of the key developmental tasks—identity, autonomy, intimacy, and sexuality—and the variables, such as gender and social class, that influence them' to propose that:

> Today's youth media technologies [are] an important social variable and that physical and virtual worlds are psychologically connected; consequently, the virtual world serves as a playing ground for developmental issues from the physical world such as identity and sexuality. (Hill 1983, 525)

This proposition is relevant in the context of this remote community. This became evident in interviewees' contributions that showed how extreme behaviour portrayed on social media played out in community life. The mother of a girl in her teens complained: 'Who writes that shit on Facebook'. This woman, who generously assisted me in the study, urged me to look closely at the popular social media site and said: 'You'll notice that on Facebook, with their comments, you notice the "statuses" that young people write and you wonder, gee, where their heads are … you know even at home'. This mother wanted me to understand that homes and family could mean very little to a vulnerable young person. They did not have to be physically isolated from familiar surroundings in the community to feel emotionally and socially isolated. Being surrounded by family did not always result in feelings of solidarity and subsidiarity. While mental and emotional isolation could build resilience in a supportive environment, in a resource-poor setting, it could cause long-term distress.

Clerkin, Smith and Hames (2013, 525) assert that the internet allows 'children and adolescents to fulfil critical needs of social interactions, self-disclosure and identity exploration'. According to Forest and Wood (2012), for young people with low self-esteem, Facebook can be an attractive means of disclosing personal information. Facebook has the potential for positive outcomes for those who struggle interpersonally; however, when used ineffectively, it can confer a negative long-term vulnerability (Forest and Wood 2012). What constitutes ineffective uses of Facebook or other social media sites? Is it the use of the tool or the conflict between the tool and Yolngu culture that creates a (potential) social trap? One of my interviewees, parodying the mannerism of a young person, said:

> You've got an iPhone and I've just got a flip phone. *Miyalk* (women), *giddy* (belonging or things), *rrupiah* (money). Even work. You think you're good because you've got *djama* (work)?

Here we see a young person blaming his peer for trying to stand out from the crowd by owning a piece of technology, engaging in intimate relationships and maintaining employment that opened up a world of material possessions, resulting in a higher social status among kin. It is a put down for acting 'white' and subscribing to the ways of the Other (see also Burbank 2011, 129).

In Yolngu society, the notion of work, income and ownership of material objects may not be linked to the same sense of achievement as in Western societies. This disconnect from the socioeconomic structure of the larger society is accompanied by young people's growing disregard for the ethos that accompanies the Yolngu kinship system. The kinship system, which provides the grounds for demand sharing and reciprocity, has long militated against the development of status and wealth difference. Social media, when combined with the rise of Indigenous corporatisation (Rowse 2012) and resultant resentment and discord, has created a platform for discourses that appear to be pushing this ethic aside, at least for the youth of this community.

Muise, Christofides and Desmarais (2009) found that high-frequency use of Facebook among young couples predicted jealousy-related feelings and behaviours, such as the regular checking of a partner's profile and suspicion of their online activity. Susan had paid close attention to the dynamics of mobile phone and social media use in her community for almost 20 years. She reflected on some of the challenges of seamless communication in a community where polygyny was the normative behaviour until the influence of Christian missionaries diminished its practice. She connected domestic violence to the use of mobile phones and social media, as they could facilitate infidelity:

> Because they jealous and they thought that you'll meet someone, it can happen to anyone, any age. Before it was opportunistic, now social media and mobile phones make it much more manageable.

Many young people form relationships and attempt to move to the next level of intimacy by swapping Facebook passwords; some even share a single Facebook profile as a means of precluding infidelity. However, a falling out in the relationship can threaten this trust, presenting the opportunity for an aggrieved partner to post intimate material and photographs online as a form of jealousy porn.

Amid their exploration of identity, sexuality and relationships, young people simultaneously search for reassurance. According to Clerkin, Smith and Hames (2013), the relationship between Facebook reassurance seeking and self-esteem is heavily implicated in the genesis of two interpersonally generated feelings: 'thwarted belongingness' (e.g. I am alone) and 'perceived burdensomeness' (e.g. I am a burden) (Van Orden et al. 2010, quoted in Clerkin, Smith and Hames 2013, 526).

A combination of 'thwarted belongingness' and 'perceived burdensomeness' has the potential to be damaging. These emotionally laden cognitions may, according to Van Orden et al. (2010) and Clerkin, Smith and Hames (2013), produce the desire for suicide. Evraire and Dozois (2011) conclude that negative online feedback as a result of excessive reassurance-seeking is detrimental to the maintenance of healthy interpersonal relationships, and Sowislo and Orth (2013) assert that young people's Facebook status updates reflect their 'offline' selves and can signal that the path into depression is not far away.

What, then, were the effects of social media on youth in this remote Indigenous setting? Here too, Facebook hosted constant calls for reassurance and attention. YouTube became a platform on which videos of street fights were uploaded and endlessly viewed. Young people trying to drown out the noise and frustrations of life in overcrowded houses turned away from face-to-face interactions and searched for meaningful relationships via social media. A perceived lack of attention and reassurance could be countered with threats of suicide. Several of the people I spoke to suggested that such behaviour had become the norm, but most also said that if someone was serious about taking their own life, they would not talk about it openly.

To increase consumption and profit, social media and mobile phones engage in a continuous cycle of improvement and innovation. Inserted into a society still reeling from its colonial history and resultant dissent and conflict, these technologies deeply influenced Yolngu youth who, due their adolescent life stage, were inherently vulnerability (e.g. Konner 2010; Schlegel and Hewlett 2011). Through the use of social media, young people already challenged with low self-esteem and social isolation became entrapped in the digital economy of the future. Capitalist values of competition and subjugation became interwoven with old behaviours of clan hood, power and domination. A clear example of how damaging these so-called technological improvements could be to remote Aboriginal youth emerged during an interview with a young man. He told me about a pornography site that was able to function with low data streaming. He was concerned about its accessibility, as even the slowest Telstra connections and Samsung flip phones could access the site. He mentioned a couple's private media that was posted on the site and said:

> If her brother has seen that, who knows what the consequences can be. Back in the day they'd probably get bashed. Maybe they were even wrong skin [incorrect marriage partners].

This technology-induced social disruption has deep implications for the healthy development of youth and their relationships in north-east Arnhem Land.

Negotiating a Globalised Identity within a Yolngu Framework

The plurality of lifestyles (Kral 2014) experienced by Indigenous youth seems contradictory to the image of the 'noble' non-materialistic Aboriginal person embedded in mainstream Australian society (Rowse 2012). Appadurai (1996, 65) has encouraged anthropologists to 'come in from the cold and face the challenge of making a contribution to cultural studies without the benefit of its previous principal source of leverage—sightings of the savage'. Indigenous people are both inspired and led by their culture; however, in most cases, they will critically reflect on their practices and relationships (Kariippanon et al. 2015) to create a better life. The use of technology in this process of reflection and action has been clarified through the work of Carlson and Frazer (2016).

Young people have redefined their value system as a result of globalisation in a post-colonial economic order. Their visual documentation of their alcohol consumption and fights, as well as peer reactions to these, on social media have turned culturally unacceptable behaviours into positive or at least normalised behaviours (Beullens and Schepers 2013). It was no coincidence that increasing levels of violence occurred at the same time as Aboriginal youths gained access to mobile phones and social media (Langton 2008; Clark and Augoustinos 2015). This can be attributed, at least in part, to the internalisation of colonial oppression and the experiences of social and economic marginalisation (Rowse 2012). Emerging in an era of self-determination, the new technology has enabled the amplification of these experiences.

For Yolngu youth with positive support systems, culture only ever acts as a guide (Deger 2006). According to my interviewees, an example of a positive support system is one in which young men have a consistent male presence in the home and experience fulfilment of kinship obligations towards one another. But culture can be changed by external influences, including those designed to perform such functions. For example, Moreno et al. (2013) have suggested that Facebook was constructed to influence user attitudes, intentions and behaviours. Could Yolngu youth be more influenced by Facebook than by their culturally grounded upbringing? It is possible that, in the face of unfulfilled relationships and the absence of positive role models, young people have become more vulnerable to the influence of such technologies. Facebook itself may have amplified the power of the dominant discourse and dominant culture on minorities, acting as a commercial engine for capitalist assimilation, creating a consumer-centric culture amid Aboriginal ways of being.

The 'Aboriginal Protector' or colonial master—a figure of dominance and control—has been reincarnated in social media through monitoring and surveillance, internalised by Yolngu youth who perform surveillance activities (Millie, Darvell and White 2011) on Facebook and Divas Chat. Unlike the findings from research conducted with non-Indigenous participants, self-esteem did not significantly predict frequent partner monitoring for Indigenous youth on Facebook and Divas Chat (Fox and Warber 2013; Senior, Helmer and Chenhall 2017). It seems that the oppressive attitudes of colonialists have been normalised and entrenched in the lives of Aboriginal people living in low socioeconomic conditions (Langton 2008). This claim is substantiated with findings of 'online public fighting' and 'jealousing' by Senior, Helmer and Chenhall (2017).

During my time with Yolngu people, I observed that, while Aboriginal identity remained within its customary boundaries, the alteration of traditional practices, often in economic exchanges, had transformed the new technology into a double-edged spear. The individualisation of Aboriginal youth, as observed in their use of a new kind of communication technology, had resulted in the formation of bicultural identities within an Indigenous structure. Martin (quoted in Rowse 2012, 116) explained that: 'There is no such thing as an autonomous arena of Indigenous values and practices, rather there is a contested intercultural field of transforming and transformed practices and values'.

The redrawing of the borders between Indigenous youth and globalised youth culture—the appropriation of hip hop alongside the sounds of the *yidaki* (didgeridoo), the desire to use the same communication tools as their non-Indigenous peers—did not signal the intention to defy or undermine Yolngu culture, but to embrace modernity. Like challenging the power and bureaucracy of Indigenous elders and Traditional Owners, this was a natural phase of identity exploration by Indigenous youth (see also Chapter 3, this volume).

The understanding that mobile phones and social media—unlike tobacco, dugout canoes and other Macassan or Commonwealth commodities—are not governed or monopolised by a gerontocracy, allowed Indigenous youth to achieve a level of autonomy from their elders: a measure of liberation from the confines of cultural conservatism. Facebook and Divas Chat supported them in their engagement with another reality, one beyond the constraints of remote public housing: cramped, unfurnished and lacking in privacy. According to Senior (2003) and Senior and Chenhall (2012), these are essential features for positive youth development. Mobile phones and social media appear to have been adopted, at least in part, as opportunities to improvise, to create order and control, and to access resources in the hope of eventually beating the internal and external forces of inequality. For example, Joe said:

> There's not whole lot for youth to be doing [here]. In the cities and stuff, unless they feel unsafe, there are plenty of things for people to be doing unlike in this region.

However, Vaarzon-Morel (2014), in her study of technology and social relations among Walpiri, reminds us that tensions in this technology have the potential to exacerbate and intensify existing social problems.

Conclusion

The use of mobile phones and social media at Yirkala is a double-edged sword. At the same time as creating opportunities, they threaten to destablise and undermine important aspects of young people's lives. The need and ability for young people to explore their identity, strive for autonomy and engage in the globalised world has enabled a process of creating and negotiating bicultural identities, furthering the development of Aboriginal modernity. The opportunity for young people to claim a place in the nation's economy and to be heard as part of dominant discourses, regardless of status and power, has been reinforced by the accessibility of online tools and excellent mobile phone coverage. Conversely, the tensions that arise from the use of social media threaten the experience of youth as they explore sexuality and intimate partner relationships. Equally, the internalisation of old power structures of community elders, Christian missions and Aboriginal protectors has created a practice of surveillance and suspicion that threatens to stifle young people's freedom of expression and innovation.

References

Appadurai, A. 1988. *The Social Life of Things: Commodities in Cultural Perspective.* Cambridge: Cambridge University Press.

Appadurai, A. 1996. *Modernity at Large: Cultural Dimensions of Globalization.* Minneapolis: University of Minnesota Press.

Altman, J. 2011. 'A Genealogy of "Demand Sharing": From Pure Anthropology to Public Policy'. In *Ethnography and the Production of Anthropological Knowledge: Essays in Honour of Nicolas Peterson*, edited by Y. Musharbash and M. Barber, 209–22. Canberra: ANU E Press. doi.org/10.22459/EPAK.03.2011.13.

Beullens, K. and A. Schepers. 2013. 'Display of Alcohol Use on Facebook: A Content Analysis'. *Cyberpsychology, Behavior, and Social Networking* 16 (7), 497–503. doi.org/10.1089/cyber.2013.0044.

Bevir, M. 1999. 'Foucault, Power, and Institutions'. *Political Studies* 47 (2): 345–59. doi.org/10.1111/1467-9248.00204.

boyd, d. 2007. 'Social Network Sites: Public, Private, or What'. *Knowledge Tree* 13 (1): 1–7.

Burbank, V. K. 1994. *Fighting Women: Anger and Aggression in Aboriginal Australia*. Berkley: University of California Press.

Burbank, V. K. 2011. *An Ethnography of Stress: The Social Determinants of Health in Aboriginal Australia*. New York: Palgrave Macmillan. doi.org/10.1057/9780230117228.

Carlson, B. and R. Frazer. 2016. 'Indigenous Activism and Social Media: A Global Response to #SOSBLAKAUSTRALIA'. In *Negotiating Digital Citizenship: Control, Contest and Culture*, edited by A. McCosker, S. Vivienne and A. Johns, 115–30. Lanham: Rowman & Littlefield.

Clark, M. and S. K. May. 2013. *Macassan History and Heritage: Journeys, Encounters and Influences*. Canberra: ANU E Press. doi.org/10.22459/MHH.06.2013.

Clark, Y. and M. Augoustinos. 2015. 'What's in a Name? Lateral Violence within the Aboriginal Community in Adelaide, South Australia'. *Office Bearers of the APS College Of Community Psychologists* 27(2): 19.

Clerkin, E. M., A. R. Smith and J. L. Hames. 2013. 'The Interpersonal Effects of Facebook Reassurance Seeking'. *Journal of Affective Disorders* 151 (2): 525–30. doi.org/10.1016/j.jad.2013.06.038.

Deger, J. 2006. *Shimmering Screens: Making Media in an Aboriginal Community*. Minnesota: University of Minnesota Press.

Eltantawy, N. and J. B. Wiest. 2011. 'The Arab Spring. Social Media in the Egyptian Revolution: Reconsidering Resource Mobilization Theory'. *International Journal of Communication* 5: 18.

Evraire, L. E. and D. J. Dozois. 2011. 'An Integrative Model of Excessive Reassurance Seeking and Negative Feedback Seeking in the Development and Maintenance Of Depression'. *Clinical Psychology Review* 31(8): 1291–303. doi.org/10.1016/j.cpr.2011.07.014.

Forest, A. L. and J. V. Wood. 2012. 'When Social Networking Is Not Working Individuals with Low Self-Esteem Recognize but Do Not Reap the Benefits of Self-Disclosure on Facebook'. *Psychological Science* 23 (3): 1–8. doi.org/10.1177/0956797611429709.

Fox, J. and K. M. Warber. 2013. 'Romantic Relationship Development in the Age of Facebook: An Exploratory Study of Emerging Adults' Perception, Motives and Behaviors'. *Cyberpsychology, Behavior, and Social Networking* 16 (1): 3–7. doi.org/10.1089/cyber.2012.0288.

Griffith, M. E. 2015. 'Downgraded to Netflix and Chill: Freedom of Expression and the Chilling Effect on User-Generated Content in Europe'. *Columbia Journal of European Law* 22: 355.

Hill, J. 1983. 'Early Adolescence: A Framework'. *Journal of Early Adolescence* 3 (1): 1–21. doi.org/10.1177/027243168331002.

Hinkson, M. 2002. 'New Media Projects at Yuendumu: Inter-Cultural Engagement and Self-Determination in an Era of Accelerated Globalization'. *Continuum* 16 (2): 201–20. doi.org/10.1080/10304310220138769.

Hinkson, M. 2017. 'Beyond Assimilation and Refusal: A Warlpiri Perspective on the Politics of Recognition'. *Postcolonial Studies* 20 (1): 86–100. doi.org/10.1080/13688790.2017.1334281.

Kariippanon, K. A., D. Garrawirtja, K. Senior, P. Kalfadellis, V. Narayan and B. McCoy. 2015. 'Ethnography and Filmmaking for Indigenous Anti-Tobacco Social Marketing'. In *World Social Marketing Conference Sydney 2015*, 21–23. Lichfield, UK: Fuse Events.

Keen, I. 1990. 'Images of Reproduction in the Yolngu Madayin Ceremony'. *Australian Journal of Anthropology* 1 (2–3): 192–207. doi.org/10.1111/j.1757-6547.1990.tb00383.x.

Konner, M. 2010. *The Evolution of Childhood: Relationships, Emotion, Mind.* Cambridge, MA: Harvard University Press.

Kral, I. 2014. 'Shifting Perceptions, Shifting Identities: Communication Technologies and the Altered Social, Cultural and Linguistic Ecology in a Remote Indigenous Context'. *Australian Journal of Anthropology* 25 (2): 171–89. doi.org/10.1111/taja.12087.

Langton, M. 2008. 'The End Of "Big Men" Politics'. *Griffith Review* (22): 48.

Marika, W. and J. Isaacs. 1995. *Wandjuk Marika: Life Story.* St Lucia: University of Queensland Press.

Millie, J., S. P. Darvell and K. M. White. 2011. 'Facebook Tells Me So: Applying the Theory of Planned Behavior to Understand Partner-Monitoring Behavior On Facebook'. *Cyberpsychology, Behavior, and Social Networking* 14 (12): 717–22. doi.org/10.1089/cyber.2011.0035.

Moreno, M. A., R. Kota, S. Schoohs and J. M. Whitehill. 2013. 'The Facebook Influence Model: A Concept Mapping Approach'. *Cyberpsychology, Behavior, and Social Networking* 16 (7): 504–11. doi.org/10.1089/cyber.2013.0025.

Morphy, H. and F. Morphy. 1984. 'The "Myths" of Ngalakan History: Ideology and Images of the Past in Northern Australia'. *Royal Anthropological Institute of Great Britain and Ireland* 19 (3): 459–78. doi.org/10.2307/2802183.

Muise, A., E. Christofides and S. Desmarais. 2009. 'More Information than You Ever Wanted: Does Facebook Bring Out the Green-Eyed Monster of Jealousy?' *CyberPsychology & Behavior* 12 (4): 441–44. doi.org/10.1089/cpb.2008.0263.

Peterson, N. 1993. 'Demand Sharing: Reciprocity and the Pressure for Generosity among Foragers'. *American Anthropologist* 95 (4): 860–74. doi.org/10.1525/aa.1993.95.4.02a00050.

Rowse, T. 2012. *Rethinking Social Justice: From "Peoples" to "Populations"*. Canberra: Aboriginal Studies Press.

Schlegel, A. and B. Hewlett. 2011. 'Contributing of Anthropology to the Study of Adolescence'. *Journal of Research on Adolescence* 21(1): 281–89. doi.org/10.1111/j.1532-7795.2010.00729.x.

Senior, K. 2003. 'A Gudbala Laif? Health and Wellbeing in a Remote Aboriginal Community—What Are the Problems and Where Lies Responsibility?' PhD thesis, The Australian National University, Canberra.

Senior, K. and R. Chenhall. 2008. 'Walkin' About at Night': The Background to Teenage Pregnancy in a Remote Aboriginal Community'. *Journal of Youth Studies* 11 (3): 269–81. doi.org/10.1080/13676260801946449.

Senior, K. and R. Chenhall. 2012. 'Boyfriends, Babies and Basketball: Present Lives and Future Aspirations of Young Women in a Remote Australian Aboriginal Community'. *Journal of Youth Studies* 15 (3): 369–88. doi.org/10.1080/13676261.2012.663890.

Senior, K., H. Helmer and R. Chenhall. 2017. ' "As Long as He's Coming Home to Me': Vulnerability, Jealousy and Violence in Young People's Relationships in Remote, Rural and Regional Australia'. *Health Sociology Review* 26 (2): 204–18. doi.org/10.1080/14461242.2016.1157697.

Sowislo, J. F and U. Orth. 2013. 'Does Low Self-Esteem Predict Depression and Anxiety? A Meta-Analysis of Longitudinal Studies'. *Psychological Bulletin* 139 (1): 213. doi.org/10.1037/a0028931.

Subrahmanyam, K. and P. Greenfield. 2008. 'Online Communication and Adolescent Relationships'. *Future of Children* 18 (1): 119–46. doi.org/10.1353/foc.0.0006.

Tofighian, N. 2013. *Blurring the Colonial Binary: Turn-of-the-Century Transnational Entertainment in Southeast Asia*. Stockholm: University of Stockholm.

Vaarzon-Morel, P. 2014. 'Pointing the Phone: Transforming Technology and Social Relations among Walpiri'. *Australian Journal of Anthropology* 25(2): 239–55. doi.org/10.1111/taja.12091.

Van Orden, K. A., T. K. Witte, K. C. Cukrowicz, S. R. Braithwaite, E. A. Selby and T. E. Joiner Jr. 2010. 'The Interpersonal Theory of Suicide'. *Psychological Review* 117 (2): 575. doi.org/10.1037/a0018697.

9

Juvenile (In)Justice in Darwin: Young People's Voices from the Don Dale Youth Detention Centre

Pippa Rudd, Kate Senior and Jared Sharp

Introduction

> The face of youth crime, until yesterday, was the one we could see. Break ins, stolen cars, wanabee teen gangsters. And seemingly endless re-offending. There has been an undeniable frustration within the community that our justice system does not break the cycle and that kids leave youth detention to resume lives of near poverty, drug use and petty crime. Where the community can be forgiven, and the NT Government cannot is that treatment of our troubled youth had a face that most of us could not see. There can be no doubt, after viewing the footage on *Four Corners*, that the brutalisation of young people within Don Dale is an overwhelming cause of that reoffending. (Smee 2016)

So ran the front page of the *NT News* on 26 July 2016. Despite several formal enquiries and a series of damning reports by Amnesty International into the Don Dale Youth Detention Centre, it was the Australian Broadcasting Corporation's (ABC's) investigative news program *Four Corners'* episode 'Australia's Shame', broadcast on 25 July 2016, that finally exposed the brutality of youth detention in Darwin. The conditions in which detainees were placed and the punishments inflicted upon them demanded an urgent response (Amnesty International 2014; Bath and Gwynne 2015; Vita 2015). That response was the creation of the Royal Commission into the Detention and Protection of Children in the Northern Territory.[1] Established in 2016, the royal commission released its report in 2017; it described the 'systemic and shocking failures' of the youth detention system, including the failure to comply with basic human rights (Commonwealth of Australia 2017).

This chapter is based on the perspectives of three Aboriginal youths who were incarcerated in the Don Dale facility three years prior to the ABC's exposé.[2] It offers an anthropological perspective on the causes of persistent delinquency and/or incarceration of Aboriginal young people in the Northern Territory. Insofar as it describes firsthand experiences of pathways into and out of youth detention, it contributes a facet of understanding that supports efforts at effective reform.[3] One of the royal commission's recommendations was to 'implement policies to incorporate Aboriginal cultural competence and safety in the design and delivery of education programs, activities and services for children and young people in detention' (Royal Commission into Protection and Detention of Children in the Northern Territory 2017, 468). As this chapter demonstrates, identifying and understanding the 'cultural' context in which young Aboriginal people begin, and too often continue, what may be a lifelong engagement with Australia's detention system, is vital for policy development and implementation. Non-Aboriginal service providers, we suggest, need more than a general understanding of what is labelled 'culture' by some Aboriginal people as well as non-Indigenous outsiders. This chapter demonstrates how a more complex anthropological view of 'culture'—one that incorporates

1 The royal commission found that:

> Many of the children who come into contact with the youth justice and child protection systems do so as a result of the underlying drivers of socioeconomic inequality including racism, remoteness, poverty, housing issues, poor physical and mental health and disabilities. This includes cognitive impairments such as fetal alcohol spectrum disorder, as well as trauma and intergenerational trauma. This forms the backdrop for many of the children and young people who get caught up in the youth justice and child protection systems in the Northern Territory and is a fundamental challenge which must be acknowledged and addressed. (Commonwealth of Australia 2017, 40).

While the recognition of such factors is an important step in addressing the problems associated with youth delinquency, we suggest that this needs to be complemented with greater understanding of how such factors work out in the lives of specific individuals.

2 Ethical clearance for this project was granted by the Menzies School of Health Research Human Ethics Committee (Ref: 2013-2093).

3 The commission's activity included interviews with adults and young people. These interviews focused primarily on experiences of family separation and detention in the Don Dale facility.

an account of the 'intercultural' and associated experiences of living within an admixture of two, often contradictory, cultural systems—expands understanding of the context of Aboriginal offenders' lives and thus, ideally, encourages and enables more appropriate treatment of both delinquent and Aboriginal youth more generally (Anthony 2013; Blagg and Anthony 2019; Blagg, Tulich and Bush 2017; White and Cunneen 2015).[4]

Stories from Inside

The interviews for these stories were conducted by Pippa Rudd, then a PhD student. Her work involved intensive observation at the Darwin Youth Justice Court as well as interviews with incarcerated young people in the Don Dale Youth Detention Centre. The interviews took place in May 2014, which can be seen as a midpoint in the timeline of incidents at the detention centre (see Appendix: Timeline). Tragically, Pippa lost her battle with cancer before she was able to complete her work. This chapter has been compiled through analysis of her transcribed interviews as well as un-transcribed audio material, with constant reference to her meticulous field notes. The following presents a selection of her interviews. Some of the speakers were interviewed on multiple occasions. The audio recordings are punctuated by the sounds of heavy doors banging and keys rattling. All the young people interviewed were 17 years old and worried about being transferred to the adult prison. Most had been in Don Dale several times before, and so described it as being 'normal' or 'alright'. This was despite the fact that all had experienced, or were currently experiencing, periods of being a 'red-shirter' (high security), which meant being denied the luxury of a fan or air-conditioning in Darwin's heat.[5]

Carmen's Story

Carmen's interviews are tough and feisty. An articulate young woman, she evidently enjoyed her interaction with Pippa. In April 2014, Carmen was worried about being transferred to the adult prison, as she would turn

4 Sociologists have also contributed important studies on these issues (see e.g. Blagg and Anthony 2019).

5 The young people were differentiated by the colour of their shirts. The most problematic young people wore red shirts and were denied privileges such as having a fan. This was supposed to be an incentive for them to change their behaviour.

18 the following August. First arrested at 14, she was a frequent detainee at Don Dale. Her arrests all appear to be due to fighting. She spoke about being bullied at school and learning how to fight to defend herself, behaviour that led to her incarceration:

> My first time was 'cos I had a fight. I had got used to fighting from being bullied at school and started defending myself. And I guess, just went overboard, you know, out of control. I thought I could give that person a hiding, teach that person a lesson. 'Cos I was the one that used to get bullied. And didn't tolerate that stuff.

She talked about the ongoing burden of being continually monitored by the police and being a focus of their attention because of her Indigenous status:

> Oh my God, that's annoying, they harass me all the time. I can't even go into the shopping centres, do my own stuff without them walking up to me and saying: 'what are you doing here, don't you have trespassing orders against the place?' And umm, I'll be like 'no, that's not me, you got the wrong person there'. Then they'll harass me, they'll be like 'don't be going stealing, we'll be watching you on camera. Otherwise you can just leave this space right now'. And I'll be like 'what are youse on about, I come here to do shopping, not come here to harass people or annoy people or start fights and anything. Or steal'. And they'll be like 'sure, we know what you're like'.

Carmen described life under constant surveillance as being 'too stressful'. This, combined with an unchanged home environment and pressures from family, provides insight into the serial recidivism of some in Don Dale:

> But the only reason I breached this time is like family business, a little bit of fighting and that. It just pisses me off. It's like every time I come out, I'm involved with shit that I don't want to be involved with. And I try to tell people oh umm, I'm out to do other stuff, not to be involved with fights and shit, because other people bring my name up. And that's when I get pissed off, I get stressed out. And yeah, that's when I'll be like, fuck it, I'm too used to being in Don Dale, I'm going back there.

The conditions of bail, which include a curfew and non-association orders, could also be difficult to comply with. Carmen talked about being 'set up to fail'. For example, her mother was homeless and so she was sent to live with other relatives. She could exert little control over these members of her family and was pulled back into criminal behaviours.

Carmen described a family life in which parents engaged in violent behaviour directed at each other and their children. Her father attacked both her and her brother, using extreme physical violence:

> C: Family fights from mother and father and smash it out, I grew up with that stuff, like domestic violence and my own brother went to welfare because of my dad. We don't get along with him, he pushed my brother out of the car, in Darwin he used to bash me and my brother around. That's when my mum got sick of it. She had to run away with us. She took off after she had her last kid with him. When I was three and that's when Jessie was born.
>
> P. That's a brave thing to do.
>
> C. He was over controlling for her. He was a druggie, alcoholic. At least my mum did that, because if she was still with him today, I'd probably be worse than I am now.

Despite this family history, longing and concern for her family are pervasive in Carmen's discourse. She speaks of wanting to shield her brothers and sisters from her situation and to prevent them from following her path:

> C: I ask my little sisters, 'You mob going to stay in school now?' 'Yes we gonna stay in school 'cos we know what will happen if we hang around with the wrong crew and we do the wrong stuff and we gonna get locked up if we break the law'.
>
> P: Do they come and visit?
>
> C: Nah, I don't want them to come and visit.
>
> P: You don't want them to do that? Why is that?
>
> C: If my family come and see me, especially those three, I just get upset and just start thinking of them and start stressing out and I get angry and take it all out on me 'cos of what I've done. And yeah, my little sisters and my baby brother shouldn't be coming in here and seeing me, in the wrong place. They should be seeing me on the outside.

Carmen's account of the factors leading up to one of the incidents at Don Dale, in which a group of young people climbed into the roof of the centre (see Appendix: Timeline), highlights the everyday humiliation and deprivations that young people were subjected to within the centre:

> One night the boss came back and he was being a smart arse and he was like: 'If youse mob wanna keep acting like animals', which we wasn't. We was just sitting there, thinking 'what the fuck are you on about?' And he was like, 'We'll start treating you like animals in pounds then'. And we got pissed off, it was like: 'What the fuck? Why would you say that to us?' So, it was like, if you want to treat us like animals, we will show you what animals are like. So that's what we did, we broke into the roof and smashed it up. But ah well, that was his fault for starting it all. They didn't feed the boys properly last night, they didn't give them much feed, most of the boys. They left them to starve on purpose. And, umm yeah we made a plan and got up in the roof.

Carmen's overall discourse may be read as one of resilience. She has given up smoking and drinking and talks about transforming her desire to fight into a formal martial art. Rationalising her experience makes Don Dale bearable:

> I guess this place is just like a little holiday camp. Makes you think of everything in here, going forwards, what you should have done, shouldn't have done. Should have stuck to this thing, should have done that thing.

Joel's Story

Joel is also on the brink of turning 18. When he is not in Don Dale, he lives with his grandmother and two brothers. Another brother is in the adult prison, Darwin Correctional Centre, for the same crime as Joel: a ram raid. The severity of his crimes has increased since he first faced court at 13 for stealing a bike. Since then, he has been to court 'so many times that I have lost count'. His first time in Don Dale was in 2013, and since then he has been frequently in and out of detention:

> Then I just be coming back after that, ever since, come in for a week get out, come in for three days get out … just back and forth … Once you've actually served time here, they know you've seen what it's like on the inside and they know, it's your choice, you know what it's like and we're going to keep sending you back. So they send you back.

According to him, the courts think that no one would willingly put themselves in a position in which they would be returned to Don Dale once they had spent time there. Assuming his interpretation of the justice system is accurate, it highlights the court's ignorance of factors affecting an individual's ability to *choose* to stay out of trouble. As Joel says, 'it just happens, you get in trouble':

> But it's not like that, you don't, you don't want to come back. No one wants to come back. It just happens, you get in trouble. You make mistakes, everyone makes mistakes. My biggest mistake is drinking.

Joel talked about struggling through school with undiagnosed dyslexia and eventually giving up because it was all too difficult:

> Nah, I started wagging and I'd just start walking out of classes when I'd get to something too hard, too embarrassed to ask for help or anything, I'd just stand up and walk off. Yeah, that's that.

Like Carmen, Joel experienced the revolving door of Don Dale because of his inability to comply with bail restrictions. He said that he would agree to all the restrictions 'but would know in the back of my head that I'm not going to go by those'. Going back to Don Dale was seen as inevitable in the pattern of his everyday life and he characterised it in the same way as smoking weed or drinking—it was too difficult to change when everyone else was doing the same thing:

> It's just like, like I'll get drunk one day and my mates will be around my house … they'll all leave and I'll be like 'fuck it, I'll just come with youse'.

Alcohol was the main undermining factor in his life:

> Everything I do is when I'm drunk. I don't go out stealing sober, I don't even, can't even, steal socks from Kmart when I'm sober. I don't, I'm not, I don't steal. When I'm drunk, I go steal stuff, just sort of motivates me. To me, it's having fun.

He spoke of his ability to drink a whole carton (24 cans) to get 'drunk, really drunk' and said that he had been a heavy drinker since the age of 12. Yet, what appears to have been a very cursory assessment of Joel by a drug and alcohol counsellor failed to effectively explore his relationship with alcohol. According to Joel, the person running the sessions commented: 'We don't target people like you for this session. You don't smoke weed, you don't smoke drugs, you drink on occasion.' Joel says that his life of drinking, stealing, selling drugs and ending up in Don Dale are just part of being young. In his words, he was 'getting it all out of his system' before he turned 18 and had to face the frightening and unknown circumstances of adult prison.

Samuel's Story

Samuel's childhood was spent in foster homes. His brothers and sisters are also in foster homes, but in a different state, and he has very little knowledge about their whereabouts or wellbeing. Samuel was ambivalent about being in Don Dale; he had run away from every foster care placement because he didn't like being sent to live with strangers. At the time of his detention, his father was serving a seven-year jail sentence in Queensland and Samuel's girlfriend was also in Don Dale. Being at Don Dale was one of the most consistent experiences in his teenage years, providing him, it seems, with sense of stability in his life. This is indicated in his discussion about being in court:

> When I sit up there, I don't even listen. I just sit there and hope for the best. I know that I've been a bad lot, last time I was here I didn't want to get out, because I thought that this was the best place to be.

At that point in time, being incarcerated in Don Dale was the best option his limited circumstances had to offer.

However, when he was interviewed by Pippa, Samuel appeared to be highly anxious about his incarceration. He was wearing a 'red shirt' (indicating he was a high security risk) because he had tried to escape at every opportunity. His father had just been released from prison, as had his girlfriend, but because of their criminal records, neither were permitted to visit him. A desire to see people he cared about may well have motivated his escape attempts:

> I don't want to be here. I've been here a month and a week now and realise this ain't what I want. My dad's been out for the first time in my life. I was real depressed and stuff and then my girlfriend got out the next days and I tried calling her last night and stuff and no answer. Tried calling my grandma to talk to my dad, no answer. Ahh so stressing out.

Samuel talked about his ambitions to reconnect with a father he had not seen for seven years and, while he acknowledged feeling anxious about this meeting, he also had high expectations for a good life with his father, an opportunity, perhaps, to reclaim some of his lost childhood:

> It's a little bit scary, I haven't seen him for seven years, I wouldn't even know if I would walk down the street and see him, I'd walk past like he was a normal person.
>
> My dad will be there 24/7 and if I wanna go anywhere he can take me with him, because I'll be allowed out with him, to play football and stuff.

Sociocultural and Psychological Factors Associated with Youth Incarceration

Carmen, Joel and Samuel came from homes that were deeply dysfunctional in which they experienced few stable adult influences. Both Samuel and Joel regarded their grandmothers as the most important people in their lives, but also recognised that their grandmothers had little ability to control them or their peers. Drug use and alcohol were ubiquitous and deeply embedded in their criminal histories and exposure to violence (Rudd 2015). All three talked about violent episodes they had witnessed or experienced during their childhoods. Child and youth policy in the Northern Territory, with its narrow focus on the early determinants of child health, regarded these young people as broken beyond repair (Nossar 2014). From this perspective, investments in rehabilitation for youth are a waste of scarce resources. According to this viewpoint, the course and outcomes of these young people's lives were set in motion well before birth, with the effects of parental stress, drug and alcohol abuse affecting the developing infant (Allen 2011; Spencer 2003). Early exposure to violence is often considered to be associated with the development of violent behaviours in youth and adults, in a so-called 'cycle of violence' (Dodge, Bates and Pettit 1990; Lisak and Beszterczey 2007). This belief makes it easy to anticipate the transition from abused and neglected infant to youth drug dealer, teenage mother or violent criminal. But, as Bourgois (2003) has pointed out, this expectation does not encourage attention to the social, cultural and psychological factors shaping these young people, including their experiences of poverty within an increasingly affluent city, and the fact that they have no middle-class parent to dismiss their often petty crimes as 'youthful mischief' and keep them out of jail. The young people's stories are filled with accounts of constant monitoring and surveillance. This is in keeping with Tuari's (2013) argument about racist profiling by the police arising from an ongoing neo-colonial culture that is responsible, at least in part, for driving high rates of reoffending.

Rather than being seen as the passive victims of external factors, Bourgois (2003, 143) recommends seeing the deviant behaviour of marginalised young people as a deliberate response to their situation, though, tragically, one that can have very painful consequences for the individual and the community:

> People ... have not passively accepted their structural victimisation. On the contrary, by embroiling themselves in the underground economy and proudly embracing street culture, they are seeking an alternative to their social marginalisation. In the process, on a daily level, they become the actual agents administering their own and their community's suffering.

At various points in their stories, the young people express ambivalence about their experiences in Don Dale; they have become accustomed to its conditions, despite their awareness of its deprivations and punishment. For Samuel, it was preferable to being placed in foster homes with strangers, a practice highlighted in the royal commission as being an important contributing factor in youth delinquency and crime (Commonwealth of Australia 2017).

Carmen and Joel said that life was easier inside than outside. The food, if not good, was at least regular and the young people were surrounded by their friends, in contrast to strangers in the foster home situation. Howerton et al. (2009) found that such perceptions were common in serial short-term prisoners, who had 'nothing at stake in the community' and the possibility of a more stable and predictable life inside.

All three young people were deeply fatalistic about meeting the conditions placed on them for non-custodial sentences and talked about agreeing to conditions that they had no hope or inclination to meet. All three were aware that the pressures inherent in their home and community lives would inevitably lead them to reoffend. Such conditions were often placed on them with scant regard for their circumstances. Samuel's contact with those with whom he perpetrated crimes was restricted by a 'non-association' condition. This prohibited personal contact with his brother, but they lived in the same house! The concept of choice—choosing not to do things that will lead them to detention—permeates their discourse, either in terms of their own resolve to do things differently or to demonstrate they have heard what people in authority have said to them. Despite considerable resolve, it is clear that the same pressures that undermined their ability to comply with parole conditions also undermined their ability to stay out of adult prison. For example, Joel gave up smoking drugs despite the fact that his whole family smoked around him. This is not an environment in which he can be expected to stay drug free.

Conclusion

In spite of the circumstances in which these three youths live, circumstances that readers might have trouble imagining, there is considerable resilience within their stories: each have made difficult choices and have managed to stick with them. But, as they teeter on the brink of an adult sentence, they remain buffeted by factors we fear may affect their resolve. Their lives are characterised by absent parents, unstable households, violence, homelessness, disconnection from education, and drug and alcohol abuse. They experience racially motivated monitoring and surveillance, making it difficult for them to be inconspicuous and stay out of trouble.

Their lives inside, although they sometimes appear to be less chaotic than their lives outside, are also violent, degrading and often deeply humiliating. They have lost contact or damaged their relationships with family members who are most dear to them, and they have lost chunks of their childhood, most poignantly expressed by Joel, who just wanted a dad to play footy with him.

Their stories of the sentencing process are permeated by fatalism and a sense that things are beyond their control—that things 'just happen'. The larger society's insistence on an agentic posture of making good choices stands in marked contrast to this lack of control. This strikes us as somewhat contradictory, especially given a policy environment heavily influenced by the notion of pre-determination with regard to delinquency. These young people appear to think that they have to make good choices to stay out of prison. The authorities reinforce this notion by asserting that they are in prison by choice: after all, who would want to go there? The reality we find in these young prisoners' texts is that choice is both extremely limited and difficult for this group whose experience to date has been one of repeated failure and who live in circumstances of deprivation and deep uncertainty.

Although the *Four Corners* report and the subsequent royal commission brought the conditions at Don Dale to national attention, there had been several previous reviews of the Don Dale facility and youth justice conducted in the Northern Territory.

In September 2014, Children's Commissioner Howard Bath launched an Own Initiative Investigation (allowed under the *Children's Commission Act 2013*) into the conditions at Don Dale. This was in response to an incident in which young inmates had armed themselves with homemade weapons and tried to escape, and guards had used CS gas (tear gas) and a prison security dog from the Darwin Correctional Centre (Bath and Gwynne 2015). This incident was also described in an Amnesty International report on 2 September 2014.

The Children's Commissioner's Report, completed by Commissioner Colleen Gwynne, was provided to the government in June 2015 and publicly released in September 2015 (Bath and Gwynne 2015). The report found major failings in the treatment of young people and breaches of the *Youth Justice Act* including:

- the use of prolonged solitary confinement of young people (up to 17 days), even though the legislative maximum allowance is 72 hours
- the housing of young people in solitary confinement cells that are unsanitary; do not have fans or air conditioners; do not have windows, natural light or ventilation; and do not have access to running water, in temperatures that can exceed 35°C
- the failure to provide young detainees with access to education or rehabilitation programs
- the use of spit hoods, even in circumstances in which young people have no history of spitting
- the use of handcuffs and foot restraints
- the housing of young people in adult prisons
- the use of dogs and chemical agents, to the extent that one young person was exposed to tear gas for a period of eight minutes

- a lack of policies and procedures to govern the use of force and restraints on young people
- the use of insufficiently trained staff to guard the youth detention centre
- a lack of accountability when excessive force is used.

One of the youth justice officers interviewed for the report did not blame the kids for 'going off'—he said that he would have done the same thing if he had been treated like they had and was 'surprised it didn't happen sooner' (Bath and Gywnne 2015).[6]

We may be surprised that, in 2016, it was clear that a royal commission was required, indicating not only an inability, or disinclination, to rectify the situation in which highly vulnerable youths were being placed, but also the complexity of the problem. These incidents provide the context and background for the stories of Carmen, Joel and Samuel.

6 The review was conducted by Michael Vita, who was the superintendent of the Reiby Youth Detention Centre in New South Wales. The terms of this review were to investigate the policy and procedures that were to be put in place as youth were moved from Don Dale into the Berrimah adult prison.

Although the terms of this review were narrower than those of the children's commissioner (who focused on youth justice more broadly and not just youth detention), the Vita review noted serious deficiencies in a number of key areas, including strategic direction, staff training, infrastructure, leadership and resourcing. A youth detention worker was quoted in the report as saying: 'It's hard to be strategic when operating in a climate of daily crisis' (Vita 2015). Vita's report highlighted the lack of staff training, with Northern Territory workers only receiving four days of training compared to 11 weeks for New South Wales prison officers and 30 weeks for New South Wales youth detention officers. The procedures manual and standard operating procedures guiding actions were found to be outdated and inadequate and needed to be 'urgently addressed'. Vita also found 'isolated cases' in which staff had used inappropriate force and/or intimidated detainees. He provided an example of an incident in August 2014 in which 'staff acted inappropriately in threatening a detainee at the Don Dale YDC and attempted to cover up the CCTV surveillance to hide this' (Vita 2015, 50). Finally, he commented on the lack of individualised case management plans and the need for offence-focused programs to be run in rehabilitation. Vita's report included 16 recommendations and emphasised the need for staff training in areas of case management, mediation and negotiation, use of force, youth behaviour, symptoms of foetal alcohol, ADHD and mental health, prosocial modelling, emergency management and cultural awareness (Vita 2015, 18).

Both Bath and Gwyne's and Vita's reports highlighted deficiencies in the training and poor practices around crisis intervention. The children's commissioner's report noted that, in April 2012, surveillance tapes depicting inappropriate and unsafe use of restraint were shown to senior staff of the Department of Justice, which incorporated Correctional Services (DOJ), and that undertakings were provided that such practices would cease. In December 2012, as noted in their report, the Office of the Children's Commissioner sent DOJ a formal recommendation regarding the review and suggested the implementation of safe intervention techniques. It appears that the 2012 recommendations were not implemented at that time or in the subsequent 18 months.

Appendix

Timeline of events at Don Dale Youth Detention Centre, 2014–15

2014

2 August: Two teenagers break out from Darwin's Don Dale Youth Detention Centre. They are on the run for almost four days. The breakout prompts the Northern Territory Government to speed up previously announced plans to move youth detainees to Berrimah Prison.

21 August: Tear gas is used on six young people, one being 14 years old, in response to a disturbance. Leading up to this incident, all six had been held in conditions amounting to solitary confinement for six to 17 days. One young person had left his cell after his cell door was left open by a youth detention officer. The other five young people were locked in their cells. All were tear gassed.

23 August: One detainee escapes his (unlocked) cell. He causes damage to windows and light fittings. Tear gas is used on this detainee and four others who were still in their cells. The five are moved to the new prison at Holtze (before adults were transferred there) as a stopgap measure.

3 September: Children's Commissioner Howard Bath announces an investigation into the tear gas incident and the response by staff. Dr Bath explained that the investigation would consider 'the management, the procedures, what were the circumstances, context of this event occurring'.

14 September: Two teenagers escape from their cells at the new prison at Holtze. They are found sitting on the roof of the prison. The two are moved to maximum security.

15 September: A teenager kicks in a security screen at a new maximum security cell in the AU$500 million new prison and escapes into an adjoining courtyard. Three teenagers allegedly overpower security guards at around 9.00 pm and steal a security swipe card at the new prison. They are found on the roof. The teenagers are moved to maximum security.

2 October: The Northern Territory Government commissions a review into youth detention by Michael Vita, Superintendent of Reiby Youth Detention Centre, New South Wales.

29 December: All youth detainees are moved to the old Berrimah prison, which was partially renovated and re-opened as the new Don Dale Youth Detention Centre.

2015

5 January: Detainees in G Block of Berrimah (not renovated) smash windows, doors and set fire to a mattress. One youth gets on the roof.

February: Vita Review handed down, cataloguing systemic deficiencies in Northern Territory youth detention.

24 February: Three youths attempt to escape by taking a tradesman's car and ramming it into a fence. One escapes over the razor wire and is quickly recaptured.

April: Two boys escape from separate correctional services vans transporting them to Berrimah.

31 May: Several youths in B Block alleged to have caused damage, and two youths escape from Berrimah. The corrections commissioner says the latest escapes are an 'embarrassment' that will not be tolerated, and announces that a new, more secure, maximum security section of Berrimah (B Block) will have anti-climb fences installed. He also says that adult prison guards will be used at Berrimah. Maximum security youths moved to C Block. The two youths who escaped return two days later by driving through the front roller door and are moved to the adult prison.

1 June: Another youth escapes from C Block at Berrimah.

12 June: Northern Territory Corrections bring an application for the two boys who had been held in adult prison for 10 days to have their imprisonment extended while renovations are completed at B Block as the only alternative place to house them, C Block, is 'not an appropriate environment'. The presence of asbestos in C Block, rust in doors, damage and other structural weaknesses in cell doors and internal and external security doors, as well as a lack of trained staff, are provided as reasons.

References

Allen, G. 2011. *Early Intervention: The Next Step. An Independent Report To Her Majesty's Government.* London, UK: The Early Intervention Review Team.

Amnesty International. 2014. 'Answers Urgently Needed about the Teargassing of Children in Darwin'. Amnesty International, 2 September. Accessed 8 June 2021, www.amnesty.org.au/teargassing-of-children-in-darwin/.

Anthony, T. 2013. *Indigenous People, Crime and Punishment.* Abingdon: Routledge. doi.org/10.4324/9780203640296.

Bath, H. and C. Gwynne. 2015. *Own Initiative Investigation Report: Services Provided by the Department of Correctional Services at the Don Dale Youth Detention Centre.* NT: Office of the Children's Commissioner. Accessed 8 June 2021, occ.nt.gov.au/__data/assets/pdf_file/0003/440832/pdf-final-investigation-report.pdf.

Blagg, H. and T. Anthony. 2019. *Decolonizing Criminology: Imagining Justice in a Postcolonial World.* London: Palgrave McMillan. doi.org/10.1057/978-1-137-53247-3.

Blagg, H., T. Tulich and Z. Bush. 2017. 'Indefinite Detention Meets Colonial Dispossession: Indigenous Youth with Foetal Alcohol Spectrum Disorders in a White Settler Justice System'. *Social and Legal Studies* 26 (3): 333–58. doi.org/10.1177/0964663916676650.

Bourgois, P. 2003. *In Search of Respect, Selling Crack in El Barrio.* New York: Cambridge University Press. doi.org/10.1017/CBO9780511808562.

Commonwealth of Australia. 2017. *Royal Commission and Board of Inquiry into the Protection and Detention of Children in the Northern Territory, Findings and Recommendations.* Canberra: Commonwealth of Australia.

Dodge, K. A., J. E. Bates and G. S. Pettit. 1990. 'Mechanisms in the Cycle of Violence'. *Science,* 21 December: 1678–83. doi.org/10.1126/science.2270481.

Howerton, A., R. Burnett, R. Byng and J. Campbell. 2009. 'The Consolation of Going Back to Prison: What 'Revolving Door' Prisoners Think of Their Prospects'. *Journal of Offender Rehabilitation* 48: 439–61. doi.org/10.1080/10509670902979710.

Lisak, D. and S. Beszterczeys. 2007. 'The Cycle of Violence: The Life Histories of 43 Death Row Inmates'. *Psychology of Men and Masculinity* 8 (2): 118–28. doi.org/10.1037/1524-9220.8.2.118.

Nossar, V. 2014. 'The Role of the Earliest Years of Life in Future Health and Development—Delivering Effective Prevention'. 6 March. amaqhealthvision.com (site discontinued).

Royal Commission into Protection and Detention of Children in the Northern Territory. 2017. *Volume 1, Chapter 18, Territory Families Recommendation.* 18.1: 468.

Rudd. P. 2015. 'State of Imprisonment: If Locking 'Em up is the Goal, NT's a Success'. *The Conversation,* 20 April. Accessed 8 June 2021, theconversation.com/state-of-imprisonment-if-locking-em-up-is-the-goal-nts-a-success-39185.

Smee, B. 2016. 'The Face of Youth Crime'. *NT News.* 26 July.

Spencer, N. 2003. 'Social, Economic and Political Determinants of Child Health'. *Pediatrics* 112: 704.

Tuari, J. 2013. 'Crime Control, Politics and Policy Production: Critical Reflections on the Demonization of Indigenous Youth'. Paper presented to Australasian Youth Justice Conference, Canberra, 20–22 May.

Vita, M. 2015. *Review of the Northern Territory Youth Detention System Report.* NSW Juvenile Justice, NSW.

White, R. and C. Cunneen. 2015. 'Social Class, Youth Crime and Youth Justice'. In *Youth, Crime and Justice*, 2nd ed., edited by B. Goldson and J. Muncie, 17–36. London: Sage.

10

Sawyer's Story: Guidance and Control of Adolescents in a Remote Aboriginal Community

Victoria Burbank

Introduction: Change and Continuity at Numbulwar

Remote Aboriginal communities in Australia have not been exempt from the rapid and radical changes that have characterised recent human history (e.g. Rowse 2017). While much of this change has resulted in improved health and wellbeing for many world populations, for others the consequences have been mixed. Drawing primarily on autobiographical material from a senior Numburindi man, this chapter looks at the effect that one of these changes has brought for Aboriginal youth over a span of 30 years in the south-east Arnhem Land community of Numbulwar. Somewhat ironically, it is the continuity of these changes—the control over Aboriginal people by an outside polity—that disables what may be a necessary and helpful control over young people. How and why some individuals respond more constructively to their current circumstances than others are questions that point to the complexity inherent in the control and guidance of youth in the intercultural spaces of remote Aboriginal Australia.

The south-east Arnhem Land community of Numbulwar was originally established by the Anglican Church Missionary Society (CMS) as the Rose River Mission. Its first Aboriginal residents were Wubuy-speaking people, known as the Nunggubuyu, or Numburindi, many of whom had previously lived at CMS missions on the Roper River and at Groote Eylandt. I have visited this community, located at the confluence of the Rose River and the Gulf of Carpentaria, on a number of occasions, first in 1977 and most recently in 2007.[1] Between these years, Numbulwar grew from a community of roughly 400 to 800 relatively permanent residents. In the early mission years, Aboriginal people were 'Wards of the State' and their activities were largely under mission control. At this time, a great many changes to their lives and livelihoods were made, changes that continued throughout the years. While the people of Numbulwar were still hunting, fishing and gathering in 2007, provisions of Western-type foodstuff, once as mission rations, later to be purchased in the 'shop', provided a major part of the diet. Marriage-related practices such as mother-in-law bestowal,[2] polygyny and a pre-menarcheal marriage age for females had all but disappeared. Senior men could no longer punish, as they once did, those who violated the 'Law'—that is, the imperatives of life established in the Dreaming, which had been challenged, if not supplanted, by Christianity and other Western beliefs. Wubuy and other languages of Numbulwar's population, such as Wandarang and Anindilaguwa, had largely been replaced with Roper/Ngukurr Kriol and, for a number of residents, Aboriginal English. Most people were supported by some form of welfare and, increasingly, Western material objects had made their way into the community. Although surrounded by Western things, social arrangements and institutions, such as vehicles,

1 Beginning in 1977, I have visited Numbulwar on a number of occasions to conduct anthropological fieldwork: 1977–78 for 18 months, 1981 for 9 months, 1988 for 7 months, 1997 for 5 weeks and between 2003 and 2007 for an approximate total of 7 months. All these projects have been undertaken with the knowledge of my research intentions and permission of the community. Informed consent has always been sought from the individuals with whom I have worked. Some of the publications from this research include: *Aboriginal Adolescence: Maidenhood in an Australian Community* (New Brunswick: Rutgers University Press, 1988); *Fighting Women: Anger and Aggression in Aboriginal Australia* (Berkley: University of California Press, 1994); and *An Ethnography of Stress: The Social Determinants of Health in Aboriginal Australia* (New York: Palgrave Macmillan, 2011). My last trip for the purpose of research took place in 2007. I was able to make a brief personal visit to Numbulwar in 2019. Permission for this last trip was granted by the Northern Land Council (NLC), as were all my previous visits. The NLC required one community member's support of my application to visit.

2 Once the Nunggubuyu/Numburindi and other language groups in Arnhem Land (e.g. see Shapiro 1981) bestowed little girls, perhaps around the age of four or five, upon a man as his mother-in-law. He would then, ideally, receive all of her daughters as wives should she give birth to girls (Burbank 1988, 51–52).

houses, a school, governing councils, town clerks and Western schedules, the people of Numbulwar identified themselves in terms of Aboriginal categories and continued to attend to some of their older laws and customs. For at least some, this would include mother-in-law/son-in-law avoidance, the custom of *mirriri* that prescribes distance and respectful behaviours between mature brothers and sisters, the use of an Aranda-type system of kin classification, circumcision of boys and attendance at various Indigenous ceremonies (see also Biernoff 1979; Cole 1982; Heath 1980).

While many discussions of the difficulties faced by Aboriginal people focus, appropriately, I think, on changes that have taken place in their lives, I want to frame this discussion, inspired and illustrated by segments of one man's autobiography, in terms of what I have mentioned as a significant continuity—the control over Aboriginal people by an external power. This control changed in some details, from the assimilation polices of the mission period through the integration, self-determination and intervention policies of the Commonwealth and Territory entities that have been in power over the years (Rowley 1977; Austin-Broos 2011). In effect, however, or so I argue, Aboriginal lives have been governed to a large extent by the policies and institutions of an encompassing polity that is largely ignorant of, and, usually, indifferent to, Aboriginal values and goals. As the circumstances created by this continuity have affected every part of Aboriginal being, it is no surprise that they have affected the experience of Aboriginal youth, and have long done so. I focus on just one aspect of this experience, the intergenerational guidance and control of adolescents.

Adolescents: An 'Old Man's' Perspective

In discussing this topic, I am guided by the words of a man in his early 50s whom I call, pseudonymously, Sawyer. Most of my work at Numbulwar has been with women and girls but, as an older woman, over the course of three of my most recent field trips, I was able to have a series of extended conversation with Sawyer. During one of our conversations in 2003, I asked him if he could tell me what he saw as the difference in his life when he was a 'young boy' and the lives of young boys at the time we were speaking. Young boys, as the reader may know, is a phrase that has been used to refer to male adolescents at Numbulwar, if not elsewhere in Aboriginal Australia. Sawyer replied to my request as follows:

> There is a lot of difference, not just one difference … I tell you about my time when I was a young boy. My time when I was a young boy had simple things that I could do with my life. And those things that I wanted to do, I was really scared in doing sometimes because when I did it I was in big trouble … Like most of the things that's wrong, like stealing … I got into trouble for that. I wasn't stealing, I just picked it up like other boys did and I got in trouble, like sugar cane, I never ate in my life. I broke a little bit to taste but I got a hiding for that. I guess I had a strict family, living with strict family mob, they never tolerated anything that I did that was wrong.
>
> Old way, you can't ever go talk to woman in our society; that is wrong. Can't even go an' take a woman away from home, and even take out on a walk or talk to her, that's wrong in my society. And sniffing petrol, I never sniffed but I watched boys that sniffed. The punishment [for petrol sniffing] had to be in public, that's how elders mob wanted it to happen if elder said, 'He did the wrong thing'. [Missionary] used to warn if [he] does it again [he'll] have to be banned from community. It was really strict in those days. Young men used to sleep long way from married couples, maybe a couple of kilometres away, not allowed to look at women. They would stay completely a long way from them.
>
> There are reasons why our young kids have gone on their own path. They broke away from our culture, they can do anything, that makes me wonder why they doing that. They can go and sniff petrol anytime they want, to smoke ganja [cannabis] anytime they want to. If they feel like smoking ganja we can't stop them; they can drink alcohol anytime they want. They can play music of the tape recorder, big stereo they can buy from the shop. They can play music loud as they like it anytime. They don't worry about the next door neighbour. They can choose whatever woman they want to meet during the day or the night. And all these things that young people does that I see them do, it's completely out of my reach. I can't hold them up and say to them, 'You should be doing that'. Us mob today, we don't have any power to do anything. Our power system was lost as soon as we lost the elders to control the community. (Sawyer, 12 November 2003)

At Numbulwar, the people adults might regard as adolescents do not fit neatly into Western categories and definitions. Their transitional life stages, for example, may be shorter than Western ones or extend beyond the teenage years. Whatever her chronological age, when a girl's breasts begin to develop she is regarded as a *ngarlanyjinyung*, a 'young girl', until she is married and has children. In past times, at least, the passage of an adolescent girl into marriage and motherhood might be a short one, while that of an adolescent boy's passage into manhood appears to have been more protracted. His time as a *wulmurinyung*, or 'young boy', begins when his body shape, voice and facial hair begin to resemble that of an adult male. As is the case with adolescent girls, he only becomes a man with marriage and children. In the past, this occurred in a male's late 20s or early 30s. Recently, however, this prolonged period of adolescence changed and boys in their teens might be married, in spite of adult disapproval. One older woman expressed this most emphatically with her scorn of a 23-year-old's marriage. He was, as far as she was concerned, still a 'young boy' (Burbank 1988, 4, 31).

The behaviour of young people appears to have changed as well; most critically, as Sawyer indicates, some, though not all, youth seem inclined to engage in acts that both concern adults and disrupt the community on a regular basis. For example, in the late 1970s, I heard the following:

> Sarah, sister's son Bentley [age 21] broke into the shop last night and took Sarah's son, Llewellyn [age 14] with him. Llewellyn took some cigarettes and two singlets but later returned them. When Sarah found out about this she began hitting Bentley on his back, yelling that he shouldn't teach her son to steal. Seeing her son beaten by her sister, Bentley's mother ran at Sarah but stopped when Sarah shouted to her about what her son had done.

Sometime later, the account of Bentley continued:

> Sarah said that when the police came to take his brother's son Bentley that her husband was angry because when they came to take him off to jail they put handcuffs on him. They didn't tell him they were coming. They told the Council and the Council didn't tell him. 'The Council got him sneaking'. She said he wanted to put the shop *gurdugurdu* [sacred] but she stopped him, but she had better get back to be sure that he didn't. Sarah came back around 4:00 PM and said that her husband had put [cursed] the shop and office, 'really *gurdugurdu*, to a really ceremony place in his mother's country. He is really boss of that place, then after him Monroe

> and Walt. They could take it off, but only if he says yes. He wants it to stay like that for a week. Everybody is asking me to tell that old man to take it off, but I said, "No". I don't know where that old man is. He put the shop and left.' (Field notes, 1978)

In his anger, Sarah's husband put what today is referred to as a 'curse' on the shop and office, rendering them sacred and thus unusable for the vast majority of the population. Numbulwar had no permanent police presence at that time, so we must presume that Bentley's theft was reported to the council, which in turn notified the police on Groote Eylandt, who then came to Numbulwar to take Bentley off to court or to jail, an act that clearly outraged his father's brother. Bentley's act, along with teaching a young teen to steal, assuming he didn't know how to do so already, led to a near fight between Sarah and her sister, for parents may fight with others, even close relatives, to defend a child of any age (Burbank 1994, 75–78). It also inconvenienced the community when the shop and office were closed as these two venues provided services relied upon by many.

On none of my visits to Numbulwar has youth-created disruption been absent. In 1988, for example, a woman mentioned that:

> The men did that business [ceremony] last night but still those young girls and young boys were sniffing [petrol] and calling out and crashing around, playing tape. We didn't sleep much. (Field notes, 1988)

Youth misbehaviour not only disturbs the adult community, it disturbs adolescents too. Here I am speaking with an 18-year-old about harassment and gossip that may have arisen from competition over a boyfriend:

> Kinsey: [My life] it's now bad. Because people growling at me, makem me upset. And making me worry about, like worry inside, making me think about my father mob. If people like growling at me and make me upset, that's why. Or talk about you behind your back and you don't know, that make you upset and worry and skinny.
>
> VKB: What's that behind the back talk?
>
> Kinsey: Anything, like maybe talk about you for anything, or they jealous to you, you know, like girl. They talk about you for anything.
>
> VKB: Other girls been talk about you?

> Kinsey: Yeh.
>
> VKB: What for that behind the back talk make you think about your father?
>
> Kinsey: Maybe they talk about me and make me upset and make my father and mother upset too. They gonna talk to them too … They talking to that girl. Like explain with them not to teasing, 'Cause you might make a big problem, your mother and father might end up fighting', with my mother and father, and stab each other. They might stab each other, eh? (Burbank 2011, 84–85)

Kinsey was not only 'upset' by her peers' harsh words and gossip, she was also concerned about her parents, that they might be injured in a fight. The concerns of this insightful teen suggest the intensely negative feelings that parents may have, and the actions they might take, when the welfare of their children is threated by others. Youth behaviour clearly adds to the unpleasant stresses of daily life that are already considerable in remote communities like Numbulwar (e.g. Brady 1992; Brooks 2011; Senior and Chenhall 2008; Tonkinson 2011). Why then, outsiders might ask, don't these communities attempt to control them to a greater extent than they do at present?

Sex, Drugs and on the Dole

Recent research on the adolescent brain suggests that the early teenage years may be an especially vulnerable time for at least some young people. This, it is thought, may be due, in part, to developmental changes that take place in the limbic system, where, along with the anterior cingulate cortex, motivation may be said to originate (Tse 2013, 187). During adolescence, the limbic system is highly sensitised to reward and the presence of peers by increases in gonadal hormones, dopamine and dopamine receptors. This sensitivity may lend itself to the risk-taking so often seen in youth behaviour, especially in the presence of peers. The wellbeing of young people, then, may depend on a degree of external adult guidance and control (e.g. Casey 2015; Chein et al. 2011; Konner 2010).

A number of pre-industrial communities appear to have discovered this. According to Alice Schlegel and Herbert Barry (1991), who undertook a cross-cultural study of adolescence in 186 societies, this is a time when peer groups may, at least temporarily, hold greater sway over an individual than the family. However, adults in some settings may be those who 'determine the activities of these groups'; it is they, not youth, who 'make the demands, provide the resources and bestow the rewards' of peer group activity (75). Youth peer groups may be appropriated for community-wide projects whether of a military, religious, economic or social nature. In the latter domain, adolescents may be responsible for organising or contributing to events such as balls, festivals, rituals, weddings and funerals. They may also be recruited as 'agents of social control' (82), overseeing both the actions of their peers and of adults. These community roles and the presence of adults (135–37) may be vital to the wellbeing of a youth cohort as the peer group at this life stage can be a major socialising force. In certain circumstances, 'it can equal the family in the enforcement of behaviour and inculcation of values' (69).

The Aboriginal people of Numbulwar may have once controlled the behaviour of their young people too, through a prolonged process of religious indoctrination for males and early, often polygynous, marriage for females. Both these arrangements, however, were undermined by mission dictates and the laws and institutional arrangements of the encroaching polity. Little by way of control of young people appears to have taken their place (Burbank 1988, 33–41). It is, then, perhaps no accident that it is largely in the peer-directed peer groups of today that many of Numbulwar's youth engage in the behaviours that so concern the older generations: substance abuse, vandalism, theft and (relatively) unregulated sexuality.[3]

In Western settings, beyond the family, youth are guided and controlled to some extent by high schools. This arrangement, however, may only be effective if students believe that the activities they are directed to undertake will enable a desired future (see D'Andrade 1992; Steinmayr and Spinath 2009). And, as many a Western parent knows to their sorrow, there are many other, more powerful, organisations working against this purpose—the automobile, alcohol, tobacco, drug, entertainment, IT and fashion industries, to name just a few institutions in consumer society that usually appear indifferent to children's wellbeing.

3 On the basis of their cross-cultural study of adolescence, Schlegel and Barry (1991, 135–37) have suggested that delinquent behaviour may, in large part, be attributed to the absence of adult companionship.

Some of Numbulwar's youths continue on to the later grades of high school. But it is unlikely that schooling holds the promise that is does for some Western youth. Here are the words of a teacher speaking in 2003:

> We're trying to educate students to a high level and what this does is raise the level of frustration and here there is no pathway, no jobs, no one to hire our students. The community doesn't have a mine, a source of money, there is nothing here. No infrastructure. I don't see where the education is leading. These kids put all this effort into education and end up on CDP[4] collecting trash. (Burbank 2011, 27)

The school is not an institution likely to control most of its students. It cannot teach the means of achieving a desired future, for who knows what that might be. Nor does initiation into the Law, the religious life of the Dreaming, have a sufficient hold on youths. As anthropologists have already noted, once the Law is challenged by other discourses, the controlling effects of initiation are weakened (see Hiatt 1985; Myers 1980; Sackett 1978; Tonkinson 1974). The Law at Numbulwar has certainly been challenged by years of mission proselytising and Western education. But, even if this were not the case, there are diminishing numbers of men to teach young boys. Too many, who once might have been their teachers, are dead, disabled or caught up in a prolonged adolescent phase of their own, so to speak, given their continuing abuse of alcohol and/or cannabis. Along with the enhanced sensitivity of the adolescent limbic system, we might see the problems of youth at Numbulwar as a mismatch between potentially controlling agents and the current environment. Neither the school nor the Law is suited for doing so in the context of this community.

Exceptions: Positive Risk

The adolescent brain may be characterised as one that is highly sensitive to environmental factors, particularly those of a social nature. Research-based accounts in cognitive psychology and neuroscience portray adolescents as acutely aware of, and affected by, sociocultural cues, including those that come from explicit teaching, social evaluation and social rejection, especially by peers (e.g. Worthman and Trang 2018, 32; Crone and Dahl

4 'CD[E]P' refers to CDEP, a Commonwealth work program designed for Indigenous communities (Sanders 2005). In the 2000s, the acronym was pronounced with a silent E.

2012, 640; Blakemore and Mills 2014, 187–89). The combination of this sociocultural sensitivity and a propensity for risk-taking can be a positive, if not essential, development in the right kind of environment insofar as it can enhance learning (Blakemore and Mills 2014, 200). And, as we might imagine, as brain development and related behaviours are not necessarily uniform across all young people, and as these differences appear to be caused, in large part, by sociocultural factors, among which are family and school environments, positive sociocultural experience may be associated with positive youth behaviour. We might also keep in mind, as some researchers have suggested, that: 'Individual differences in neurobiology can determine how sensitive an adolescent is to their social context indicating that identical social environments might affect different individuals in different ways' (Foulkes and Blakemore 2018, n.p.).

Sawyer appears to have been one of those adolescents whose brain was put to good use. Petrol sniffing was present in his youth, but he was not one of the sniffers. And there are, of course, young people at Numbulwar today who do not vandalise or steal, take to petrol, alcohol and drugs, or conceive children, sometimes with incorrect partners according to local marriage rules, at an early and unhealthy age. We may assume positive experiences for some of Sawyer's 'family', that is the large extended 'family' of 'close' relations, and, perhaps, of the education they receive from the school's teachers and/or the community's ritual leaders. We may also assume a kind of neuropsychological development that assists a positive view of the social environment whatever it might be.

Sawyer would have been born around the time that Numbulwar was first established as Rose River Mission in 1952, but he did not live there until he was nine or 10 years of age. His first years of life were spent in the bush around cattle stations like Tanumbirini and on the settlements of Borroloola and Ngukurr. Here is an excerpt from the story of his early years:

> I never went to school until I was about this high [about a metre tall]. I went back to Ngukurr, only place I went to school. Missionary said, 'You have to start school from the very start, we have to move you back to kindergarten. That's the Law … Older kids from the school used to tease me, big boys who said, 'What's a big boy doing in the kindergarten?' Every day they came to tease me. That made me think very hard. This is my voice, 'I can't stop teasing. I gotta work hard as I can to learn education, learn hard to write, learn hard to read, all, all this, they do in school'. Promise

> I made to myself. So from then I did just that. I learned how to read, write, I learned ABC. I worked very hard at sums … I came to Numbulwar. I went to school … But I was still studying very hard, not only white man side of things. I was also sitting down listening to elder people, stories from our parents, telling stories around the fire. I didn't get involved in any ceremony yet, only corroboree and stories why they sing corroboree. Then I been learn how to survive out bush, what kind of spear you need to catch fish. If you need to cut meat without a knife, you need stone axe. All the studying our culture way of doing things. Mostly learning how to survive when in the bush. They taught me all that. When I went into first circumcision ceremony, I was about 10 years of age. And after that I been study very hard why they do circumcision. We don't make it up, it's been there for centuries. Then I been learning big heavy laws for men when I was 12 and 13 and I been go though the other two big ceremonies. But one thing I've learned since I was 10 or small boy,[5] I been learn about respect. (Sawyer, 20 November 2003)

Some people, of course, take to Western education more readily than others, perhaps due to abilities that make learning the three Rs more satisfying (Steinmayr and Spinath 2009). In Sawyer's case, an additional incentive might be found in his equation of success at school with respect from his peers. But why would his peers have chosen school level as a reason for teasing? This act suggests that at least some value was placed on Western education by these young students. For as long as I've been acquainted with Numbulwar, school attendance has always been a problem. And I suspect this was the same at Ngukurr at that time. School does not appear high on the list of many children's priorities, nor, I suspect, on that of their families. It is, however, a whitefella thing and whitefella things are admired (see also Musharbash 2008). Sawyer, for example, thinks highly of refrigeration:

> There are a lot of good things *munanga* [whitefella] way. You can look at keeping food for a number of months. Flour, bread, meat can be put in the fridge to keep for two or three months. Good way of living, *munanga* way. (Sawyer, 2004)

5 Calculating age chronologically is a relatively new practice in parts of Aboriginal Australia and numbers given may only provide a rough estimate (see Burbank 1988, 10–11).

At least some Aboriginal people, I suggest, see an association between literacy and whitefella wealth. In 1978, for example, several adults saw proposal writing as the means of acquiring Land Rovers and other desired goods. Whether we are speaking of the clothes, vehicles and houses of the mission period or the mobile phones, computers, iPods and CD players of more recent times, school may be a symbol of whitefella power, a power that might be achieved by anyone who can learn what it has to teach. However, this belief might have been more likely in the early days of Numbulwar's settlement when firsthand experience may not have complicated ideas of how whitefella power was acquired.

Yet, Sawyer appears to have found meaning in more than just Western learning. The Law also holds value for him. He equates knowledge of his culture with both respect and survival. We should ask why this might be so in a setting in which the Law's value is undermined by Christianity and other Western discourses. Here I would suggest that an early and intensely emotional experience in which Aboriginal beliefs were central, motivated, at least in part, his dedication to the Law:

> When my mother passed away we were at Rosy Creek … There was a stock camp there. My mother and father travelled all the way from Borroloola, going to Rosy Creek … but my mother got sick. My father didn't want her to stay in hospital in Borroloola. She was really sick. She passed away, we were in the middle of nowhere. No telegraph, no telephone to ring up my mother's sister to come out. My mother's sister was staying at Tanumbirini, they used to work there, stock hand, to catch more bullocky [cattle], we call them. She stayed there, my mother's sister, Sarrri. When my mother died, nothing to get in touch to ask her to pick me up. We had no car, no plane … I had a little brother too who was already born but he was too small, he could only eat breast milk. The other ladies there had no breast milk and maybe they were too scared to ask for powdered milk or goat's milk.[6] That night my brother passed away too. So I had two deaths. And when my mother passed away, this is the incredible thing that she did. She said, 'I better go to my sister'. She went to Tanumbirini. This was the last thing she did because she really loved and cared for me and my younger brother. She knew those old ladies there couldn't help. So she went to Tanumbirini and when she went there and old Sarri was sleeping. And she came out in the room where they

6 In another telling of this account, Sawyer mentions that the old ladies thought they might be shot if they approached a whitefella.

> were camping and said to Sarri, 'You don't have to look at me, this is me, your sister. You gotta leave tomorrow early. If you can't leave early tomorrow both of my sons will pass away. You have to go straight to Rosy Creek cause that's where you'll find them.' She said to her, 'Go ask the manager to give you spare horse to go'. And when old Sarri listened to her she cried because she knew her sister died. Early next morning she went to the manager and she said, 'I need you to give me some horse, I gotta save two boys, they might end up dying'. I was a lot bigger than my younger brother. She packed up the horse and left, took three days and three nights to reach us. She travelled, no rest, to reach us. If I had a map here, I could show you how far she travelled. When she got there my younger brother passed away. She was a day late. I was still alive, still running. I still ran to meet her when she came. It's an incredible story. At least she save my life. If she had come a day earlier she would have saved my brother. I would have a brother with me. At least she saved me. (Sawyer, 20 November 2003)

I do not know when and how Sawyer learnt the story of his rescue, a distinctively Aboriginal discourse. It may have been told just once or repeated throughout his childhood and adolescence. Or it may have been one he remembered, at least in part, or created and told himself. Whatever may be the case, it appears to be an important part of his autobiography. The events it details are the source of Sawyer's salvation, his survival in spite of an absence of Western forms of communication or Western assistance. Hence, I think, his willingness to take the Law seriously, to see his 'culture ways of doing things' as a means of staying alive and thus worth learning.

In his youth, Sawyer could be described as a risk taker, but one who appears to have largely engaged in its positive forms if we can agree that he was taking risks in pursuing both Western and Indigenous knowledge. It is members of a boy's 'family' who decide that he is ready to be circumcised and begin his engagement with the series of rituals that are a male prerogative. However, a child's behaviour may be such that a family daren't approve of his participation, for if a new initiate does not follow the Law, punishment may be severe. As the following conversation we had on youth delinquency reveals, Sawyer was well aware of the dangers associated with ritual participation:

> All the stages you go through after circumcision, you will be learning. Small boys are told they can't do anything wrong. And when they go to second stage, really really strong, they are told again. They are out there two, three months, taught it, have to be

> reminded every day, 'This is the Law, can't break Law'. And once come out of the thing they are warned, 'We will be keeping an eye on you. We. You do anything wrong, even if you argue with parents, you will be punished'. (Sawyer, 4 August 2004)

Western education may have also involved some risk from Sawyer's perspective:

> So I thought in my young days that I was an electrician. That's what I really loved, that was the choice I had when I was in school. So I did go into Darwin to do electrician course. I been there twelve months, one year, and I received the certificate. (Sawyer, 20 November 2003)

Although Sawyer doesn't say so, he, like youths from Numbulwar who find schooling in Darwin difficult, may have been homesick and lonely during that year. I once asked eight women if they would like to live in a place like Darwin and all replied in the negative, six of them using the words 'homesick or boring'[7] in their replies. We can imagine that young people might find it even more so. One adolescent girl even saw the city as dangerous:

> Something night happen [in the city]. Car accident or someone gonna stab me with the knife. It's dangerous. If you go and see the Long Grass People [who go to Darwin to drink or take drugs], they give you shit for money and they stab you with the knife. They got the knife in the pocket. You gotta be careful to yourself. (Kinsey quoted in Burbank 2011, 167)

Sawyer, though, was prepared to return to Darwin after his first year there, however lonely and homesick he might have felt:

> I was top man on the exam so the teacher said, 'I think you need more training'. So I went [back to] Darwin for [another course] ... Then after that they came to tell me there is no more money to fly you into Darwin.[8] That was a waste. I had to come back to

7 The word 'boring' as it is used at Numbulwar has a social component not usually found in its whitefella usage. For example: 'It's boring, nobody walking around, it's too dead' (in Burbank 2011, 167; see also Musharbash 2007).

8 In 2004, when retelling this part of the story of his education, Sawyer said:

> Then I received the certificate ... I came back here but before I was going to Darwin, I had bad news, bad story, because government changed. The new government put up different things, the department looking after us, I think it was Welfare, had a different policy. Not enough money to take me back to do the apprenticeship. That was a big loss. But I didn't give up. I got a job as assistant electrician. (Sawyer, 1 September 2004)

> this community and started work here as electrician. And from that time, I been picking up and learning as much as I could learn. I've worked in the work shop. I was there when you came here, first time [1977–78], I remember. (Sawyer, 20 November 2003)

Sawyer might be regarded by some as a near orphan, his mother dead by his early years, his father often absent, at least during his childhood. He may have also seen himself in this way:

> I never started school, preschool. In those days I was living out bush, living with one family, not my family, this family that looked after me. I was looked after by a lot of family really, when we lived out bush. (Sawyer, 20 November 2003)

I think that here Sawyer is attempting to communicate the distinction between his biological parents and more distant relatives to an outsider, whom he cannot assume is familiar with the way in which 'family' is calculated. But it is notable that he was making this kind of distinction, one that, as I have demonstrated elsewhere, is made at Numbulwar (Burbank 2018). He was, however, being cared for by 'family'; therefore, others would not have considered him to be an orphan, a *wangulu*, in the local scheme of things (Burbank 2011, 151–52). Eventually, he was 'rescue[d]' by people who appear to have been closer kin:

> I went to school at Ngukurr. My father was there. [Two other clansmen and] Old Sarri came up and rescue me. I owe her a lot. I owe her my whole life ... That's why I've lived at Ngukurr, four, five years. I been at school. But inside my heart I miss my mother and my brother and sisters. I had a space inside my heart; really want to be with them. I got lucky. My father was taken [away for prolonged medical treatment]. Umbakumba people came with the work boat, brought supplies from Groote to Numbulwar and Roper and they seen me there at Ngukurr. I was at the river for a swim. Maybe I was on the swing. 'Hey, is that Sawyer?' ... They recognized me because I been to Groote, Umbakumba, when I was a kid. 'You can't stay here. Your father [away getting treatment], you can't stay here. Too many *mulunguwa* [murderers, usually from outside a community] here. We gotta take you back' ... I guess when [a woman] got off here [at Numbulwar from the transport] she been start yelling top of her voice, calling [to one of Sawyer's kinsmen]. 'Sawyer here'. [Two of his clansmen] came out running and Old Sarri heard too ... and as soon as I saw them I was really happy, I had a mother. That's the one thing I was missing in my life. She's my mother's elder sister. So that was my

> destiny and I lived here ever since. When my father came back from [his medical treatment] he wanted me to meet the plane. I went to airstrip on the tractor. He said to me, 'I'm not going to take you away'. He went to Roper, worked and came back here. (Sawyer, 8 September 2004)

What most strikes me about this part of Sawyer's narrative is how it is presented in accord with the story of his mother's death and attempt to save her sons. In neither account does he focus on any kind of neglect; rather, he paints his kin as his saviours and emphasises, in the former story, his mother's love for him and, in the latter, his appreciation of his 'mother' Sarri. This may be a form of impression management, of course, but I think it more likely reflects how Sawyer really felt, or wanted to feel. That is, I propose that Sawyer's view of his life, in particular of the family environment of his formative years, is as much a consequence of his social need, intelligence and persistence as a reflection of what it really was. Sawyer has subsequently led a life unlike many others at Numbulwar with the benefits of two seemingly incompatible forms of education. This, I think, is largely due to the idiosyncrasies of his life history, to the particularities of his social environment, and of his psychobiological make-up, which is, of course, a product of his social environment as well as of his genotype (e.g. Konner 2010, 159–201; LeDoux 2002, 65–96).

Conclusion

There is more to say about the guidance and control of youth in remote Aboriginal communities. This conversation might include the necessary attributes of adults for their presence in young peoples' lives to be a beneficial one, the effect of family culture on youth behaviour and the complications of both these factors in remote Aboriginal Australia. What I want to emphasise here, however, is the complexity of individual human lives and life chances. Other children may have intense Aboriginally redolent experiences and so be protected from outside challenges to the Law. Other children at Numbulwar may have Sawyer's kind of intelligence and find delight in reading and what they learn at school. They may have his interest and drive and thus be susceptible to the healthy control that these two forms of education have a potential to exert. They may have the kinds of family relationships (or see their family relationships to be of the kind) that encourage them to follow their dreams and take positive risks. If we are to be of any help to Aboriginal communities in their attempts to enable the healthful development of their youths, it is for anthropologists to abstract the components of idiosyncratic life histories that may be replicated in other youths' lives, and to understand their relations with aspects of the encompassing sociocultural environment.

References

Austin-Broos, D. 2011. *A Different Inequality: The Politics of Debate about Remote Aboriginal Australia.* Crows Nest, NSW: Allen & Unwin.

Biernoff, D. 1979. 'Traditional and Contemporary Structures and Settlement in Eastern Arnhem Land with Particular Reference to the Nunggubuyu'. In *A Black Reality: Aboriginal Camps and Housing in Remote Australia*, edited by M. Heppell, 153–79. Canberra: Australian Institute of Aboriginal Studies.

Blakemore, S-J. and K. Mills. 2014. 'Is Adolescence a Sensitive Period for Sociocultural Processing'. *Annual Review of Psychology* 65: 187–207. doi.org/10.1146/annurev-psych-010213-115202.

Brady, M. 1992. *Heavy Metal: The Social Meaning of Petrol Sniffing in Australia.* Canberra: Aboriginal Studies Press.

Brooks, D. 2011. 'Organization within Disorder: The Present and Future of Young People in the Ngaanyatjarra Lands'. In *Growing Up in Central Australia: New Anthropological Studies of Aboriginal Childhood and Adolescence*, edited by U. Eickelkamp, 183–213. Oxford: Berghahn Books.

Burbank, V. 1988. *Aboriginal Adolescence: Maidenhood in an Australian Community.* New Brunswick, NJ: Rutgers University Press.

Burbank, V. 1994. *Fighting Women: Anger and Aggression in Aboriginal Australia.* Berkeley: University of California Press.

Burbank, V. 2011. *An Ethnography of Stress: The Social Determinants of Health in Aboriginal Australia.* New York: Palgrave Macmillan. doi.org/10.1057/9780230117228.

Burbank, V. 2018. 'Of Mothers, Adoption and Orphans: The Significance of Relatedness in a Remote Aboriginal Community'. In *Focality and Extension in Kinship: Essays in Memory of Harold W. Scheffler*, edited by W. Shapiro, 203–24. Canberra: ANU Press. doi.org/10.22459/FEK.04.2018.06.

Casey, B. 2015. 'Beyond Simple Models of Self-Control to Circuit-Based Accounts of Adolescent Behaviour'. *Annual Review of Psychology* 66: 295–319. doi.org/10.1146/annurev-psych-010814-015156.

Chein, J., A. Duston, L. O'Brien, K. Uckert and L. Steinberg. 2011. 'Peers Increase Adolescent Risk Taking by Enhancing Activity in the Brain's Reward Circuity'. *Developmental Science* 14 (2): F1–F10. doi.org/10.1111/j.1467-7687.2010.01035.x.

Cole, K. 1982. *A History of Numbulwar*. Bendigo, Vic.: Keith Cole Publication.

Crone, E. and R. Dahl. 2012. 'Understanding Adolescence as a Period of Social-Affective Engagement and Goal Flexibility'. *Nature Reviews Neuroscience* 13: 636–50. doi.org/10.1038/nrn3313.

D'Andrade, R. 1992. 'Schemas and Motivation'. In *Human Motives and Cultural Models*, edited by R. D'Andrade and C. Strauss, 23–44. Cambridge: Cambridge University Press. doi.org/10.1017/CBO9781139166515.003.

Foulkes, L. and S-J. Blakemore. 2018. 'Studying Individual Differences in Human Adolescent Brain Development'. *Nature Neuroscience* 21: 315–23. doi.org/10.1038/s41593-018-0078-4.

Heath, J. 1980. *Nunggubuyu Myths and Ethnographic Texts*. Canberra: Australian Institute of Aboriginal Studies.

Hiatt, L. 1985. 'Maidens, Males, and Marx: Some Contrasts in the Work of Frederick Rose and Claude Meillassoux'. *Oceania* 56: 34–46. doi.org/10.1002/j.1834-4461.1985.tb02106.x.

Konner, M. 2010. *The Evolution of Childhood: Relationships, Emotion, Mind*. Cambridge, MA: Harvard University Press.

LeDoux, J. 2002. *Synaptic Self: How Our Brains Become Who We Are*. New York: Viking.

Musharbash, Y. 2007. 'Boredom, Time and Modernity: An Example from Aboriginal Australia'. *American Anthropologist* 109 (2): 307–17. doi.org/10.1525/aa.2007.109.2.307.

Musharbash, Y. 2008. *Yuendumu Everyday: Contemporary Life in Remote Aboriginal Australia*. Canberra: Aboriginal Studies Press.

Myers. F. 1980. 'The Cultural Basis of Politics in Pintupi Life'. *Mankind* 12: 197–214. doi.org/10.1111/j.1835-9310.1980.tb01192.x.

Rowley, C. 1977. 'White Settlement and Interaction'. In *The Australian Encyclopaedia*, 3rd ed., 52–61. Sydney: Grolier Society of Australia.

Rowse, T. 2017. *Indigenous and Other Australians Since 1901*. Sydney: UNSW Press.

Sackett, L. 1978. 'Punishment as Ritual: Man-Making among Western Desert Aborigines'. *Oceania* 49: 110–27. doi.org/10.1002/j.1834-4461.1978.tb01382.x.

Sanders, W. 2005. 'CDEP and ATSIC as Bold Experiments in Governing Differently: But Where to Now?' In *Culture, Economy and Governance in Aboriginal Australia: Proceeding of a Workshop of the Academy of the Social Sciences in Australia Held at the University of Sydney 30 November – 1 December 2004*, edited by D. Austin-Broos and G. Macdonald, 203–12. Sydney: Sydney University Press.

Schlegel, A. and H. Barry. 1991. *Adolescence: An Anthropological Inquiry*. New York: Free Press.

Senior, K. and R. Chenhall. 2008. 'Lukambat Marawana: A Changing Pattern of Drug Use by Youth in a Remote Aboriginal Community'. *Australian Journal of Rural Health* 16: 75–79. doi.org/10.1111/j.1440-1584.2008.00956.x.

Shapiro, W. 1981. *Miwuyt Marriage: The Cultural Anthropology of Affinity in Northeast Arnhem Land*. Philadelphia: Institute for the Study of Human Issues.

Steinmayr, R. and B. Spinath. 2009. 'The Importance of Motivation as a Predictor of School Achievement'. *Learning and Individual Differences* 19: 80–90. doi.org/10.1016/j.lindif.2008.05.004.

Tonkinson, M. 2011. 'Being Mardu: Change and Challenge for Some Western Desert Young People Today'. In *Growing Up in Central Australia: New Anthropological Studies of Aboriginal Childhood and Adolescence*, edited by U. Eickelkam, 213–38. Oxford: Berghahn Books.

Tonkinson, R. 1974. *The Jigalong Mob: Aboriginal Victors of the Desert Crusade*. Menlo Park, CA: Cummings Publishing Company.

Tse, P. U. 2013. *The Neural Basis of Free Will: Criterial Causation*. Cambridge, MA: MIT Press. doi.org/10.7551/mitpress/9780262019101.001.0001.

Worthman, C. and K. Trang. 2018. 'Dynamics of Body Time, Social Time and Life History at Adolescence'. *Nature* 554: 451–57. doi.org/10.1038/nature25750.

www.ingramcontent.com/pod-product-compliance
Lightning Source LLC
Chambersburg PA
CBHW050808270326
41926CB00026B/4637

* 9 7 8 1 7 6 0 4 6 4 4 4 8 *